Running A One-Person Business

Other Books by Whitmyer:

Mindfulness and Meaningful Work: Explorations in Right Livelihood (editor, Parallax Press, 1994)

In the Company of Others: Making Community in the Modern World (editor, Tarcher/Perigee, 1993)

Other Books by Rasberry:

Marketing Without Advertising (Nolo Press, 1987, with Michael Phillips)
Honest Business (Random House, 1981, with Michael Phillips)
The Briarpatch Book, (editor, Volcano Press, formerly New Glide, 1978)
The Seven Laws of Money (Random House, 1974, with Michael Phillips)
Rasberry Exercises (Freestone Publishing, 1970, with Robert Greenway)

Running A One-Person Business

SECOND EDITION

Claude Whitmyer and Salli Rasberry

Ten Speed Press
Berkeley, California

1☯

TEN SPEED PRESS
P.O. Box 7123
Berkeley, CA 94707

Cover design by Fifth Street Design
Text design by David Charlsen

Library of Congress Cataloging-in-Publication Data

Whitmyer, Claude.
    Running a one-person business / Claude Whitmyer & Salli Rasberry. — Rev.
        p.   cm.
    Includes index.
    ISBN 0-89815-598-3
    1. Self-employed.   2. Small business—Management.   I. Rasberry, Salli.   II. Title.
    HD8036.W45   1994
    658'.041—dc20   93-50577
                                                                          CIP

SECOND EDITION, FIRST PRINTING 1994
Printed in United States of America

    3   4   5 — 98   97   96

Dedicated to

Gail Terry Grimes and Michael Eschenbach,
our beloved life partners,
and to Miles Dylan Marshall, Salli's grandson,
and Arek Corbin Whitmyer, Claude's son.
May this book serve our progeny for generations to come.

ACKNOWLEDGMENTS

Many people were important in the creation of this book and we hope we have remembered to thank each of them personally, as well as in print. Thanks to you who rubbed our backs, cooked us dinner, took time from your busy lives to be interviewed, were understanding about deadlines, and offered words of cheer when we felt under pressure.

We were deeply touched by the concern for the environment and the commitment to community and service expressed by everyone we interviewed. Each interview was important and added richness and depth to the book. Thanks to Don Anderson, Liz Baldwin, Kate Bishop, Sherri Brautigan, Patti Breitman, Clifford Burke, Sharon Cahn, Catherine Campbell, Debra Lynn Dadd, Bill Dale, Tom Ferguson, Pam Glasscock, Alexandra Hart, Helen Hendricks, Harrison Judd, Bernard Kamoroff, Alicia Bay Laurel, Suzanne Maxson, Davida Milborn, Bill Morehouse, Eileen Mulligan, Catherine Osterbye, Yana Parker, John Parry, Malcolm Ponder, Norman Prince, Roger Pritchard, Ted Rabinowitsh, JoanAnn Radu, Deborah Reinerio, Robert Rovin, Diane Stuart, Paul Terry, Nadine Travinski, Lydie Van Gellder, Charlie Varon, Bob Wachtel, Dorothy Wall, and Teri Joe Wheeler. A special thanks to Padi Selwyn for her help with the marketing chapter, and Roger Pritchard, Pat Wagner, and Leif Smith for the information on networking and support. And bouquets to Sasha Marshall for her beautifully transcribed interviews.

Amy Hill, we appreciate your lending a hand during a holiday. And Barry Jaeger, thanks for being such an inspiration!

A special word of gratitude goes to Sharon Kehoe and Jo Anne Coates for their help in managing the Master of Arts in Business program which made it possible for Claude to do the final editing of this book.

A special note of thanks to our book designer, David Charlsen, to George Young, who is still the perfect publisher, and to Christine Carswell for shepherding the whole flock of us to completion.

They say a good friend is someone you can call at four in the morning. A good planning buddy doesn't even think that's odd. Salli would like to acknowledge the support, encouragement, and understanding of her two planning buddies, Jim Sullivan and Robert Kourik. And Claude acknowledges Paul Terry and Deborah Reinerio for their roles as support persons extraordinaire.

Much love and appreciation to our mates, Michael Eschenbach and Gail Terry Grimes, for their love, patience, and support. We couldn't have completed this job without them.

And finally, thanks to the readers of the first edition who took the time to write to us with feedback and critiques, especially Joan Leslie Taylor, E. Allan Paul, and Katie and Roy Whitehead.

CONTENTS

Foreword

by Tom Peters

Working people are scared to death. Job security has vanished. Temporary employment soars. Wild technological changes are still picking up steam. And global competition—for my position and yours—is a way of life from now on.

Some people are responding, from the Russian steppes to Paris's arrondisements, by voting for radicals who promise to close the borders and turn back the clock. Some are pulling up their turtlenecks and hiding beneath their desks, in hopes that the bearers of the next list of job cuts will overlook them somehow.

And some are taking their destinies into their own hands, and discovering matchless opportunity amid the turbulence.

"People do realize that job security is gone," wrote Professor Homa Bahrami, of the University of California at Berkeley, "but many don't realize what it's been replaced by. The driving force of a career must come from the individual, not the organization." Smart individuals on corporate payrolls are beginning to act as though they were independent contractors. Bahrami quotes a saying at perpetually volatile Apple Computer: "Your sense of job security lies in your employability."

The wise employee, with the mind of an independent contactor and an eye on her or his market worth, works each day at developing contracts on or (especially) off the company payroll, improving skills, and delivering services that are of demonstrable value to "customers" inside the organization or out.

But a growing number of workers are going the next big step and saying, in effect, "Hey, the lot of the self-reliant individual, on or off the payroll, isn't all bad." Enter Claude Whitmyer and Salli Rasberry's *Running a One-Person Business*. I came across it two years ago in a variety store in Occidental, California. I started reading it as my wife, Kate, drove us up the Northern California coast. I kept reading her longer and longer excerpts. I was hooked in a flash.

"For those who feel life is more than making money, the one-person business is an exciting business form," the authors, who have advised hundreds of one-person enterprises, begin. "It is business as lifestyle—business as a statement about who you are and what you value." The book is a fabulous testament to creating a rewarding lifestyle through your work, whether as a gardner, physicist, or dressmaker. It's also a no-nonsense, one-step-at-a-time primer to getting there from here.

Though Whitmyer and Rasberry emphasize the humanness of the one-person enterprise, they spare no detail in helping you set up a book of accounts, draft a business proposal, or make the decision about whether to use an answering machine or answering service (the importance of first impressions and all that). In fact, believe it or not, the authors go a long way toward helping the nonnumerate realize that installing and using simple financial control systems can actually be a kick.

British business consultant Charles Handy is rated by many (including yours truly) as the most thoughtful observer of tomorrow's workplace. The new career, he claims, will typically consist of several mini-careers, on and off company payrolls. I'm certain Handy's right. Hence the book's value for the current corporate denizen with an eye on tomorrow, as well as the pioneer ready to make the jump.

But the fact is, I think the greatest rewards will accrue to those who are already struggling to make it on their own. I've been in business for myself for over a decade now (though my company's payroll is a bit more than just me), and I can tell you that I learned an enormous amount from *Running a One-Person Business*. I just wish I'd had it on that lonely day in November 1981, when I first wiggled out of the corporate cocoon and began my liberating adventure.

Introduction: Business as Lifestyle

For those who feel life is more than making money, the one-person business is an exciting business form. It is business as lifestyle—business as a statement about who you are and what you value.

The one-person business is rapidly becoming the boom industry of the 1990s. A large-scale nationwide economic reorganization is afoot and it appears this is only the beginning. In recent years, the media has pointed repeatedly at research findings showing that self-employment is growing at a faster rate than wage- and salary-paying jobs. Government sources estimate that at least one million new businesses are started each year. The American Home Business Association claims that there are at least thirteen million home-based businesses, representing 11 percent of the U.S. work force, and *Entrepreneur Magazine* estimates 18.3 million people operate businesses from their homes. Neither of these figures includes one-person businesses with offices outside of the home.

To put this massive change in historical perspective, it's important to remember that individual business ownership was in fact the early foundation of the U.S. system of private enterprise. Then, as more and more people began to depend on working for others for their livelihood, self-employment slowly became a dying lifestyle. Joining an existing business or corporation became the clear choice for most Americans and, by 1970, less than 7 percent of the population was self-employed. In contrast, by the early 1990s, the number of self-employed had nearly doubled, with the ranks of one-person businesses at about twenty million and growing. Without fanfare, the one-person business has quietly become one of the most significant social revolutions in America.

What's the Attraction? People who brave the uncharted world of the one-person business are looking for many things, among them a greater degree of personal autonomy and self-expression than is possible within other career structures. They start one-person businesses for a variety of reasons, but at the top of the list is the desire to be their own bosses, without the responsibility of overseeing others. This autonomy offers them the opportunity to restructure their lives in an inventive way, and, at the same time, maintain their personal independence.

Running a one-person business is not only flexible, challenging, and creative, it is also a liberating and effective way to respond authentically and gracefully to the changing face of life in the 1990s. It also seems that a growing number of people are sick and tired of just living for the weekend, for two weeks of vacation with pay, and for the increasingly ephemeral promise of the good life after retirement.

One of the most fascinating aspects of the family of one-person-business options is the incredible range of lifestyles and goals it embraces. While some, for whatever reasons, want a lot of money, others prefer few possessions and a simple lifestyle. Some work only to make a living; others view work itself as a positive value. Whatever style of life you prefer, it can be supported by running a one-person business.

Running a one-person business is about creating a life while making a living. From the owners of such businesses we often hear a startling fact: they don't want their businesses to grow large and they are not interested in becoming wealthy. "Wealth is not the goal," says master horticulturist Robert Kourik, who runs several adjacent one-person businesses. "All the business books are filled with the same few examples of highly successful (read 'rich') entrepreneurs. Less than 5 percent of us will ever become really affluent. Most of us have to be happy just making a living. It's the quality of the process of making a living that counts—and it's the chance to define 'quality' for yourself that's critical."

But Why Fly the Corporate Nest? Since the first edition of this book appeared in 1989, the very way business is conducted has been in constant flux. According to *USA Today*, U.S. employers are laying off workers at the rate of 2,200 a day. Salaries are being frozen, health benefits have been scaled back, and pension plans are shaky. Business icons are beginning to topple as major structural changes occur, resulting in increased insecurity in the workplace.

In a *Time/CNN* poll reported in November 1993, two-thirds of the respondents believed that job security had deteriorated over the last two years and 53 percent of those respondents felt it was a long-term problem. Surveys show that people are also feeling increasingly uncomfortable with the disparity between what they feel is important and the work they do. About the same time, a Roper survey showed that only 18 percent of Americans find their careers rewarding and more and more people are searching for ways to integrate their work with the rest of their lives. More startlingly, a Hilton Hotels Time-Values Survey showed that people were even willing to give up the security of a steady paycheck in exchange for more control over their life and work. Seventy percent of those earning $30,000 or more a year, and 48 percent of those earning $20,000, would give up a day's pay each week for an extra day of free time!

Why this Book? This book is for those of you who are daydreaming about the possibility of running a sole proprietorship or who are working for someone else as you make the transition to becoming your own boss. It's also for those who are knee-deep in the first year of being your own boss and for those who are old hands at it but who need specifics and refinement to help you remain a one-person business. This book is for all who suspect or already know that it is possible to create fulfilling work and integrate it with all that is important in your life.

The one-person business has distinct characteristics that make it very different from other businesses. Historically, most business schools have treated the one-person business as some kind of stunted version of regular business, suitable only for gaining experience on the way to a bigger enterprise. This attitude misses the point that many people actually prefer this unique form of business. We wrote the first edition of this book to respond to the needs of clients and students starved for information that spoke to their situation as one-person-business owners. At the time, no such books existed. The only information that came even close to satisfying the needs of one-person businesses was in publications aimed at the hobbyist or home businesses. So we decided to fill the void with a book liberally sprinkled with both nuts-and-bolts practical advice and words of inspiration from people who were actually running successful one-person businesses.

Since then, we have continued to refine and hone our knowledge and to listen to and learn from our students, clients, and the diverse community of one-person businesses. For the last fifteen years, we have had the privilege of advising and teaching several hundred one-person businesses from around the world. To write this book, we felt it would be valuable to conduct in-depth interviews to supplement those years of experience. These interviews gave us the chance to delve into the highly effective systems that these businesses had worked out over the years. Like all the one-person businesses we have known, those we chose to examine more closely were run by individuals whose incomes varied as widely as their goals and lifestyles. They represent a variety of fields and live in different parts of the United States (one lives in Scotland). In our discussions, we captured many insights about the real meaning of success and how it relates to social issues.

In this second edition of the book, we show readers how to incorporate personal and social needs gracefully into the whole business picture. We also show you how to apply sound business practices, such as the diligent use of effective record-keeping systems, regular activity measurements, and careful planning of daily work strategy, to the management of a one-person business.

Although we wrote this book primarily as a practical guide, it seemed to us that all really good "how-to" books give the reader confidence—a sense of "I know that" or "I was on the right track" and "I am not alone." We don't deny the fragility of one-person businesses. In fact, we stress just how difficult running one can be and spend considerable time explaining what it takes to succeed and what to do if you find yourself short of the prerequisites. In addition, we suggest many ways to reduce the inherent risks—experiences drawn from our own work and the work of our colleagues and interviewees. Our hope is that this book will allow you to determine if the one-person-business form is for you, and, if so, to run your one-person business in an efficient, profitable way while remaining true to your social and ethical values.

Remember, as the owner of a one-person business, you're part of a growing group of entrepreneurs who can act as a positive social force. You can't be fired and, once you've learned to make your business work, you can be secure enough to take strong moral, ethical, political, and environmental stands, if you choose. Running a one-person business can provide you with a decent living, make your personal life more meaningful, and give your social and civic life a level of excitement and interest that working for someone else seldom delivers.

Welcome to the growing community of one-person business owners! You represent both a vital force in American business and one of the most significant social revolutions occurring today!

One-Person Business Owners—
A Unique Group

One-person businesses are found nearly everywhere, and they earn a wide range of incomes. Consider the oil traders who buy and sell drilling rights worldwide and deal in millions of dollars from their home phones. Or the arbitragers and bond dealers working on investment portfolios of their own, with just a telephone and a rented desk in the back of some brokerage office. These one-person businesses are often major forces in the financial market.

In the political realm, a lobbyist and a private consultant specializing in policy analysis are among the best-paid and most influential people in our nation's capital. Both run quiet, behind-the-scenes, one-person businesses in Washington, D.C.

Professional one-person businesses include realtors, consultants, accountants, speakers, trainers, free-lance editors, psychotherapists, and tax preparers.

Some one-person businesses are retailers, such as the flower shops, juice bars, and shoe repair stores that flourish in many cities. A fellow in Seattle, Washington, motors his little boat around Lake Union selling espresso and croissants to houseboats, ships at anchor, and shoreline offices. And we've encountered many a homey resort-town gift shop catering to the tourists who drive through each year.

Traditionally, many service trades have been run as one-person businesses, including housekeeping, beauty salons, shoe-shine stands, tailoring, plumbing, carpentry, fortune-telling, child-care providers, and mechanics. The last twenty years have seen a proliferation of service providers, as more and more women join the workforce and households with two wage earners become the norm. As Americans work longer hours and are under more stress, many new market niches have been created in the personal-service and alternative-healing fields, including: herbalists, personal trainers, acupuncturists, aura and angel readers, channelers, and practitioners of biofeedback.

Regardless of the field, it takes a certain turn of mind, some unique skills, and a big dollop of realism to successfully run a business on your own. As we said earlier, a one-person business is not primarily a stepping-stone to a bigger enterprise, though you could use it in that way. People run one-person businesses because they *prefer* that form of business. They like the opportunities and freedom it gives them—to enjoy more flexible and expansive personal lives, to express their political and ethical values, to play a larger role in their communities and, in some cases, to pioneer new fields.

Having control over their work plus the joy and security that comes from expressing their internal vision are two important reasons why people choose to start a one-person business. Increasingly, people are feeling the need to make a difference and take charge of their lives, as is testified to by the statements of some of the people we interviewed for this book:

> A lot of my friends who are employed are scared to death they're going to lose their jobs. I have a friend who has been unemployed for two years and can't find a job. She was laid off after fourteen years. I feel there's a lot more security in being self-employed. My business can go up and down, but no one's going to fire me. I'll always have a job.
>
> I have control of my life and my time, the rhythm that seems right to me on a daily basis, and I don't have to answer to someone else. Being self-employed means I can say yes or no to projects I want to work on. As an employee, no matter how many of your own projects you're impassioned about there will always be the boss saying you gotta do this; I'm assigning it to you.
>
> I think part of why other people think of running a business as such a risk is that it's not part of their life. To me it's a natural extension of what I do anyway. It doesn't feel like I'm working when I'm working. It's an incredibly good feeling to know that what I'm doing has an impact, that I am helping people achieve peace and health and harmony in their lives. I no longer feel the separation that I had when I worked for someone else and had a work life and a personal life and there was a line down the middle. Now that line is totally blurred. It's really nice. I feel like my life and my work are of a piece.
>
> —*Patti Breitman*, book agent

> Being self-employed—once you're successful—the real benefits are almost boundless. Even though there are none of the traditional benefits. There is no

time and a half, no vacation pay—there's none of that. I have to salt money away for that. But I personally wouldn't trade working on my property out here in the country—looking at the redwoods, watching the birds in the feeder in my wife's garden with my children running around—for anything. I don't know how I could have a better life, really. I'm crazy about what I'm doing. I have my moments of frustration and then I think: Would I rather be working for another lab? and boy, I get my priorities straight. I all of a sudden realize how great it is in spite of the few frustrations here and there. It could be a lot worse, and it couldn't be a lot better.

—Don Anderson, Anderson Dental Studio

I think having a one-person business is about having control of your life and your time—not having to answer to someone else. While I was getting my master's degree I worked at a bookstore, and for those three years I had the experience of being an employee. Although I liked being part of a group and the sense of having colleagues and going someplace and seeing people every day, I hated the fact that when I was tired and ready to stop I couldn't. At four in the afternoon, when I was ready to exercise and go have dinner, I had to keep working. I was not efficient during that time, and it didn't make sense. I couldn't pay attention to my own body rhythms, I couldn't work when I was best able to and most productive—I had to work according to *their* time clock.

I just think I'm the luckiest person in the world when I wake up in the morning to have the flexibility, the control of my time, the time to write, the time to exercise in the afternoon, walk, and do yoga. I never commute. I stay home if it's gray and rainy and I don't want to go out. If I don't want to go to the office, I don't. It's wonderful. Who can complain?

Dorothy Wall, writing consultant

There are times almost every day that I get this little chill that runs through my body and I go: Wow! I'm really enjoying this day. I'm having a good time. I make some money; I'm in control of my life doing what I want to do, not what someone else wants me to do. What more could you ask for? I feel like I've gotten to a place I've always wanted to be. It's great. Sure, I could make more money if I went to work for Hewlett-Packard or someone like that, but why? The money is not what it's all about, for me at least. It's about having that feeling every day. Where you're driving down the road and you're sitting there thinking: "I'm as happy as I can be and I'm working. I'm being a productive member of society and enjoying it and getting paid for it."

John Parry, Solar Works

I have two kids and there's no question that my priority is to be a good mother. Everything about my work would probably be *more* if I didn't have children, but it's very important to me to do a good job raising them. And I think, compared to friends of mine who have other kinds of jobs and have the same juggling act to do, I feel really lucky because I'm flexible in my hours. I can take the boys to a soccer game and get up a little earlier so I have my time in the studio, or pick them up from the soccer game and then go out to my studio. I have that kind of flexibility, that a lot of people who are more connected to an institution or some kind of job can't have.

Pam Glasscock, fine artist

My work is very preventative and helps me be in tune with something bigger than myself. I guess it is the spiritual aspect of preventative medicine—something more than you—not just your little self. It does use the biological as a way to the spiritual, but there is nothing churchlike about it.

The fact that it is in service of something cogent that rebounds back to me and is also serving something bigger than myself is very satisfying. That satisfaction and the freedom of choice can also be hugely distressing. I'm learning how to enlarge my capacity for not knowing and being in chaos and turmoil. By my actions I learn what comes back very quickly, and it's usually in a way that is salutary. It gives me a great sense of well-being.

Robert Rovin, Rosen bodyworker

In this chapter we will talk about the personal attributes and market perspective needed to create and sustain a one-person business. We will focus on the two factors that are essential to the success of a one-person business: *tradeskill* and *market focus*. Then we will introduce ten people who are running successful one-person businesses, each in a different field.

TRADESKILL

Popular business magazines often carry glitzy profiles of real-life businesses that read like fairy tales: success stories that shrink years of work into "started making cookies in her trailer and ended up with a multimillion-dollar business." The emphasis is on making a pile of money and being in the right place at the right time, implying that if you work hard and have a great idea, you, too, could be one of the people in these articles. The skill it takes to run a business is never addressed.

Creating a one-person business and keeping it going involves what we call *tradeskill*. This is a term coined by Salli Rasberry and Michael Phillips in *Honest Business* to describe a whole cluster of behavioral attributes that are vital to running a business. Most of these, if you already have these attributes, chances are you learned most of them when you were young.

As Paul Hawken noted in his book *Growing a Business*, "While we recognize 'natural' musical and athletic abilities, business ability on the whole is still considered something that you can acquire as an adult. But I believe tradeskill, like many skills, is easy to acquire when young, harder to get the knack of when you're older. Tradeskill is what you learn as a kid while running the paper route, working in your uncle's store, or starting an over-the-counter market in baseball cards. The smaller the business, the more important tradeskill becomes."

You can go to the most prestigious business school in the country and you won't find anyone talking about tradeskill. Chanting mantras, practicing visualization, or taking a workshop won't help you acquire tradeskill, and it won't rub off on you by reading this or any other book.

You picked up tradeskill from your parents or from someone else you spent a lot of time with who was in business. Tradeskill is like riding a bike, ice skating, and being lovable: it's much easier to learn when you're young. You usually know whether you have tradeskill or not, just as you know if you have a "green thumb" or are good with children.

Tradeskill is quite different from being skilled in a trade. Being a talented dress designer doesn't mean you will succeed at running a dress-designing business. Being a good cook does not ensure success in the restaurant business. Being a skilled carpenter does not automatically make you a competent contractor. Being a competent artist does not ensure you will succeed as a gallery owner.

Success in business is not an inalienable right bestowed at birth to every United States citizen. It's actually more like raising a child or getting married. While everyone *thinks* they can do it, few actually know what 'it' is. It is beyond this book to deal with marriage and child-rearing. But the fact is that not everyone can start a one-person business and expect to succeed.

Running a successful one-person business requires tradeskill. Tradeskill means that not only do you have to be competent in your field, you also have to be good at business. Of course, if you don't have the knack of running a business it's all right to use trial and error as a way to learn, as long as you have not used your home as collateral or borrowed heavily from your in-laws.

Do You Have Tradeskill?

How do you know if you have tradeskill? Over the years we have identified the following seven attributes as being necessary to run a successful business: *being persistent, facing the facts, minimizing risks, being a hands-on learner, being good with numbers, being organized, and being able to read carefully.*

Being Persistent Rasberry and Phillips describe it this way:

> The persistence attribute seems to lead to an awareness of the slow process by which things occur in the world and to the realization that time increases the likelihood of success.
>
> Persistence consists of being willing to keep trying something long after your energy is used up, long after your enthusiasm has waned, and certainly long after other people have lost interest in helping you. The people who can't make it in business are the ones who give up easily or divert their attention from the long, hard parts to do the easier, more glamorous parts. Everyone who succeeds in starting and running a business has the attribute of persistence.

Persistence is the ability to push ahead, to put one foot in front of the other. You have persistence if it's four in the morning yet you are determined to finish those frames for tomorrow's gallery opening. This despite the fact that your honey's been in bed for hours and your eyes feel like sandpaper. You have persistence if you finish that landscaping job even though it's seven-thirty on a drizzly evening and you long for a bath and a hot brandy. And being persistent also means having what it takes to plug away a little bit at a time, day after day, until the job is done. The people who succeed in running a business all have this ability to "hang in there" long after others would have given up. Successful businesspeople are not easily pulled off course from those inevitable long, hard parts of running a business.

Facing the Facts   Again, from Rasberry and Phillips:

> Being willing to let go is of course what facing the facts is about. It involves the ability to learn constantly from empirical evidence and the willingness to change your behavior when the weight of the evidence tells you to change. This aspect of tradeskill is different from the quality in people that leads them to change their behavior because of new ideas, convincing arguments, pride, or whim.
>
> The sense in which we use "letting go" does not refer to quick responses to everyday pressures or to blowing in the wind. Rather it refers to a willingness to let go of belief systems found only at a very high level of functioning. It refers to letting go of one's personal patterns and beliefs. It is a pragmatic behavior and it is difficult for many people.

Facing the facts means having the ability to change your behavior when your personal patterns and beliefs are not working for you. It means being flexible. It means having the expectation that better decision-making information comes with time. People who face the facts understand that wisdom is gained by the constant reevaluation of life experiences. If you love white asters and keep featuring them in your landscape design, despite the feedback that your clients don't like them, you are *not* facing the facts.

Minimizing Risks   What happens in your business on any given day is not going to be that important over time. People good at minimizing risks remind themselves every day that it is the bigger picture that must be considered when making decisions, not any individual crisis. Rasberry and Phillips put it this way:

> When looking at new businesses, most tradeskill people we've known were very open about looking at completely new ideas and strategies, but when the implementation period came, they methodically went about reducing the risk. They find fall-back plans and alternative solutions in the event the main thrust of their venture doesn't work. They constantly think of alternative uses for the equipment they are using, or for subletting their location if their plans don't work.

Risk and tradeskill are surprisingly connected. People with well-developed tradeskill minimize risks! If forced to choose a gambling game, they would favor roulette where the odds are close to 50/50, and avoid slot machines where the odds are worse than 25/75, although the payoffs are higher. They would avoid gambling in the first place, and own the casino when they had that alternative.

Being a Hands-On Learner People with tradeskill have the hands-on learning attribute of wanting to participate in the total process of their business, paying attention to detail and being involved in understanding every aspect of the business. According to Rasberry and Phillips:

> People who succeed in starting and running small businesses have the hands-on attribute very visibly before they start a business. They learn by touching and doing. They are hands-on people who gain confidence in their decision making by participating in all the processes that relate to the decision. Such people pay close attention to details. They carefully look at contracts before signing them. They read legal notices that come in the mail and they invariably go back to look at the new wiring that the electrician put in before the wall is sealed up. Most people we know with tradeskill like to do their own books, and they pay daily attention to financial material. This tendency seems to be a direct result of the hands-on learning attribute, since the books give a hands-on, comprehensive feeling of the business.

Being Good with Numbers In his book *Growing a Business*, Paul Hawken echoes the opinion of Rasberry and Phillips: "Numbers express relationships," he says. "Any business, whether manufacturing, service, or retail, consists of hundreds and thousands of relationships that can be expressed, analyzed, and conceptualized through numbers. Many people in business with little or no education or training nevertheless succeed—in good part because they have an intuitive sense of these numbers."

Being Organized and **Able to Read Carefully** In *Small-Time Operator*, Bernard Kamoroff echoes this point about numbers ability, but adds two more elements of tradeskill to the list ahead of it. He calls them the "basic characteristics that you've got to have or be willing to develop if you're going to start a business," but it is clear that what he is talking about is tradeskill:

> The first and most important characteristic is a clear head and the ability to organize your mind and your life. The "absent-minded professor" may be a genius, but he will never keep a business together. In running a small business, you are going to have to deal with many different people, keep schedules, meet deadlines, organize paperwork, pay bills, and the list goes on. It's all part of every business. So if balancing your checkbook is too much for you, or you just burned up your car engine because you forgot to check the oil, maybe you're not cut out

for business. The work in a small business is rarely complicated, but it has to be done and done on time. Remember, this is going to be your business. It's all up to you.

A second important characteristic is the ability to read carefully. Most of your business transactions will be handled on paper, and if you don't pay attention to what you're doing, you could miss out. You may receive special orders for your product. You will be billed by your suppliers in all kinds of ways, sometimes offering discounts if you are prompt in paying. You will have to fill out a lot of government forms. Government agencies can't exist without forms, and the instructions for these forms are sometimes tricky. If you mess up, these agencies have the most aggravating way of casually telling you that you're going to have to do it all over again.

"A third important trait," Kamoroff concludes, "is, if not a 'head for numbers,' at least a lack of fear of numbers. Tax accountants get rich off of people who look at a column of six numbers and panic. It doesn't have to be that way. The math involved in running a small business is mostly simple arithmetic—addition, subtraction, some multiplication."

In recent years we have identified three more elements we think are crucial to business success: *self-starting energy, cooperation,* and *consistency in behavior.*

Self-starting Energy This is the ability to get going without stimulants or pressures from others. It is closely related to persistence and is probably the source of the energy that we draw on when we are hanging in there.

As Don Anderson puts it, "I'm highly motivated. You have to be to be self-employed. Who's going to make you get up and do your work? There is nobody motivating me to go do the lab work. My wife doesn't wake me up in the morning and say 'Time to get to work, honey.' She will not do that, so I have to stay on top of it and look at the due dates, estimate how long I need. I have to stay on top of my business day by day."

Cooperation Most of the successful one-person businesses we know prefer cooperating with others to isolating themselves, and that makes perfect sense. It is difficult to get and keep customers if you are too isolated.

In our culture, business has often tended to be selfish, cutthroat, secretive, and warlike in its competitiveness. Practitioners of such behavior like to think of it as a form of Social Darwinism, in which survival of the fittest has some ultimate social good. While competition and aggression were once important to our survival as a species, they are no longer appropriate behavior in many aspects of our lives. Businesses of all sizes are coming to realize that competitiveness is part of a worldview that is no longer viable. Viewing business as a hostile and competitive arena doesn't feel good and uses up a lot of energy.

Cooperation, on the other hand, is a healthy force in the marketplace. The logic is straightforward: By being cooperative you get more help from everyone. The benefits that smaller businesses reap from helping each other are most evident in the widespread formation of referral services for professionals and health-care providers, now commonly listed in phone books across the country. Such businesses recognize that helping others in their field helps individual practitioners as well. The same is true for continuing education, which is supported by more and more fields of business.

Cooperation plays an important role in the life of Kate Bishop, a dress designer whose long vacation gave her a fresh perspective. "Being in an environment where there were no artists for a year made me realize how much I missed my artist friends and how much I depend on my whole social circle as a network for creative input. It seems like in the ordinary course of my life more and more of my work is becoming integrated with my life. So many of my friends are artists, and we all have something to offer each other. We'll talk about the kids and we'll talk about our lives and work and some technical information will be exchanged. It just seems to happen very naturally now. In the beginning it was more work. I had to make a project of finding something out. Now it's just part of the flow."

Author Robert Kourik goes further in his analysis of the importance of cooperation to a one-person business: "Running a one-person business is not about competition—even though it will feel like it some of the time. The natural order appears to be highly competitive, but in reality it more often includes coevolutionary strategies, niche development, genetic diversification, and extinction (which isn't necessarily due to predation). If it feels like competition, you're in the wrong niche or you have lost your creative edge."

Cooperation, then, is an essential ingredient for the success of a one-person business. If you are not part of a community of other one-person businesses, you will find it extremely difficult to make it in the long haul. All businesses are communities. One-person businesses thrive in the company of others to whom they can turn for emotional support, for referrals, and whom they can hire as suppliers or subcontractors.

Consistency in Behavior Here we are referring to what people sometimes call "emotional stability." Actually, there is no such thing as emotional stability. Emotions rise and fall. Sometimes we can figure out why and sometimes they just seem to be there for no particular reason. To ensure success in business, however, we must do what needs to be done next, regardless of how we feel. So-called emotional stability is actually consistency in behavior. Our customers and clients come to experience us as being present and engaged, most of the time. And so they are willing to rely on us to deliver our products or services when they need them.

In summary, then, these are the ten elements of tradeskill that you must have or cultivate if you are to maximize your success as a one-person business: (1) being persistent, (2) facing the facts, (3) minimizing risks, (4) being a hands-on learner,

(5) being good with numbers, (6) being organized, (7) being able to read carefully, (8) self-starting energy, (9) cooperation, and (10) consistency in behavior.

People with tradeskill look ahead to future opportunities and are poised to handle the unexpected. Malcolm Ponder, an accountant who sees a few hundred clients a year, observes: "Change is coming faster than you can imagine. I advise my clients to analyze the changes that are occurring now and what that might mean for their business in the future. To use the vision part of their mind to see the changes that are happening and to keep a step or two ahead of reading about them in the paper."

What If You Don't Have Tradeskill?

So what do you do if you really want to run your own one-person business and you don't have tradeskill? Despite much of the popular literature, merely being passionate and doing what you love is usually not enough. There are several options: First, you might find a partner who does have tradeskill, one that complements your strengths and makes up for your weaknesses. This requires being very honest with both yourself and your prospective partner. Second, since there are no tradeskill training schools you might create your own 'school' by getting a job in a small business with the goal of taking on increased responsibility over time. Another alternative is to become an apprentice, working closely for a number of years with someone who does have tradeskill.

We urge you to consider these options rather than just jumping in, because in a one-person business there is no partner to pick up the slack and no whiz bang employees either. There's just you.

Writing consultant, Dorothy Wall, states it well, "The main thing about running your own business is having the right skills for it. Being persistent, facing the facts, being a hands on learner. You don't easily give up and you believe in yourself, believe in your skills and what you have to offer, you're a hard worker. You always operate at the top level, at your best at all times. You are professional. You have to have all those qualities and if you do have them great! Some people are not suited for this kind of thing at all and I think it's important for people to be realistic. You also have to have an idea that is viable, something that is truly marketable. You have to be realistic both about what your skills and capabilities are and have a viable product."

MARKET FOCUS

Market focus means finding and focusing in on your appropriate market niche. Fortunately, the number of market niches for a one-person business is many times larger than for any other business form. This is so because consumers are becoming much more sophisticated. Greater consumer awareness is leading to an increase in businesses that match goods and services to the consumers who need them. While the globalization of big business is leading to mass-produced items and generalized services, there is a simultaneous increase in the demand for products and services that are more suited to individual wants and needs.

A particularly interesting example of a one-person business fitting this description is auto brokering. Auto brokers are individuals who will buy your car for you. You specify your budget and the features you are looking for. The auto broker shops for you, gets you the best deal, and delivers to you a car complete with insurance and registration.

Increased awareness of nutritional needs and the broader availability of specialized cooking utensils and specialty restaurants has led to a demand for cookbooks, cooking newsletters, cooking classes, food delivery services, caterers, and so forth. A delivery service, Waiters On Wheels, has printed up its own menus listing particular items from about thirty local restaurants. You call Waiters On Wheels to place your order and they pick up the feast of your choice from the restaurant and deliver to your door.

Still other examples of market-focused one-person businesses include helping people select, install, and learn to use a wide variety of appliances, such as computers, VCRs, or microwave ovens. Consultants, newsletters, and classes abound on subjects ranging from environmental toxins to sports training regimens. We heard recently of a one-person business that does housecalls to program VCRs. They also install and consult on buying home entertainment systems.

Less obvious but equally viable market niches can be found in more traditional occupations. Chiropractors, massage professionals, home-care nurses, plumbers, gardeners, painters, and professional house-sitters all can offer some unique approach or a specialized service in their field. Not to mention the increased demand for handcrafted and ethnic goods.

And of course, each of these special service or product businesses needs the support of accountants, lawyers, graphic artists, printers, photocopy stores, word processors, researchers, and others who cater to one-person businesses.

PROFILES OF SUCCESSFUL ONE-PERSON BUSINESSES

Of the twenty people we interviewed for the first edition of this book, we chose eight to profile. For the second edition we conducted several new interviews, did follow-up interviews of the first group, and added Roger Pritchard and Patti Breitman to the group of one-person businesses profiled in this chapter. The subjects in this section are not particularly more successful or more erudite than any other one-person business we have encountered but we chose them to represent the broadest range of locations and fields.

Like all the one-person-business owners we have come across, these ten individuals have defined success in their own terms and have figured out how to live their lives in their own ways. On the other hand, they live rather ordinary lives. Another consistent trait is that all are committed to their communities and strive to provide them with quality goods and services. They each exhibit most of the elements of tradeskill as well. In our opinion, these ten people are representative of successful one-person businesses everywhere. You can learn a lot from them, especially that it is possible to create the meaningful work that you are good at, and to make a living doing it.

Malcolm Ponder, Accountant

Malcolm's business has evolved over the last fifteen years from a financial consultancy to tax preparation work for over two hundred clients. He does personalized taxes for individuals and small businesses.

"I used to do a few corporations. I realized that you can't do a few of anything and do it well. You have to do a lot of something because there are so many changes, so many new laws. So I am concentrating on what I do best.

"I have somewhat fewer clients so it isn't as frenetic in that forty-five-day period approaching April 15 as it used to be. I don't want to go beyond what I've got now. I want it to work easily and painlessly, and I want to work with basically the same people and do a high-quality job. In terms of moving my business to a shopping center or expanding, it doesn't make sense. It works right the way it works now. If I went into expensive quarters, anything more than my small office just a few feet from my home, then the overhead would go up dramatically.

Malcolm is Salli's accountant and tries to help her and all his clients keep an eye on their business or personal finances. "Quality is my aim. I try to prepare a totally accurate, perfectly done tax return. I also try to do more than just fill out a tax return. In addition to sitting down with my clients to get the necessary information to do the proper tax return, I'm also asking, 'Why are you spending so much in this category?' And, 'Let's talk about your overhead and other expenses.' I want to help my clients with the overall financial part of their business or personal life. I can provide an analysis of clients' numbers so that their numbers are working *for* them while helping to educate them in terms of what they can do to improve their business or keep it from sliding. That's the kind of information I have tried to put into the business from the beginning based on my experience as a banker and treasurer. I'm attempting to provide more than just a liaison with the IRS."

Malcolm believes that community involvement is vital. As he puts it, "Anybody who is in business in any size town ought to be putting a bunch back into the town and community. A by-product is that you get back out of it proportionate to what you put in. When I first started my tax preparation business, I was president of the community center in my area and everybody knew I was reliable. When a fund-raising event came around, I took care of the money, which was a relief to the other people because no one else wanted to worry about that aspect. The bulk of any one-person-business clientele comes from your community base. So not only do you want to be a major part of that community, to help the good things happen, but by being part of that community you'll become known and people will grow to trust you."

A former wholesale banker for Bank of America, Malcolm lent money to corporations and wealthy individuals. He got hired away by a mining and shipping company and was their assistant treasurer for four years. During his fourth year, he was in Brazil with high officials in his company. Malcolm remembers, "I was the only one that wasn't at least a senior vice president. I started studying these people at the top, the people whose jobs I wanted in five or ten years. They were away from their families twenty-six weeks a year minimum, and lots of them were drinking heavily and carousing. I came back from that trip to our house in Bolinas, California, and realized I wanted out. My wife had died when my kids were very small, and my housekeeper had been raising them. The kids were getting to know her real well, and I was this guy who came and visited occasionally. So I got out, and have worked out of my home ever since."

Tom Ferguson, M.D., Writer and Lecturer

Tom is a self-care pioneer, health futurist, and award-winning author based in Austin, Texas. Although Tom has a medical degree from Yale, he is by practice a writer and lecturer. He founded the influential journal *Medical Self-Care* and is the editor of the medical section for the upcoming *Millennium Whole Earth Catalog* (HarperSan Francisco, 1994) and recently wrote a chapter for the book that accompanied the Bill Moyers series on mind/body medicine.

The central thread of his work deals with the self-care approach to health. According to Tom, "I went through medical school and decided that I was not entirely enthralled with the exclusively professional orientation of most of the health-care system. Having had contact and experience with the folks who put out the *Whole Earth Catalog*, I got very interested in applying their self-sufficiency paradigm to medicine. And since medical school I have focused full-time on helping people to take care of themselves, rather than taking care of them myself."

Tom is presently helping to shape an exciting new field that will set the stage for an industry designed to help consumers use computers to gain access to the information they need to better manage their own health. He recently organized the first national conference on "consumer health informatics"—consumer-operated computer applications in health care—at the National Wellness Institute of the University of Wisconsin.

He is doing a lot of work with smoking cessation based on a stop-smoking method he developed that doesn't "nag, pressure, threaten or blame." "Our method is dramatically more successful because we give people what they say they want," Tom notes. "It's a nice example of market research in terms of business terminology. What we did was conduct initial interviews asking people what they wanted and then we ran many sessions of a class and asked for feedback. We kept refining and listening to people's feedback and incorporating all their suggestions until basically they said, 'We can't imagine how this class could be any better.' We're getting ratings of 9.8 on a scale of 10. Our method empowers rather than embarrasses the smoker."

Tom also conducts teaching and training workshops and seminars for health professionals in an effort to expose them to a new way of looking at the health-care system in which the central person is not the physician but the individual. He provides free services to the community of health professionals. "I believe that health care is changing," he says. "We are moving away from an old system built around the physician to a new system built around the layperson. I feel I have a special mission to bring this word to health professionals. So I do free consulting and speaking, particularly with medical and nursing students, as well as people in training to be medical professionals."

Pam Glasscock, Fine Artist

Pam paints flowers in watercolors, slowly and painstakingly creating almost botanical renderings. A successful artist, she sells her work mostly to galleries and through her shows and occasionally from her studio.

Glasscock, her husband, and two young children live simply in a rural area in Northern California. "I grew up in a family that had a strong ideal of making the world better and didn't care too much about money. The important thing was to be a good person and to do quality work. Quality is something I think about every second I am working. When I reach a certain level, I want to go a little farther, and I always have that in mind when I start a new painting.

"I have a need to do my work and I get pleasure from it—a sense of meaning and spiritual reward. It's an appetite that I have. I have to go to my studio and do my work. I'm preoccupied with what the painting looks like and how much of myself I put into it and the very personal concerns that have to do with making a work. I'm striving to do really good paintings. They are not perfect, but they're trying to be. Things have progressed on a slow upward trend despite the recession. Every year I've had the best year so far. Including this year.

"I went to New York just out of school because I was very serious about being an artist and I was attracted to the galleries and museums. It was the first place I had been where when you said you were an artist, people responded as if you had said you were a brain surgeon—or better. In many parts of the country the response is more, 'Oh. That's really nice. How do you get away with that?'

"Someone asked me once when I was in college, 'What do you care about: Life or Art?' It was a challenging question. Are you going to be an artist or are you going to have a nice life? I feel like I just walk the line in the middle. I would say I do sacrifice things for my work but I have a full life on the outside of it. In fact what I would like right now, what I have a real hunger for, is to sacrifice more of it. I want to have days where I wake up in the morning and I don't have anything else but work to think about. And I will have those days."

Alicia Bay Laurel, Musician, Floral Designer, Wedding Packager

At the age of nineteen, Alicia wrote the best-selling book *Living on the Earth*, for which she is listed in *Who's Who in America*. When we first interviewed Alicia, who is a longtime resident of Maui, she was a one-person business playing the guitar and singing—performing mostly jazz, pop standards, and Hawaiian music.

The founder and owner of Maui's only wedding-music agency, Alicia became much in demand for her performances at weddings. "I would learn particular songs for people, even if I didn't like the songs, because I wanted to provide exactly the service that was wanted. People like to hear songs they're familiar with, the songs they fell in love to."

In 1988, Alicia decided to combine her business acumen with her eye for design and her ear for music. She started A Wedding Made in Paradise, a wedding-package business that has coordinated over six hundred weddings for tourists coming to Maui. Her company specializes in the Vacation Wedding where "All you have to do is show up."

"I currently have a bookkeeper, a secretary, and a typist who comes in for approximately one hour at night. You can't really run a high-quality business like this with the volume I have without employees. When you are out putting on the wedding, someone has to answer the phone and be working on the details of the next wedding. I'm selling the business. I just decided I prefer doing it all myself. I'm going back to being a one-person business again! I'm an artist, floral designer, a writer, and a musician. I'm an overflowing fountain of creative stuff all the time. So I want to sell. Instead of the action of renting tuxedos and making sure they fit, and renting condominiums for people, and lining up photographers and videographers and all the other things a wedding planner does, I want to just go direct and sell my art, my music, and my writing. Now that I feel fully confident about running a business I'm going to sell my stuff. I've got half a dozen back-burner books I'd love to get started on. I've got so many different things I could do.

"Right now the real estate market is good. I've got the money and I'm going to go get myself a piece of land and do the sensible thing. Make myself a land base. When I did *Living on the Earth* I *was* living on the earth. I want to get back in the country. What I love most about my business is the creative part. I love doing the flowers and I love playing the music and I love writing my brochure and I enjoy going to the weddings and pulling them off. Especially the complicated ones, which I consider a big multimedia project. Here I am with music and different types of visual arts. The cake table is a visual art. I've pulled together all these diverse elements to make an artistic statement that lasts a couple of hours. It's really great when I can wow them and then they hug me and we are friends. That part of it is so nice. And it's spiritual and it's about love. Those elements in the wedding business are really wonderful. To do something that celebrates love and to celebrate it in a spiritual way is really great."

Paul Terry, Small-Business Advisor

Paul describes himself as someone who "helps, facilitates, and advises through a business-planning process that includes dealing with marketing strategies, financial projections and statements, and management issues such as personnel and time management." He considers what he does a small-business advisory service rather than a management-consulting business, because it truly concentrates on micro- or small businesses.

Paul Terry & Associates provides strategic support and planning for small businesses as well as for business enterprises that are run by nonprofits. He works with nonprofits with a social mission and small businesses that he feels are having a positive impact on the environment or the economy or are being democratically managed or run in an ethical, honest way. "I find that because of the screening system I have set up, I rarely get anyone who is doing a multilevel marketing business or a business that exists for profit alone. Ninety-five percent of my business is referrals from previous clients that I have worked with that fit that basic criteria of being openly, honestly, and democratically managed."

When Paul found it necessary to move his office out of the flat below his home and into a commercial area, he found another business to share the conference room and the facility support along with the kitchen and waiting room. Paul's local chamber of commerce awarded him a one-year contract that required complex administration. "I needed to do two things: (1) I needed to immediately build a larger stable of consultants and associates. I already had four associates that I have worked with regularly for ten years, but they weren't enough. I needed at least six more. And (2) I needed an administrative assistant to manage the billing and tracking. I justified having the employee because the money went directly to that employee and I couldn't have taken the contract that helped my business grow without her."

Paul has these words of wisdom about running a business: "Being successful is not just connected to making a lot of money. It's having an impact through services offered and products sold. The way a business is run is as important as the fruit it bears."

Bernard (Bear) Kamoroff, CPA, Author, Publisher

"Life isn't just earning money. Life is doing what you need and want to do with the world," states Bear. "Earning money should have some real value to the world. I think selling pet rocks is up the wazoo. There should be some use to what you are doing. It ought to be providing someone with something worthwhile and it ought to be quality."

Bear and his wife and four daughters live "in the middle of nowhere," and his office is in the barn behind their house. "I walk out back, and it's about a thirty-second walk to the office and there I am!"

In 1974, Kamoroff wrote and published *Small-Time Operator: How to Start Your Own Small Business, Keep Your Books, Pay Your Taxes and Stay Out of Trouble*. He has been selling a yearly updated version to book wholesalers, libraries, bookstores, mail-order distributors, individuals, and schools ever since. His operation involves a lot of mail and telephone orders but no direct contact or manufacturing because someone else prints his books for him. "You don't have to worry about appearances, what road you are on, or accessibility," he says. "If you have a telephone, a mailbox, and access to a UPS truck, you can run this type of business anywhere."

Bear has tradeskill in abundance and makes changes in his business only after careful consideration. In the past two years he has made three such changes. "I recently hired a subcontractor who runs a free-lance secretarial shipping service because I was tired of filling the book orders and being the mail person. I spent years doing everything myself, and I could afford to hire somebody, and I said, 'Why do it all myself?' I reached a point where I was ready to let some of my business go. It's time after all these years not to be a shipping clerk."

Small-Time Operator also has a new look. "In order to stay popular, a book has to stay with the times," Bear feels. "The cover of the book had a look that was appropriate for the time it came out but is no longer appropriate. It's still kind of cartoony, but it's a little more elegant. Now that we are in the nineties it's a little more eighties. Nice colors. I've gone to high quality laminated covers because the books travel a lot and require that kind of protection. It's on 100 percent recycled high-quality paper. And of course I'm doing all my typesetting myself now that I have a computer.

"The computer really made a big difference in the book business for me because I can do all my typesetting myself and get it just the way I want. The word-processing programs that are out on computers now can lay out pages beautifully. You don't need page-layout programs or any of that complicated stuff. I get the book pages and the ads and the brochures and everything exactly the way I want them."

Kate Bishop, Clothes Designer

Kate defines success as freedom. She says, "I like to remember the words of Christopher Marlowe: 'There is only one success: To be able to live your life in your own way.' I feel successful because I can make a living doing the work I like to do. Working for myself, I can set my own schedule, choose the people I want to work with, and live where I want—which is in the country, far from the hysteria of the fashion industry."

Kate believes so much in living life in her own way that she and her husband, Grady, and two young children took thirteen months off to sail down the west coast of Central America, through the Panama Canal, and up to Florida, where they hauled the boat out and put it in storage. "We don't know when the next long vacation will be," Kate says, "but we tend to work real hard and take real long vacations. The last time we went cruising we stayed out two and a half years."

Kate has been supporting herself by designing garments for eighteen years. She started out wholesaling to stores and found that many of her accounts didn't pay, which is, sadly, not unusual in her line of work. The overhead she had to cover included salaries for nine seamstresses. Ten years ago she decided to keep two retail accounts that paid on time and become a one-person business specializing in custom work. For Kate the transition was very smooth and one of the best decisions she ever made. "I dress women for the role of 'beautiful woman.' Most women that I know, including myself, spend most of their time in the role of either businesswoman or mother. These are satisfying roles in a lot of ways, but they are distinctly lacking in romance and glamour. So I provide the romance and glamour. When you go out in one of my dresses you don't talk about work or the kids."

Since her trip, Kate has made another significant change regarding her business. "We love traveling so much that when I returned from this trip I decided to try out a partnership where each of us runs a one-person business while the other is having a vacation—where the two of us run the business as one. That idea really appeals to me. My new partner and longtime friend, Jill, is a one-person business who does basically the same thing I do. Our work has become so similar in the time that I was gone that we would be competing with each other if we each pursued it individually.

"I'll still be doing what I've always done and she will do what she's always done and each of us will try to do the part that we do best. I think that from what I've seen in the last year it's a good time for me not to be risking a lot of money— not to have a lot invested in my business—not to be building a lot of inventory that I *hope* will sell. This is a time to produce *now* what I'm going to sell tomorrow. I'm still working out of my scrap boxes. I have lots and lots of scraps from ten years ago when I was producing a lot and creating a lot of waste. And so I'm producing smaller things, fewer of a kind. I'm being more creative and using my scraps and I really like that.

"My business has always been, and is becoming more and more, a forum to talk to women about whatever they are thinking about. So, if I just do whatever I feel like doing then the people who are attracted to it will be women I feel like talking to.

"I feel much more integrated with the people around me and with my family. My work is more integrated with my life than it ever has been. I am more interested in making things that people can just pick up and put on and walk away and feel comfortable instead of having to build a whole occasion around my work. When I see my friends I'm talking to them about my work, my kids, sailing. Everything that's important to me comes up, and my life and my work are just continuous now. There's not a strong division between them."

Bill Dale, Computer and Training Consultant

Bill's consulting company, WADALE Associates, is closely associated with other consultants who specialize in market research, finance, computer-based training, and so forth. Thanks to these trusted subcontractors, Bill's business can marshal forces larger than just one-person. This enables him to handle a wider variety of projects and gives him more credibility with the multinationals that are his biggest market.

WADALE Associates supplies consulting and training services to high-tech companies in the computer and information-systems marketplace. The focus is on strategic issues, management development, sales, and marketing.

As Bill explains, "My training modules are like tailor-made software developed from a set of standard modules. Generally 90 to 95 percent of each module is the same and is then word processed to fit the client. I do this by picking the relevant modules from my list and editing them by changing names and other details. This cuts down the amount of development needed and allows me to produce a high-quality product tailored to each client at a price that is closer to that of standard training. I win, the client wins!"

Although Bill feels that focusing on quality may decrease performance in the short term, he believes it is a necessary balancing act for the long-term survival of the business. "If you don't do a quality job, your reputation will suffer and you will lose business. It's ultimately self-defeating to cut corners on quality. Consulting and training are intangibles, and if you don't project an image that promises quality, then people will think you can't do the job. This is particularly important before you get to know someone. Quality and high standards of performance go hand in hand. I don't like doing a job unless it is a quality one."

Recently Bill disconnected his modem because "when something comes by way of electronic mail there is a tendency to reply immediately." He feels that some things require more thought than instant communication allows. Instead of spending twenty minutes contemplating how to carefully reply, he tends to make instant decisions, which he sometimes regrets. Bill now prefers to write a letter, phone or, even better, meet face-to-face with clients. Because his business is international, Bill is very conscious of the world going through what he calls a "step-change," or paradigm shift. He has been working with business transformation, process improvement, business reengineering, mass customization, time-based management, and other ideas to help people during the transition. "You are either on the wave, or in danger of being drowned by the wave," he believes. "Cutting back older employees because they are paid more and thinking of the short-term is flawed and has not only lowered the quality of work by decreasing loyalty to the employer, but has caused a lot of people to just think of themselves rather than working as a team. There is no longer much value left in the traditional organizational structure, and customers will get the best quality by dealing with a one-person business."

Roger Pritchard, Socially Responsible Financial Advisor

"If you're doing what you love to do, a substantial part of your life should be tax deductible. One of the strongest elements for me in my success has been living simply and stepping out of the consumer economy as a goal of my business. I'm not in business to push myself hard and have a high standard of living.

"I've learned that my business is both service and making a living. And in fact, making a living is easier through service than doing anything else because I'm happy doing it, and therefore the quality of what I do is high. People like it and tell their friends and their friends become clients. It's a system that works." Roger's consulting work includes small-business advising, personal financial management, and what's now called socially responsible investing—with special emphasis on community economic development.

"I think it's very important to break the stereotype that you get an idea, you develop it, you turn it into a business plan, and off you go. I think that's fairly unusual. I think that's a minority of people who do that. Knowing the truth that you learn by trying and failing and trying again is really important.

"I've had to stay on my toes all the time because it's absolutely true that from year to year and even quarter to quarter there are shifts. One quarter when the economy was going downhill I quickly learned about bankruptcy and started to look at 'right living in tough times' and 'living simply' and began consulting with people on that. I always try to provide good information to support people in whatever cycle the economy is in. Not to just respond. I can make money when things are getting economically tough as well as when things are getting better.

"I was able, starting over a year ago, to give up my car and to rely on my bicycle and mass transit. That is to say, I decided not to accept any clients that weren't prepared to have me show up on my bicycle with a backpack as a business consultant. It worked. It also brings me back to my roots, because growing up I always rode my bike to school from when I was about twelve years old.

"I have a cape in the winter. I'm totally prepared. After all, I came from England. *Not* riding in the rain is unusual. Clients also come to me. That really helps.

"I think it's quite easy to be ideologically pure and rather sloppy in practice. I think it's an important discipline to make sure you review on a regular basis whether your business practices are consistent with the values and ideology that you're putting out. I pay attention on a regular basis to what I'm using and how I'm doing it across the board. The most dramatic example in the last year is the bicycle and restructuring my business around biking and public transit. I use recycled paper."

Patti Breitman, Book Agent

As a book agent, Patti Breitman acts as an advocate and spokesperson for authors. She helps them fine-tune their proposals and manuscripts and presents their books to the appropriate editors and publishers. Patti plays the role of a business manager so that the author-editor relationship can stay creative and focused.

"Being an agent is a vehicle for my life purpose. My goal in life is to proselytize about vegetarianism and to get the whole world to become vegetarian. Being an agent helps me, because most of the books I represent are in that field. I represent a lot of leaders in the field. My goal is to publish so many books that when you go to find a cookbook the odds are the one you pick is going to have more vegetarian recipes than meat recipes.

"A lot of the books I represent have to do with human potential and human growth, with getting the world to be a little bit more gentle and a little bit more healthy and a little bit more calm. And even if they don't mention vegetarianism they are about being happier, being more fulfilled.

"My husband once asked, 'What would you do if we didn't have to work, did not have to earn a dime?' I said I wouldn't do anything differently. My life is what I want to be doing. And the money and the agenting is all secondary. It's nice that I can make a living doing it, but I'd have found a way to do this even if it weren't a career. In my spare time I write a newsletter for vegetarians in Marin. I run a support group that meets every month. I'm doing it anyway.

"It's just this natural instinct in me to want to share vegetarianism with everyone. I've always been like that. I was always the cheerleader type. If I discover something the world has to hear about it. That's why I was in publicity. So now I've discovered all these people—it's not just me—there are physicians all over the country saying it's the best way to eat. And there are animal-rights people saying fish suffer when there is a hook in their mouth. I'm just their voice. I'm trying to help them get a louder voice, helping them find a platform for their message. Those are the kinds of books that, if I were a writer, I'd be writing. I love that I can be their cheerleader and get it out in the world and sing its praises and dance about it and make noise about it and make sure they are heard."

RESOURCES

Brodsky, Bart, and Janet Geis. *Finding Your Niche: Marketing Your Professional Service.* Berkeley: Community Resource Institute Press, 1992.

Hawken, Paul. *Growing A Business.* New York: Simon & Schuster, 1988.

Kamoroff, Bernard. *Small-Time Operator*, 17th ed. Laytonville, Calif.: Bell Springs Publishing, 1992.

Phillips, Michael, and Salli Rasberry. *Honest Business.* New York: Random House, 1981.

2

Bookkeeping

Bookkeeping is the most important part of any business. The first business system to put in place is your books. Most people focus on marketing first, but this is a dangerous strategy. Why? Because almost anything you do to promote your business will work. And the better you are at promotion the more business you can get. But without smoothly functioning financial and organizational systems in place, the increase in volume can swamp you and put you out of business overnight. The worst possible response would be to provide lower-grade services or products because you are unable to keep up with the demand. So focus on your financial and organizational systems first.

In many thriving one-person businesses, the only bookkeeping is a checkbook and a file folder with receipts. In our experience, businesses with such casual bookkeeping practices are usually unable to grow to an efficient size or respond effectively to changes in market demand. They also operate without the elegance and perfection that is readily achievable in a one-person business. The level of skill needed for bookkeeping in a one-person business is low by any business standards. Although we recommend that you use the simplest method you can, even the simplest requires some thought, care, and attention. In this chapter we talk about basic bookkeeping methods and tools, inventory records, and accounting principles—

and about the importance of deciding whether to do your own books or hire an accountant.

BUSINESS—A SET OF MEASURABLE EXCHANGES

From its historic meaning of an exchange between friends, neighbors, or tribes to its modern sense encompassing the interactions of giant corporations and governments, the word business expresses the idea of a set of measurable exchanges. Contained within the historical meaning of business is the idea that the exchanges will be mutually beneficial. This idea can still be found in many small businesses, and it is the cornerstone of any successful one-person business venture. The measure of this benefit is the money (or some other standard of value) that is received and spent in making these exchanges.

Business does not have to involve money, although most people have forgotten this and equate the two. Money is a yardstick of business: the measurement tool that indicates how well or how poorly the exchanges are faring. But it is not the only measurement tool, and the upswelling of private barter systems in recent years, as well as the continual exchange of goods and services under the table by many businesses and individuals, testify to this fact.

In addition, an increasing awareness of environmental and social issues in business has lead to the development of the new field of *social auditing*. Social auditing is concerned with observing and reporting the social and environmental impacts of business exchanges. Two excellent sources of information on social auditing are *Rating America's Corporate Conscience* (Redding, Mass.: Addison-Wesley, 1987), put out by the Council on Economic Priorities, and *EcoManagement* (San Francisco: Berrett-Koehler, 1993), sponsored by the Elmwood Institute.

For any business, the comprehensive and objective way of measuring success known as bookkeeping is essential. Bear Kamoroff, a mail-order publisher, is also a certified public accountant. He speaks from experience when he says, "You've got to know bookkeeping well, and it's simple to learn. There is nothing simpler in the world; it just sounds mysterious. Bookkeeping is just keeping track of money coming in and money going out, the money owed you and the money you owe, and how much is in the bank. That's it."

Book designer Clifford Burke concurs, and stresses that bookkeeping is the best way to eliminate money as a problem. "I'm becoming more committed to having my books in order. Although I refuse to put money as my first priority, I've come to see that the best way to keep it in its proper place is to keep track of it, and that doing this doesn't need to take a lot of time. Good bookkeeping really helps. I believe in getting your books right and keeping them right. It doesn't mean you have to be any different about the way you do anything else. Business is money, after all. It's not just for fun, and it's not just for good works in the world. It really is to make a living."

Eileen Mulligan, a landscape gardener, doesn't like keeping books at all, but she understands the importance of it. "I do my own monthly bookkeeping even though I hate it. That way I know how much money is going through my books. At first I didn't know what I was doing, but now my bookkeeping system is pretty clear. It's straightforward enough that I can deal with the IRS, and that is a major consideration. I have an intuitive sense of how much money is coming in and from where. I still look over my records once a month, however, because I must always be on top of how much each client is costing. I resent spending the time on putting all those numbers together and moving papers around and keeping them in files. I sit there and look out the window, and it's a nice day and I'd rather be doing something else. But I continue because I feel that organized records and bookkeeping are absolutely essential. They're the one thing that will make a business fail or succeed."

Alexandra Hart, a desktop publisher, keeps thorough records on all aspects of her business, but her systems are quite simple. "I keep careful track through a checkbook system. At the end of the year, I put all my figures into the ledger. I use a simple double-entry system. I don't construct a profit/loss statement. When I'm really concerned about how things are changing, I do a simple cash-flow chart for the next three months. Then I can see how everything is shifting a little. Redoing the cash-flow and seeing how it has changed is really helpful to me.

"I keep records project by project," Alexandra continues. "In many cases I have to estimate costs ahead of time. I note down the client's name, our agreements, my billing quotes, and whether something will be farmed out. I record the dates and places I go and a description of what I do for the hours billed. I record if I spent money on a typesetter, etc. At the end of the job, if I have underestimated, I eat it and get better the next time. If my estimate was off because of the client, then I try to communicate that and change the amount billed. I keep six to eight income columns in my double-entry system, and I can see that my workshop line has no entries or that my writing line is bringing in more. Once a year I look at what works."

BOOKKEEPING BASICS—MONEY IN, MONEY OUT

In business, your books are the map of your territory. You can wander around in the territory without a map, but you will make much more intelligent management decisions about which way to go if you have a good one.

Single Entry or Double Entry?

The two common forms of bookkeeping used by small businesses are single entry and double entry. Most one-person businesses need only single-entry bookkeeping. But if your business has a large inventory (such as an import-export company), if you are a manufacturing business with equipment (such as a one-person cosmetics

The Importance of Keeping Good Financial Records

Bernard Kamoroff, "Bear" to his friends, is one of our personal heroes. He speaks eloquently on behalf of being a one-person business and does a good job of running one. Because he is an accountant and the author of the best-selling *Small-Time Operator*, we think it is especially useful to quote him on keeping good financial records:

I keep track of all my expenses on a simple expense ledger. These are broken down by categories that are important to me and my tax return. I keep track of total income, of people who owe me money, of bills I have to pay, and of how much cash there is in the bank account to make sure it's enough. It's very simple bookkeeping. My total bookkeeping takes me in the neighborhood of two days of work a year. Maybe three at the very most.

I recommend that people do their books as regularly as possible so that paperwork doesn't back up. This is real important. The problem with bookkeeping is that when the paper backs up, it becomes a nightmare. An hour a day or whatever it takes, do it so it won't pile up.

The most important information I need to know is who owes me money. I keep track of that constantly. I know who owes me money and keep a watch on it because my business involves a lot of direct credit. Many of my customers call on the phone and get thirty-day terms or ninety-day terms or whatever. Some of them pay regularly and some need to be nudged. There are a lot of people who need to be nudged in order for me to get paid. I don't like that, but I've learned to live with it because they are good people and that's just their way of doing business.

Another reason for looking at my books is to keep track of my inventory. I basically am selling one book, so I don't have a lot of products. Since I've been watching sales each month for several years and I know how long it takes to reprint, I know from experience when it's time to reorder.

People need to find some way of keeping track of their inventory —what they have, what they don't have, when they need to add to it. Some people don't need records; they can do it just by looking around. Some people need very elaborate inventory records, especially if they are manufacturing something or putting a lot of different raw materials together. They need records so they can figure out how much their product really costs to produce. If they don't keep track, they'll wind up not being able to figure out what to sell their product for.

manufacturer), or if you have a number of investors, you should consider a double-entry system. It provides arithmetic cross-checking that will keep your investors happy and your own confidence high with respect to the figures that your checkbook and cash-receipts records generate. Bear Kamoroff explains it this way in *Small-Time Operator*:

> Double entry is a complete bookkeeping system that provides cross checks and automatic balancing of the books, that minimizes errors, and that transforms business bookkeeping from a part-time nuisance into a full-time occupation. In double-entry bookkeeping, every transaction requires two separate entries, a debit and a credit. These terms originated in double-entry bookkeeping, along with the expression "balancing the books": total debits must equal total credits for the books to be "in balance."

Single entry differs from this, as its name suggests, by only requiring one entry per transaction. There are no debits or credits to deal with. The trade-off is that you lose the error-checking of double entry. But for most one-person businesses, the number of transactions is so small that double entry is just overkill.

Cash versus Accrual

For either double-entry or single-entry bookkeeping, there are two methods of keeping track of the cash coming into and going out of your business: cash and accrual.

You are using the *cash* method of accounting if you make an entry in your books only when you actually receive some income or pay for some expense. You are using the accrual method if you offer your customers or clients credit (that is, the opportunity to receive a product or service and to pay for it later) and you enter that income into your books before you actually get it, or if you buy supplies or inventory on credit and enter the cost into your books before paying for it.

Any business with a physical inventory of products or parts is required by the IRS to use the accrual method to keep track of its inventory. This means counting the inventory on hand at year end, even if it has not been paid for yet. Aside from this requirement you can choose to use either method, but once you have begun using the accrual method, you cannot go back to the cash method without filing a special application for a change in accounting method, which must be approved by the IRS.

Regardless of what the IRS requires, if you are a business that buys and sells a product inventory, you should use the accrual method. Even if you are a professional-service business, strongly consider using the accrual method, since it will give you a more accurate picture of the financial condition of your business.

Chart of Accounts

All small businesses that are not incorporated are required to file a Schedule C: Statement of Profit or Loss with the IRS at the end of each year. In keeping track of your financial information, a good place to start is with the questions you need to answer on the Schedule C. However, bookkeeping is not intended just to answer questions for the IRS, but to answer your questions too.

The so-called *chart of accounts* is an organized way to keep track of all the questions you might want to ask yourself about the financial condition of your business. Following is a chart recommended by the American Institute of Certified Public Accountants; you can adapt it for your own use (see figure 2.1). Don't be thrown by the numbers, which are simply meant to help you in making entries in your books. If you like, you can use words or abbreviations of the actual categories, such as those shown from the computer software program *Quicken*, in figure 2.2.

It is not as important that you make a chart of accounts as that you make a list of questions. Among these questions might be some as simple as, "How much rent do I pay every year?" Rent is a question you need to answer for the IRS. But you might have other questions as well: "What are my three top sources of income?", "How much do I spend on my newsletter each issue?", "How much do the sleeves for my videotape product cost me each month?", and so forth.

You can go back to the original invoices and receipts any time you wish and figure out these answers. It would be much easier, however, if you had made a category in your checkbook, or a column in your check journal, labeled Newsletter. You could have created three categories in your income record for your top three sources of income, say, Consulting, Teaching, and Book Sales. And in your expense record you could have created a category called Cost of Goods Sold, breaking it down into Videotape Sleeves, Videotapes, and any other costs related directly to the assembling of your videotape products.

Fig. 2.1 Chart of Accounts

	Account No.
BALANCE SHEET (Accounts 1 through 500)	
ASSETS (1-300)	
Cash (1-50)	
Petty Cash (Cash on Hand)	11
Cash in Bank – General (Regular Bank Account)	21
Cash in Bank – Payroll (Payroll Bank Account)	31
Receivables From Others (51-100)	
Notes Receivable	51
Accounts Receivable – Customers	61
Accounts Receivable – Others	71
Inventories (101-150)	
Inventory – Goods for Sale	101
Inventory – Supplies	121

<u>*Account No.*</u>

Prepaid Expenses (151-200)

Prepaid Advertising	151
Prepaid Insurance	161
Prepaid Interest	171
Prepaid Rent	181

Property and Equipment (201-250)

Land	201
Buildings	211
Buildings – Allowance for Depreciation	212
Automobiles and Trucks	216
Automobiles and Trucks – Allowance for Depreciation	217
Furniture and Office Equipment	221
Furniture and Office Equipment – Allowance for Depreciation	222
Machinery	226
Machinery – Allowance for Depreciation	227
Tools	231
Tools – Allowance for Depreciation	232
Leasehold Improvements – (Rented Property Improvements)	246
Leasehold Improvements – Allowance for Amortization	247

Miscellaneous Assets (251-300)

Organization Expenses (Business Starting Costs)	251
Deposits (Advance Payments)	261

LIABILITIES (301-450)

Notes and Amounts Payable to Others (301-350)

Notes Payable – Short Term	301
Accounts Payable (Bills Payable)	311
Sales Taxes Payable	321
FICA Tax Withheld	331
Federal Income Taxes Withheld	332
State Income Taxes Withheld	333

Expenses Owed to Others (351-400)

Accrued Wages (Wages Owed)	351
Accrued Commissions (Commissions Owed)	356
Accrued Interest (Interest Owed)	361
Accrued Federal Unemployment Taxes (Fed. Unemployment Taxes Owed)	371
Accrued State Unemployment Taxes (State Unemployment Taxes Owed)	372
Accrued Real Estate Taxes (Real Estate Taxes Owed)	381
Accrued Referal Income Taxes (Federal Income Taxes Owed)	391
Accrued State Income Taxes (State Income Taxes Owed)	392

Account No.

Long-Term Obligations (401-450)
  Notes Payable – Long-Term   401
  Mortgages Payable   411

OWNERSHIP EQUITY (451-500)

*Capital Investment (Investment in Business)   451
**Capital Stock (Stock Issued)   461
*Drawings (Cash Used Personally)   481
 Retained Earnings (Profit Not Spent)   491

  *For use only by sole owners or partners
  **For use only by corporations

PROFIT OR LOSS STATEMENT (Accounts 501-999)

Sales and Other Income (501-550)
  Sales of Merchandise   501
  Sales Returns and Allowances   502
  Cash Discounts Allowed (Discounts to Customers)   503
  Service Charges   511
  Rental Income   521
  Cash Discounts Taken (Discounts from Suppliers)   531
  Miscellaneous Income   541

Cost of Goods Sold (551-600)
  Cost of Merchandise Sold   551
  Freight on Purchases   561

Cost of Business Operations (601-700)
  Wages   601
  Labor from Agencies   602
  Supplies   611
  Tools   612
  Rental of Equipment   621
  Repairs to Equipment and Machinery   631
  Repairs to Trucks   632
  Truck Maintenance (Gas and Oil for Trucks)   641

Selling Expenses (701-750)
  Advertising   701
  Automobile Expenses – Salesmen   711
  Commissions   721
  Entertainment Expenses   731
  Travel Expenses   741

<u>*Account No.*</u>

Administration Expenses (General Expenses) (751-800)
Salaries	751
Office Supplies	761
Postage	762
Telephones	763
Dues & Subscriptions	764
Insurance – Miscellaneous	771
Group Insurance	772
Workmen's Compensation Insurance	773
Automobile Expense	781
Professional Services	786
Bad Debts	791
Interest	796

Miscellaneous Expenses (801-850)

Building Expenses (851-900)
Rent	851
Repairs to Building	861
Utilities	871

Depreciation (901-950)
Depreciation – Buildings	911
Depreciation – Automobiles	916
Depreciation – Furniture and Office Equipment	921
Depreciation – Machinery	926
Depreciation – Tools	931
Depreciation – Rented Property Improvements	946

Taxes (951-999)
FICA Taxes	951
Unemployment Taxes	952
Real Estate Taxes	961
Miscellaneous Taxes	962
Federal Income Taxes	991
State Income Taxes	992

Income and Expense Records

Any bookkeeping system has two basic parts: a *record of income* and a *record of expenses*. There are many different ways of keeping these records, but we will talk about a simple way that saves time and still provides the information you need to make day-to-day and long-term decisions.

Fig. 2.2   Chart of Accounts from the *Quicken* Computer Bookkeeping Program

---

Income Categories

Name	Description
Gr Sales	Gross Sales
Other Inc	Other Income
Rent Income	Rent Income

Expense Categories

Name	Description
Ads	Advertising
Car	Car & Truck
Commission	Commissions
Freight	Freight
Int Paid	Interest Paid
L&P Fees	Legal & Professional Fees
Late Fees	Late Payment Fees
Office	Office Expenses
Rent Paid	Rent Paid
Repairs	Repairs
Returns	Returns & Allowances
Taxes	Taxes
Travel	Travel Expenses
Wages	Wages & Job Credits

Tracking Income   A record of income is commonly called the *income ledger*, *sales journal*, or *cash receipts journal*. At the very least, you must enter the date, a description of the transaction (such as the check number and customer name), the amount of the transaction, and an indication of the category it goes into from your chart of accounts.

With some creative thinking, you could even adapt a simple check ledger, like the one that you get with the checks you order from your bank (see figure 2.3). Or you can order deposit slips in what is called a "two-up," or "side-by-side," format, slip a piece of carbon paper in, and make your record that way (see figure 2.4). If you want to go an extra step and use actual ledger paper, the accompanying illustration shows what your page might look like (see figure 2.5).

Tracking Expenses   For expenses you need exactly the same information: date, description, amount, and category. Again a simple checkbook ledger from your bank can serve this function (see figure 2.3), or you can have a more elaborate system, such as a *cash disbursements journal*, which allows you to summarize the most important items by "spreading" them in columns to the right of the basic information (see figure. 2.5).

Fig. 2.3 Checkbook Ledger

PLEASE BE SURE TO **DEDUCT** ANY PER CHECK CHARGES OR SERVICE CHARGES THAT MAY APPLY TO YOUR ACCOUNT

NUMBER	DATE	CHECKS ISSUED TO OR DESCRIPTION OF DEPOSIT	(−) AMOUNT OF CHECK	✓ T	(−) CHECK FEE (IF ANY)	(+) AMOUNT OF DEPOSIT	BALANCE
							3174 96
364	2/12	TO/FOR Sol Columbus / Deposit on Flyers [Printing]	110 00				BAL 3064 96
365	2/20	TO/FOR U.S. Post Office / Stamps for flyers [Postage]	97 50				BAL 2967 46
366	2/24	TO/FOR Sol Columbus / Balance on Flyers [Printing]	110 00				BAL 2857 46
367	2/28	TO/FOR Tom Hargadon / March ofc Rent [RENT]	200 00				BAL 2657 46
	3/1	TO/FOR SF SPCA ck #4188 / IV #4301 [Consulting]				600 00	600 00 BAL 3257 46
	3/2	TO/FOR Gail Grimes ck #304 / Books [Book Sales]				34 57	
	3/2	TO/FOR Terry McHugh ck #412 / OPB Workshop [Tuition]				140 00	454 57 BAL
	3/2	TO/FOR Gail Grimes ck #303 / OPB wkshop [Tuition]				140 00	BAL
	3/2	TO/FOR Joan Taylor ck #314 / OPB wkshop [Tuition]				140 00	BAL 3712 03
368	3/3	TO/FOR Whole Earth Access / Ans Machine [ofc exp]	153 74				BAL 3558 29
		TO/FOR					BAL
		TO/FOR					BAL
		TO/FOR					BAL

REMEMBER TO RECORD AUTOMATIC PAYMENTS / DEPOSITS ON DATE AUTHORIZED.

Many people use credit cards to make purchases. This can be convenient, but it can also get out of control if you neglect to post credit card receipts in your expense record. We recommend that you not use credit cards for business purposes. Then they won't be a problem, and you won't have to pay the high interest rates. If you must use credit cards, keep a record of your purchases just as though you had paid cash. If you record these purchases in the same ledger as your actual cash expenditures, give them a separate page or column, or otherwise clearly distinguish them

Fig. 2.4   **Deposit Slips**

DEPOSIT TICKET

NOTICE: A HOLD FOR UNCOLLECTED FUNDS MAY BE PLACED ON FUNDS DEPOSITED BY CHECK OR SIMILAR INSTRUMENTS. THIS COULD DELAY YOUR ABILITY TO WITHDRAW SUCH FUNDS. THE DELAY, IF ANY, WOULD NOT EXCEED THE PERIOD OF TIME PERMITTED BY LAW.

ADDRESS _____

Date ____ *who* ____ *check #*

		DOLLARS	CENTS
CURRENCY			
COIN			
CHECKS LIST SEPARATELY			
1	*4B*		*1 19*
2	*Ten Speed*	*194*	*05*
3	*Noreen*		*2 42*
4			
5			
6			
7			
8			
9			
10			
11			
12			
13			
14			
15			
16			
17			
18			
19			
20			
21			
22			
23			
24			
25			
26			
27			
28			
29			
30			
31			
32			
33			
34			
35			

3/16
3/18
3/20

⑈⑆⑆⑆⑆⑆ (routing) ⑈ ⑆ ⑆ ⑆ ⑆ ⑆ ⑆ ⑆ ⑆

TOTAL DEPOSIT

CLAUDE F. WHITMYER

TOTAL
PLEASE ENTER TOTAL HERE

DEPOSIT TICKET

NOTICE: A HOLD FOR UNCOLLECTED FUNDS MAY BE PLACED ON FUNDS DEPOSITED BY CHECK OR SIMILAR INSTRUMENTS. THIS COULD DELAY YOUR ABILITY TO WITHDRAW SUCH FUNDS. THE DELAY, IF ANY, WOULD NOT EXCEED THE PERIOD OF TIME PERMITTED BY LAW.

ADDRESS _____

DATE _____

		DOLLARS	CENTS
CURRENCY			
COIN			
CHECKS LIST SEPARATELY			
1	*11-24*	*18*	*77*
2	*90-0049-4*	*2000*	*00*
3	*11-24*	*120*	*00*
4			
5			
6			
7			
8			
9			
10			
11			
12			
13			
14			
15			
16			
17			
18			
19			
20			
21			
22			
23			
24			
25			
26			
27			
28			
29			
30			
31			
32			
33			
34			
35			

⑈⑆⑆⑆⑆⑆ (routing) ⑈ ⑆ ⑆ ⑆ ⑆ ⑆ ⑆ ⑆ ⑆

TOTAL DEPOSIT *2307 77*

CLAUDE F. WHITMYER

TOTAL *2307 77*
PLEASE ENTER TOTAL HERE

Fig. 2.5   Income and Expense Ledger

		1		2	3	4	5	6	
	CK					BAL FORWARD 3174.96	ACCOUNT	AMOUNT	
	NO	DATE	CK AMT	DEP AMT					
1	Sol Columbus	364	2/12	11000		306496	Printing	11000	1
2	US POST OFFICE	365	2/20	9750		296746	Postage	9750	2
3	Sol Columbus	366	2/24	11000		285746	Printing	11000	3
4	Tom Hargadon	367	2/28	20000		265746	Rent	20000	4
5									5
6	SF SPCA		3/1	60000	60000	325746	Consulting	60000	6
7	Gail Grimes		3/2	3457			Booksales	3457	7
8	Terry McHugh		3/2	19000	45457		Tuition	14000	8
9	Gail Grimes		3/2	14000			Tuition	14000	9
10	Joan Taylor		3/2	14000		371203	Tuition	14000	10
11	Whole Earth Access	368	3/3	16374		355829	OFC EXP	16374	11
12									12
13							SUMMARY		13
14									14
15							INCOME		15
16							CONSULTING	60000	16
17							BOOKS	3457	17
18							TUITION	42000	18
19								105457	19
20							EXPENSES		20
21							Printing	22000	21
22							Postage	9750	22
23							Rent	20000	23
24							OFC EXP	16374	24
25								61124	25
26									26
27							PROFIT	44333	27

as credit card purchases. This way you will avoid entering them twice (*double posting*) when you make the actual payment to the credit card company. Another simple approach is to pay the entire balance due on each monthly statement (thus avoiding interest charges), allocating the various purchases to their proper categories in the spreadsheet columns of your cash disbursements journal.

Preprinted Ledgers   Most office supply stores sell simple bookkeeping systems that you can use by filling in the blanks. The two most common are Ekonomik and Dome. These come in formats that are laid out for specific businesses—beauty parlor, gas station, retail store, real estate agent, construction firm, and so on—one of which may be suitable for your business. The main difference between them is that the Dome format is vertical, while Ekonomik's is horizontal. As most people find it easier to read numbers laid out across the page, we prefer the Ekonomik system. But either system will make your bookkeeping life much simpler.

One-Write Systems   A one-write check-writing system (also known as a pegboard system) can save a lot of time. With the writing of each check, all records that you need are made. It consists of special checks that have a strip of carbon on the back, about ½-inch wide, running the length of the check. You place the check on your check ledger page and fill it out. As you write, a carbon copy is being made in the ledger. At the end of a page or the end of a month, you simply get out the adding machine and total up the columns for a summary of your expenditures for a certain period. It takes a little practice to keep the checks lined up with the correct line of the ledger, but before long you will find yourself spending half as much time on check writing. Most of the vendors that sell these systems also offer window envelopes. If you use these, after filling out the name and address lines on your one-write check, you can just slip it in a window envelope and mail it.

Most one-write systems provide areas for deposits and running cash balances. Many businesses use these journals as their entire bookkeeping system. They give the totals to their tax preparer at the end of the year, thus avoiding the marathon of pain that otherwise awaits them in April.

Systems for keeping track of clients and vendors are also available. If you write more than thirty checks each month but you are not ready to move up to a computer program, one-write is the system to use.

Computerized Bookkeeping   There are many easy-to-understand and easy-to-use computerized bookkeeping programs available on the market today. But if you have a manual system that is working and doesn't require much time, you have to ask yourself "Why bother?" The big disadvantage of computerized bookkeeping is that installing, customizing, and learning to use even the simplest of computerized bookkeeping programs can eat up more time than you can ever imagine. The major advantage, of course, is that once the data has been carefully entered you can create many different types of reports with just a few keystrokes. The key words here are *data has been carefully entered*. In the computer world they have a telltale acronym: GIGO, or "Garbage In, Garbage Out."

If you are someone who loves machines or if you have a lot of transactions in your one-person business, you may want to consider computerizing your bookkeeping. We will talk more about this in Chapter 8.

INVENTORY

For a service business with over $500 worth of office supplies, and for any business that sells a product, it makes good sense to keep a written record of supplies and products on hand. If there are few items, you need only count them periodically and write the number down. You will quickly note any discrepancies between what is supposed to be on hand and what you counted. But when you have more than a dozen items, it helps to create a more systematic method of tracking your inventory.

Manufacturer's Inventory

Because their profit margins are so much smaller, manufacturers need a different level of detail in their inventory-control systems than retailers or distributors. Many manufacturing businesses are seasonal and have alternating peak periods of sales demand followed by slow periods. Sales trends must be carefully monitored so that there is just enough inventory on hand to meet the minimum production-cycle requirements. This is tricky, which is why it's important to build inventory systems into the business from the start.

Let's say that you sell a mustache grooming kit, made up of mustache wax, a mustache comb, a high-quality pair of trimming scissors, and the packaging materials. You know that you can sell five thousand units for Christmas. With a good inventory tracking system, you would know from previous years that most of the orders for the Christmas retail season are received by July. You would also know that you need to order the primary ingredients, beeswax and fragrance, sixty days before you want to begin assembling the order. The bottles and caps need forty-five days, and the comb and scissors might require thirty days of lead time. The labels also take thirty days. You need two weeks to put together the five thousand kits. So you must order wax and fragrance for delivery in early August; bottles and caps for mid-August; comb, scissors, and labels for early September; and so on. Notice that you have allowed yourself less than two weeks of grace in the event that something goes wrong.

Clearly, this is a complicated set of variables. To add to the complication, you have only two other peaks, neither as big as Christmas, but each big enough to merit attention: Valentine's Day and Father's Day. You have to repeat the same evaluation and staggered ordering process for those two holidays. You know how many kits you might sell this year, from the sales records you kept last year and previous years. You know the quantity of beeswax, fragrance, bottles, and labels you have on hand from the inventory tally sheets you completed last week. You know the lead times on additional ingredients and packaging from your accounts payable records. You know how long it takes to assemble the kits from the work record you keep, or from the invoices of the subcontractors you hired to do the assembly last time. With all of these pieces, you can foresee your needs and make management decisions based on what has worked in the past.

Retail and Distributor Inventory

Retailers and distributors, on the other hand, can make purchasing decisions based on a much simpler set of records. Their profit margins are larger than those of manufacturers, they carry many more items for sale, and they often see small changes in the inventory count on any given item. The tracking method most commonly used by retailers and distributors is to count the inventory every three months, keeping a paper record of subtractions from and additions to inventory during the intervening months. Every time the inventory is counted, the actual number can be compared with the paper number to see what has been lost or broken, which is called "shrinkage." Beyond this record, rates of sale can be made on an item-by-item basis.

Whether yours is a manufacturing, retail, or wholesale business, the general organization of your primary inventory record can be something like that shown in figure 2.6.

FINANCIAL STATEMENTS

Summarizing your bookkeeping and inventory records into financial statements will give you important information about the condition of your business. The two most common financial statements are the *income statement* and the *balance sheet*. Because they are drawn from your written record of the money going into and out of your business, they are not difficult to create. By preparing and reviewing financial statements regularly you can get the answers to such questions as, "How profitable is this business?", "What do the business assets look like?", "What changes have taken place between months or years?", "Which costs are a problem?", and "How much is owed on debts of various kinds?"

For efficient use of your financial statements, put them on the wall where you can refer to them easily and regularly. This is the best way to gain a real grasp of what is happening in the day-to-day operation of the business. At the same time you will begin to see the weekly, monthly or yearly patterns unique to your business.

The Income Statement

An income statement (sometimes called a *profit and loss statement*, or simply a P&L) shows the sources of income, the costs and expenses of running the business, and the amount of profit or loss left over (see figure 2.7).

Fig. 2.6   Inventory Worksheet

INVENTORY WORKSHEET							
DEPARTMENT:[1]							
VENDOR:[2]							
TAKEN BY:[3]							
DATE:[3]							
CALCULATED BY:[4]							
ITEM[5]	Our Cost[6]	Beginning Inventory[7]	Goods Received[8]	Ending Inventory[9]	Extension[10]	Rate of Sale[11]

To use this worksheet, fill in the blanks as follows:

1. This field is used if you want to track different sources of income or to make ordering easier. A grocery store might have dairy, dry goods, meat, liquor, and so forth, as departments. A wood-stove distributor might have stoves, stovepipe, and fireplace accessories.
2. For ordering purposes, you should keep a separate inventory sheet for each vendor. Use this field to tell them apart.
3. Inventory is such a big job that often you will need help to make the job easier. Whoever does the actual physical counting of the items listed on each sheet should sign here. This person should also fill in the date that the count is made.
4. Whoever uses the adding machine to make the calculations in the Extension and Rate of Sale boxes should sign off here.
5. This field describes the inventory item. You can use the vendors' ordering codes and/or make up descriptions that make sense to you.
6. This field is the unit price that your supplier charges you for this item.

7. This field is for recording how many units of the item were in inventory when you completed last period's inventory calculations. Each beginning inventory is always equal to each previous period's ending inventory.
8. This field is for recording how many units you received of each item during the period since the last inventory calculations.
9. This field is for recording the number of units of each item that is counted on this date.
10. This field is for recording the product of multiplying Field 9 by Field 6. This product is the value of the inventory on hand at the time of counting.
11. This is the field for recording how many units you sold during the last period. You will add the figures in Fields 7 and 8 and subtract the figure in Field 9 from that sum. The rate of sale equals beginning inventory plus goods received during the period, minus ending inventory.

The Balance Sheet

A balance sheet shows what the business *owns* and what it *owes*. What you own is reported in various categories, such as Cash in Bank, Accounts Receivable, Furniture & Fixtures, and so forth. These are known as *assets*. What you owe is reported in categories such as Accounts Payable, or Long-Term Notes Payable. These are known as *liabilities*. The balance sheet also shows your claim against the business as its owner. This claim is known as *owner's equity*.

The balance sheet is connected to the income statement by the fact that owner's equity increases and decreases by the amount of profit or loss that the business makes over time.

Other Financial Statements

Two other statements can be useful to small businesses. A cash-flow statement shows all the money flowing into and out of the business and the use it was put to. It is similar to the income statement, except that it goes a step further to include additional capital or loans, that is, money brought into the business that is not income from sales. It also shows all *capital expenditures* (on furniture, equipment, and so on) as well as *owner's draw* (the money taken from the business by the owner). The cash-flow statement is discussed in detail in Chapter 3.

A *statement of retained earnings* shows how much the net income was, what portion was taken out or distributed, what portion was used by the business, and how much is still available for use. This statement is rarely used by a one-person business, because they are usually small enough that the information contained in a statement of retained earnings is easily seen in the cash-flow statement.

DO YOU NEED A TAX ACCOUNTANT?

Ted Rabinowitsh of Rabinowitsh and Stuart, property managers, prepares his own taxes. "I use a Macintosh program. When they're finished, I go to a really top-flight accountant. I ask him questions I have, and he makes suggestions. Maybe I'm not doing something quite right or not looking at something. Sometimes he helps me with details—sometimes with whole strategies for doing things."

We think Ted's approach is a sound one. In the past, most people with basic arithmetic and the willingness to persevere could figure out their taxes, set up their books, and even incorporate themselves. In fact, doing your own books and taxes was, and is, the surest way of understanding how your business really works.

CPA Bear Kamoroff agrees, but thinks that an accountant may be a good idea because of how difficult it has become to keep up with the tax laws. "For most businesses who have any money coming in, an accountant will probably save them more than it will cost them. Also, how many hours do you want to spend struggling through tax laws as opposed to paying a couple of hundred bucks to an

Fig. 2.7 Profit and Loss Statement

```
                              LIVING LIGHTLY, INC.
                            Statement of Profit and Loss
                            4 Year Summary
```

	1994	1995	1996	1997
INCOME				
SALES	$2,505	$21,489	$52,730	$289,025
(Returns & Allowances)	–	(155)	(233)	(8,176)
NET SALES	2,505	21,334	52,497	280,849
COST OF GOODS SOLD	1,927	16,530	40,382	181,625
GROSS PROFIT	578	4,804	12,115	99,224
GROSS MARGIN	23%	23%	23%	35%
EXPENSES				
Advertising & Promotional	147	1,668	2,039	13,974
Auto & Truck	–	–	–	1,319
Bank Charges	11	–	–	1,588
Cash Short/(Over)	–	–	–	2,791
Depreciation & Amort.	44	126	178	1,105
Dues & Publications	8	–	–	213
Health Benefits	–	–	–	370
Insurance	–	–	–	1,120
Office Supplies	192	783	1,248	3,081
Payroll - Taxes	–	–	–	8,000
Payroll - Wages	–	–	–	26,506
Professional - Leg. & Acct.	5	–	–	1,532
Professional - Other	–	–	–	1,588
Rent	250	1,315	3,750	22,100
Repairs & Maintenance	–	204	–	282
Taxes & Licenses	–	583	1,345	614
Telephone	33	–	–	3,073
Travel & Entertainment	–	–	230	1,380
Utilities	–	518	451	1,760
Miscellaneous	–	38	963	879
TOTAL EXPENSES	690	5,235	10,204	93,275
NET PROFIT/(LOSS)	(112)	(431)	1,911	5,988
CUMULATIVE PROFIT/(LOSS)	(112)	(543)	1,368	7,356

accountant? If you're not making any money, you can't afford an accountant, maybe. And then you've got to struggle through it yourself.

"When *Small-Time Operator* first came out years ago, tax law for small business almost never changed. And then starting maybe eight to ten years ago, they brought in this massive change in the law. Since 1986, every single year, with rare exceptions, they've made significant changes to the tax law. It's silly because the bottom line is not a whole lot of dollars different for small business and taxes. But keeping up with those laws is quite a job."

Bear makes a good point. We still recommend that you do your own bookkeeping (although, when the volume gets big, you may want to subcontract a competent bookkeeper to do your regular posting). But we have had to reexamine the feasibility of small businesses doing their own tax returns.

As Bear explains, the new tax laws make tax preparation so difficult that it may be smarter to hire a professional than to attempt doing your returns yourself. Admittedly, tax professionals have a vested interest in a recommendation like this.

Fig. 2.8   Balance Sheet

LIVING LIGHTLY, INC.

December 31, 1997

Balance Sheet

Current Assets:

Cash On Hand	300.00	
Cash In Banks	(6,450.52)	
Accounts Receivable	24,287.02	
Inventory	65,890.56	
Security Deposits	4,218.00	
Total Current Assets		$88,245.06

Fixed Assets:

Furniture & Fixtures	7,597.64	
Total Fixed Assets		7,597.64

TOTAL ASSETS		$95,842.70

Liabilities:

Accounts Payable	52,330.80	
Payroll Taxes	5,716.84	
Sales Tax	7,984.15	
Notes Payable-Officers	4,560.00	
Accrued Salaries	5,150.91	
Total Liabilities		$75,742.70

Capital:

Common Stock	20,100.00	
Retained Earnings	0.00	
Current Profit/Loss	0.00	
Total Capital		20,100.00

TOTAL LIABILITIES & CAPITAL		$95,842.70

Even in the past, however, we have seen the advice of professionals pay off in tax savings over time, for instance, for people who had several ventures that greatly complicated their tax situation, or for people who had too little time to stay current on tax laws. So, after careful consideration, we think the wisest course today is to hire a tax professional. At the same time, you should know all the records a tax preparer needs so that you can have completed most of the work yourself, thus keeping your costs to a minimum.

RESOURCES

Books

Anthony, Robert N. *Essentials of Accounting*, 5th ed. Redding, Mass.: Addison-Wesley, 1993. An excellent, self-paced programmed accounting workbook to help you quickly learn the basics of bookkeeping and accounting.

Kamoroff, Bernard. *Small-Time Operator*, 17th ed. Laytonville, Calif.: Bell Springs Publishing, 1992. This is the best small-business book available. It covers business start-up, bookkeeping, and becoming an employer in much more detail than we do. Has the best explanation of single-entry bookkeeping.

Tax Guide for Small Businesses, IRS Publication No. 334 (revised yearly). Covers every aspect of small-business taxes. Available from any IRS office.

One-write Systems

There are many companies that sell one-write systems. Here are the names of a few:

Ekonomik Systems
P.O. Box 11413
Tacoma, WA 98411
206-475-0292

Safeguard Business Systems, Inc.
455 Maryland Avenue
Fort Washington, PA 19034
215-641-5000

New England Business Systems
500 North Main Street
Groton, MA 01471
800-225-6380

Standard Accounting Systems
P.O. Box 20609
Portland, OR 97220
800-547-9972

McBee Systems
151 Corlandt Street
Belleville, NJ 07109
201-759-6500

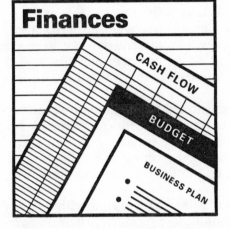

3

Financial Management and Control

If your business were a house, bookkeeping would be the foundation and financial management the framing, plumbing, and wiring. Without a good set of books, good financial management is impossible. Once you have your bookkeeping systems in place, you have the tools to begin building a sound financial-management program.

Financial management helps you look at your one-person business with a larger picture in mind: Where does your income come from? Where does it go? How are you doing compared to last month or last year? How are you measuring up to your budget? Do you have a "slow" season? If so, what strategies will help you to make it through that season? The well-being of your business is largely determined by your skill in asking and answering such questions in a timely and knowledgeable manner.

There are three key instruments you can create and use on a regular basis that will give you the most control over the financial management of your one-person business: (1) a *cash-flow statement*; (2) a *personal budget*; and (3) a *business plan*.

In this chapter we begin with cash flow, including a description of how to construct and read a cash-flow statement. Then we introduce the important topic of business and financial planning and discuss your *personal net worth*, your personal budget, and why and how to create a business plan. We conclude with a discussion of *working capital* and *types of financing.*

UNDERSTANDING CASH FLOW

Just as there are a variety of reasons for choosing to be a one-person business, there are many different goals that each of us has for our business. In addition to expecting a minimum level of income to cover our personal expenses, we want some sort of return on the capital we have invested, not to mention the blood, sweat, and tears. Other goals might be control over our time and the ability to make creative choices. In any event, you need to think about the future if you expect to make your business work.

Once you have envisioned the future you want for your one-person business, you'll need a plan to make that future come true. A projection based on the *cash-flow statement* is the easiest way we know to plan your financial future. This *cash-flow projection* is an organized estimate of the financial flows of your business such as future sales, marketing and overhead expenses, fixture and equipment needs, and so forth.

The obvious disadvantage to working with a cash-flow projection is the time and energy (and, potentially, lost productivity or revenue) that it takes to create and maintain one. The obvious advantage is that it allows you to look at your business in great detail, which makes it possible for you to make better decisions. Just as you wouldn't go on a long cross-country trip without a road map, you shouldn't try to run your one-person business without a cash-flow projection.

Cash flow is the term used to describe the pattern of all money coming into and going out of your business. A cash-flow projection is different than a simple profit and loss or income statement, which lists only your business income and expenses. The cash-flow projection also includes any money you put into the business from your own pocket, from loans, or from investors; any money you take out of the business for your personal needs, to pay off loans, or to give investors a dividend; and any borrowing you anticipate.

To really use a cash-flow projection and understand why it is so important, you need to know how to read one. Fortunately, this is not difficult to learn (see figure 3.1). Once you get the hang of it, you'll be able to see the ups and the downs of your business well in advance. Eventually, using the creative marketing solutions we suggest in Chapter 9, you'll be able to create a smoother cash flow and keep surprises to a minimum.

A well-managed business *always* uses a cash-flow projection to make decisions about how and when to spend money, cut costs, or increase income. Usually you will create one that covers income and expenses on a month-by-month basis for a whole year. Once you get in the habit, you'll wonder how you managed without it.

There are two sets of factors to keep in mind when you are constructing your cash-flow projection: *internal* and *external*. Internal factors that bear on your calcula-

---

Fig. 3.1   How to Read a Cash-Flow Projection

The clearest cash-flow projection is an expanded and modified version of the standard income statement. It includes cash to be raised and loans to be repaid. Most one-person businesses raise cash through loans or investments from family or friends. For purposes of simplification, the following cash-flow projection shows only a single quarter, although you would usually construct one for an entire year.

Notice that for each month there are two columns to fill out: one for "projected" cash flow and one for "actual." This is so you can fill in what actually happens as you go along. Projections represent your goals. Knowing how your projections compare with what actually happens allows you to become better at accurately predicting the future of your business.

A cash-flow projection begins with your guesses and calculations based on a set of "what if" assumptions about the future of your one-person business. Given these assumptions, you will project your expenses and the income you will need to make a profit. After calculating your projections, you will compare what actually happens with the projection, usually month by month. You might construct a cash-flow projection weekly for a business with a lot of transactions, such as a retail store or mail-order business. Or you might only do it quarterly for a small, slow-moving sideline business, such as handmade knives.

Start your calculations by writing down what your fixed expenses will be, things like rent and utilities. Estimate a certain amount for marketing and promotion, and calculate, as best you can, the increase in income that you believe will come from that expenditure. You probably have a pretty good idea what the lag time will be, so you can fill in the new number for income in the month in which you anticipate it occurring. Do these calculations month by month, remembering to include any increase in variable expenses, such as postage, telephone, travel, and so on, that might occur as a result of the increased marketing activity and sales.

To get a better idea of how this works, examine the following cash-flow projection closely. Be sure to read the footnotes, which explain the assumptions behind the figures.

---

tions include planned marketing and promotion, changes in the type or quality of your product or services, anticipated price changes, restrictions on the availability of products from suppliers, the need for help from subcontractors, and the amount of working capital available. The most critical external factors to consider are holidays, seasonal periods, special events that coincide with your product or service offerings, weather, what others in your field are doing, changes in consumer behavior, and changes in the makeup of the community in which you run your business.

Business advisor Paul Terry reviews cash flow regularly. "I have a business checking account and a manual single-entry bookkeeping system. I have not computerized my bookkeeping system, except that once a year I do financial projections

Cash-Flow Projection
April through June, 19--[1]

	Apr		May		June		YTD[4]	
	Projected[2a]	Actual[2b]	Projected	Actual	Projected	Actual	Projected	Actual
BEGINNING Cash Balance[3a]	2,000	5,500	2,000	-1,462[3b]	2,000	-726	6,000	3,312
CASH IN[5]								
Receivable Payments	4,000	2,289[2c]	4,000	6,111	4,000		12,000	8,400
Net Sales	13,000	10,678[2d]	14,000	12,000	15,000		42,000	22,678
Loans	0	0	1,500[2j]	0	1,000		2500	0
Investors	0	0	0	0	0		0	0
Other	0	0	0	0	0		0	0
TOTAL Cash Available	17,000	12,967	19,500	18,111	20,000		56,500	31,078
CASH OUT[6]								
Accounts Payable	7,000	7,522[2e]	7,000	6,497	7,000		21,000	14,019
Direct Labor	0	0	0	0	0		0	0
Other	0	0	0	0	0		0	0
Selling Expense	650	534[2f]	700	600	750		2100	1134
G&A	7,150	5,873[2g]	7,700	6,600	8,250		23,100	12,473
Asset Purchases	0	0	0	4,498[7]	0		0	4,498
Loan Payments Due	500	500	600[2k]	642	600		1,700	1,142
Dividends Due	0	0	0	0	0		0	0
TOTAL Cash Out	15,300	14,429	16,000	18,837	16,600		47,900	33,266
ENDING Cash Balance	1,700	-1,462[2h]	3,500	-726	3,400		8,600	-2,188
CAPITAL NEEDED								
Loans	0	1,500[2i]	0	1,000	0	0	0	2,500
Investments	0	0	0	0	0	0	0	0
Other	0	0	0	0	0	0	0	0
TOTAL Capital Needed	0	1,500	0	1,000	0	0	0	2,500

1. This projection is for a hypothetical spring quarter in any year. Be sure to label your work with the current year. This will be helpful when you look back to build long-range projections in the future.
2. Each month has both a "projected" and an "actual" figure. **2a.** The *projected* figure is your most realistic guess as to how things will turn out. The more experience you have, the more accurate these guesses will be. **2b.** The *actual* figure is what actually happened. Surprise, surprise! The people who owed you money didn't pay as much as they should have (**2c.** Receivable Payments); you didn't sell as much as you expected (**2d.** Net Sales); and you had to pay more bills than you anticipated (**2e.** Accounts Payable). That's

the bad news. The good news is that you had fewer selling costs (**2f. Selling Expense**), and your operating costs were lower than you calculated (**2g. G&A**). In the end you were $1,462 short of your needs (**2h. Ending Cash Balance**). You will have to find the cash to make up that shortage, so you decide to take out a loan for $1,500 (**2i. CAPITAL NEEDED: Loans**). You then immediately post the amount of this loan to May's projected CASH IN: Loans (**2j**) and you increase May's projected Loan Payments Due" (**2k**) by $100, the amount of the new loan payment principle (interest is part of G&A).

3. Cash balance (**3a**) is always brought forward from the previous month. Notice that the actual Beginning Cash Balance for May (**3b**) is the same as the Ending Cash Balance for April (**2h**). Ending Cash Balance of the previous month always equals Beginning Cash Balance of the following month.

4. YTD stands for the totals so far this year, or Year-to-Date. These two columns help you see the quarter as a whole. The "actuals" for this quarter can help you in planning the next quarter and the second quarter of the next year. The YTD numbers can help you see the larger picture. For example, perhaps you have been using your credit cards to borrow the small $1,500 or $1,000 amounts needed this quarter. But realizing that you may also have a similar cash flow next quarter and that you might need $2,500 or more, you decide to apply to your bank for a lower-interest line of credit.

5. CASH IN is a summary of all of the sources of cash flowing into your business. This included the payments people make to you if you have extended them credit (Receivable Payments), the cash, checks, and credit card vouchers you have collected for work done or products sold (Net Sales), money you have borrowed or raised to grow the business or make up shortfalls (Loans and Investors), and so on. The sum of all this money coming into your business is called Total Cash Available.

6. CASH OUT is all of the money that flows out of your business. It includes the payments you make to your suppliers and those who provide you with goods or services (Accounts Payable); any workers you pay whose labor is directly involved in the production of what you sell (Direct Labor); any other expenses related to producing what you sell (Other); the money you spend marketing and selling your products or services (Selling Expense); what you spend to keep the business open, such as rent, utilities, phone, office supplies, etc. (G&A, or General and Administrative; interest on loans is included here); purchases of equipment or furniture (Asset Purchases); payments of the principle portion of loans (Loan Payments Due); and any dividends you must pay to your investors (Dividends Due).

7. In this hypothetical case, a computer system has been purchased because the old one crashed. That is why it was not part of the projections. This is the kind of unexpected event that can often occur in a one-person business.

on my computer for the four or five income categories that I have and the ten or fifteen expense categories. I also have allocations for taxes and projects, so I can see what income I might expect and then track it on a monthly basis.

"I need to make a certain amount of income every month. I ask myself questions about whether I am going to make that amount or not, who it's coming from, what's the frequency of repeat, and so forth. Looking at the income ledger and getting that kind of information is something I do at least monthly, if not more often.

"Expense categories make income tax preparation very simple, because everything is up to date by the end of the year. Every month, I bill about a dozen clients, so I have a system to send out an invoice, keep a copy of it and, when the payment comes in, check the copy as having been paid. I'm always very current on who owes me money and very rarely get stuck not getting paid. It's happened a couple of times, and it was due to my own lack of skill."

Musician Alicia Bay Laurel uses a cash-flow projection whenever her need for cash changes. She gathers the numbers from a simple but elegant tracking system. "I have a calendar, and when someone asks me to do a gig I write down the date and I write down the amount of money I'm going to be paid with a little circle around it. Then if the event comes off as scheduled and I make the money, I take my pink highlighter and put a pink dot over that circle. At the end of each month I know exactly what days I played and how much I made on each day. Every three months I pay my quarterly excise taxes. I take my calculator and go through my records for the past three months, add them up, and pay my 4 percent. In addition I pay state taxes and personal income taxes.

"As far as my business expenses are concerned, I have an accordion file that is broken down into musical instruments, car repair, and so on. As the receipts or canceled checks come in, I put them in this file. At the end of the year when I'm doing my income taxes, I can go through each section and total it up. That's how I do my finances.

"If I'm in a period where my cash needs are greater than usual, I write down everything about my financial situation. This includes what I have in the bank; everything I have in cash; a list of all the upcoming gigs and what I can expect to make from them; and the money that I'm owed. Then I make a list of all the expenses that I have and prioritize them. These are things that have to be paid right away as well as things that I feel I can buy next month or in two months. This way I have a picture of everything. Then I can say, maybe I don't really need to make that purchase, etc. From a sheet like this I can get an idea of how to allot my money for the coming period of time."

It is vitally important to both hold expenses down and allow for an increase in the costs related to your efforts to increase income. You need to constantly regulate spending, anticipate future cash-flow needs, and measure the rise and fall in your business activity across time. A cash-flow projection allows you to create an ever-changing picture of your unique business.

Some one-person businesses have such simple income and expense records that their owners feel safe carrying the relevant figures in their heads. If you have been in business a long time, you too may feel comfortable with this rather intuitive approach.

We recommend, however, that you always write your figures down rather than keeping them in your head. Writing things down is a way to keep yourself honest. It is too easy to remember that you expected $5,000 in July when the original projection in your head was $5,500. So, receiving $5,100 may mean that you are actually doing worse than you expected rather than better.

With expenses, lapses in memory are even more likely. At the beginning of the year you might expect expenses to average $43 a client by year end; by November, however, when your actual client expense is $47, you might remember the $47 figure as what you actually calculated. It's easy to transpose numbers in your mind, especially if it makes you feel better or safer. The truth in this example, however, is that you're doing worse than you expected and you don't even realize it because your memory "helped you out." In our experience, when written records are compared to recollections, recollections are invariably inaccurate.

Another reason for a written cash-flow projection is that it's a good tool to use when getting outside support and advice from peers and friends. Your peers and supporters can use your cash-flow projection as a starting point to ask relevant questions about the way your business is developing. Someone might say, "John, your budget shows that by this month you expected $3,300 a month in revenue from twelve clients and a variable cost per client of $42, but revenues are $3,000 from fourteen clients with an average cost of $55. Do you know why? And does this projection still reflect the way you want to run your business?" This kind of question is useful, and it depends on having a written cash-flow projection. If your supporters and advisors can see what your expectations and goals were, they can be much more helpful when assisting you to evaluate your current situation. Furthermore, they can provide needed emotional support. "The $4,200 in revenue last month is wonderful, Susan, especially since costs were below projections. Congratulations! Keep up the good work!"

BUSINESS AND FINANCIAL PLANNING

To be successful over the long haul, every one-person business needs to do some planning. The more organized the planning the better the choices you will make. It is not necessary for you to have a full-blown business plan, like the ones used to raise hundreds of thousands of dollars for the start-up and growth of businesses with a lot of employees. For the one-person business a *simple business plan* will suffice.

Do you really need a business plan? Small-business advisor Paul Terry says: "It really depends on the nature of your business. A business plan is a product, and if you see it that way, whether you're in a service business or a product business, you will begin to see the value to the product. Like a product, a business plan is only valuable if it's used. A business plan is really an objective written estimation of what you think is going to happen in the future based on your understanding of the current situation and what has happened in the past.

"As you accumulate a history in business, whether you know it or not you begin to accumulate knowledge and data on who your market is. You also accumulate financial information even if you do not have financial statements.

"The importance of doing a business plan is the process in and of itself. It's not because I say you have to do it or a bank says you have to do it, though that may be one way to use it. The reason to do a business plan is that the very process of going through a series of questions about your business will force you to audit the current situation and think about the future—to think strategically."

Whether it's used for starting a new business or growing an existing one, the first step in any business plan is to become familiar with your personal financial condition. What is your net worth? What does your personal budget look like? How much do you need to feel financially secure? The second step is to begin looking at how much cash you will need to start or expand. Is it a realistic amount? Where can you raise the cash you need? With the answers to these questions in hand, your final step is to incorporate them into the business plan itself, which will become the blueprint for the future of your business.

Calculating Your Net Worth

One of the most powerful steps you can take to understand your financial condition is to calculate your net worth. If our economic life is about the accumulation of wealth (as economists say it is), then to understand our economic life we need to understand our wealth: where it comes from, what forms it takes, and how much of it is available for us to use in starting and running a one-person business.

Accountants have come up with a quick and simple way to help us understand our personal wealth. It's called the *balance sheet statement*, or *statement of net worth*, or, as we often say to clients, "What you *own* and what you *owe*." Basically, the statement of net worth is created by writing down the value of everything you own and everything you owe and then subtracting what you owe from what you own to see what the difference is. This difference is called your *net worth*.

The form in figure 3.2 is provided to simplify the process of calculating your net worth.

Creating a Realistic Personal Budget

The next step in understanding your personal wealth is to create a realistic budget of your monthly personal expenses. This is important, because the sum of your expenses is the minimum level of profit that your one-person business needs to make.

Please keep one rule in mind when creating your personal budget: *Beware of deprivation.* It is easy for most people to imagine doing away with all optional expenses—the ones that bring us pleasure and comfort, such as having a facial, getting a massage, going to the movies, taking a vacation, and so forth. This would be a big mistake. Cutting your budget so low can stimulate the alternating behaviors of binging and purging. You go as long as you can, doing without the little pleasures of life. Then, when you can stand it no longer, out comes the credit card and off you go on a buying binge, spending money you don't have. Later, feeling guilty about your spending binge, you return to the deprivation budget, cutting your lifestyle expenses to an even lower level, in an effort to make up for what you have done. And so it continues—the cycle of binging and purging. It is much better on your psyche and your pocketbook to calculate a deprivation budget and then raise it a couple of notches. Cut the facials from twice a month to once a month. Go to one movie a week instead of two or three. Take a shorter vacation. And so forth.

The form in figure 3.3 is provided to help you create a realistic personal budget. The categories are self-explanatory.

After learning your net worth and creating a realistic personal budget, you are able to calculate the cash needed to launch or to further develop your one-person business.

Knowing your net worth allows you to think about how much of this amount you can afford to invest in your business. If you divide the amount of your net worth that you are willing to invest by your monthly budget, you get a kind of "level of security" represented by the number of months you could, if you had to, go without sufficient income from your business to pay your bills.

Estimate the Money Needed

With your personal financial needs in mind, you can now calculate the cash you will need to launch or maintain your one-person business, plan how and when to sell your products or services, determine what it will cost to keep your business open (overhead), and determine what you must charge to pay for everything and still make a profit. An understanding of these basic financial questions will be the basis for your business plan, which we describe next.

YOUR BUSINESS PLAN

There are many important questions that your business plan will help you to answer. If you have a good idea for starting a new business, then the plan can help tell you if you should go ahead. If you can't convince yourself that your idea will work, then how will you ever convince your prospective backers and customers? Once the idea is down on paper, it becomes much easier to calculate the actual cash you will need to get started. And now you have a written record to compare

Fig. 3.2   Your Statement of Net Worth

I OWN	
Cash[1]	
Checking[2]	
Savings and money markets[3]	
Securities: quick-sale value[4]	
Real Estate: quick-sale value[5]	
Furniture: quick-sale value[5]	
Car: quick-sale value[5]	
Cash value of life insurance[6]	
Savings bonds[7]	
Keoghs & IRAs[7]	
Other assets[8]	
Receivables[9]	
TOTAL	
I OWE	
Current household bills due[10]	
Balance due on installment contracts[11]	
Car	
Appliances	
Personal loans	
Other	
Real estate mortgage (describe)[12]	
Other loans (describe)[13]	
Balance due on credit cards[13]	
Insurance premiums due for balance of year[14]	
Taxes due for balance of year[15]	
Other debts (describe)[16]	
TOTAL	
BALANCE SHEET SUMMARY	
What I OWN[17]	
Less what I OWE[18]	
Equals my NET WORTH[19]	

1. *Cash* means cash. The dollars and cents in your pocket, wallet, or mattress.
2. *Checking* is the balance of your checking account(s) on the day you are doing this exercise.
3. *Savings and money markets* is all money you own that has been deposited with a financial institute in order to earn interest.
4. *Securities* is stocks and bonds you own. Quick-sale value means the cash you could raise if you had to sell quickly, rather than waiting for the highest price you could get.
5. *Real estate, furniture,* and *car* are self-explanatory. Even if you owe money on these, they still have a quick-sale value. This field is the amount you sell them for less the balance you owe. Needless to say, it is easier to sell a car or furniture than real estate.
6. *Cash value of life insurance*: Some life insurance policies earn interest on a portion of the premium. Any unused premium plus accumulated interest equals the cash value of the policy.
7. *Savings bonds, Keoghs, and IRAs* are special ways of saving money. Keoghs and IRAs are specifically for retirement.
8. *Other assets* is anything else you own like jewelry, stamp collections, antiques, etc.
9. *Receivables* is money others owe you.
10. *Current household bills due* includes things like rent and utilities that you owe at the moment you are filling out this form.
11. *Balance due on installment contracts* is what you owe on things you've bought on credit or money you have borrowed.
12. *Real estate mortgage* is the balance owed on your mortgage, if you have one.
13. *Other loans and balance due on credit cards* are for loans or credit not covered under *Balance due on installment contracts*.
14. *Insurance premiums due for balance of year*: Insurance is often paid in installments. The policy is in effect even though you still owe further payments. Put the value of the premiums left to pay for the balance of the current year here.
15. *Taxes due for balance of year*: This is any tax you owe from last year as well as your quarterly self-employment payments that you must pay in advance for this year.
16. *Other debts* is for anything not covered above.
17. *What I OWN* is the total from the I OWN box.
18. *What I OWE* is the total from the I OWE box.
19. *Equals my NET WORTH*: Net worth is calculated by subtracting what you owe from what you own.

Fig. 3.3   Your Realistic Personal Budget

REGULAR MONTHLY PAYMENTS	
House payments (including taxes) or rent	
Car payments (including insurance)	
Appliance-TV payments	
Personal loan payments	
Credit card payments	
Health plan payments	
Life insurance payments	
Other insurance payments	
Miscellaneous payments	
TOTAL	
HOUSEHOLD OPERATING EXPENSE	
Telephone	
Gas and electricity	
Water	
Garbage	
Other household expenses, repairs, maintenance	
TOTAL	
PERSONAL EXPENSE	
Clothing, cleaning, laundry	
Drugs, cosmetics, sundries	
Doctors and dentists	
Dues and education	
Gifts and contributions	
Travel	
Newspapers, magazines, books	
Auto upkeep and gas	
Spending money and allowances	
TOTAL	
FOOD EXPENSE	
Food, at home	
Food, away from home	
TOTAL	

TAX EXPENSE	
Federal and state income taxes	
Other taxes	
TOTAL	
BUDGET SUMMARY	
Regular monthly payments	
Household operating expense	
Personal expense	
Food expense	
Tax expense	
MONTHLY TOTAL	

the results of your management efforts against your ideas of what will work. Will the plans you have for promoting the business, when implemented in a timely fashion, actually bring the response needed to make a profit?

If you're already in business, such a plan gives you a chance to develop and improve your overall business idea. It also helps you figure out the best ways to beat the odds against success that most small businesses face. Most important, it can be a way to check your pricing and delivery systems to see if they are the best they can be, making it possible for you to maximize both your profits and the quality of your products or services. Finally, the plan is the best way to stay on top of your day-to-day operations while still maintaining the bigger picture you have for how the business should look tomorrow, next year, and in five years. We will discuss the most important parts of a business plan below, but you may need additional help with the details as they apply to your particular business. An excellent source of help is Mike McKeever's *How to Write a Business Plan*. You may also want to work with an accountant or business consultant who specializes in business planning.

Your business plan will include the cash-flow projection we discussed earlier, as well as a statement of your personal net worth. In addition, it will describe the following five key areas of your business: (1) the *business* in general, (2) your *market*, (3) your *"competition,"* (4) your *marketing plan*, and (5) your *financing plan*.

Your Business

It is obvious that how you describe your business is important for your marketing efforts, but it is also important in planning your financing. There are four areas of primary concern: (1) the *products or services* that you offer; (2) your *location*; (3) your *business type*; and (4) your *personnel*.

Products or Services You should have your customers in mind when you create a marketing description of your products or services. When thinking about financing, however, you must also include a description of profitability. It is not necessary to make a big profit on your products or services, but you must have a carefully reasoned plan explaining how you can make the profit that you project. Usually, if your profit margin is low you must sell a large number of units, while if your profit margin is high you can sell fewer units to generate the cash needed to keep the business open and meet your personal financial needs. This concern with profitability makes *pricing* one of the most important things for you to think about, and we cover it in some detail in Chapter 4, "Financial Strategies."

Location For many of us, the location of our one-person business is a matter of chance. For many others, it is in our home. And, while that may be a cost-cutting necessity, it is wise to think about the best location for what we want to do and to create a plan to eventually be in that location.

There are many factors to take into consideration when you are choosing your location, but two are generally of concern to every small business: *reach* and *site*.

The *reach* of your business is how far your customers come to obtain your products or services. Words like *international* and *national* describe reach, but are not very specific.

Until the early seventies it was very difficult to move capital from one country to another, so businesses tended to be oriented toward localized reaches. With the beginning of deregulation in 1973, capital began moving between countries, making it possible to create organizations that could standardize their products and serve a global market. The establishment of these global companies, along with the rapid spread of communications technology, created reliable, affordable distribution channels that even small companies could take advantage of. So in reality, almost every small business now has the potential to be global in its reach.

Globalism notwithstanding, the reach of most one-person businesses is the immediate population of clients or customers to whom they can deliver products or services and still make a profit. Let's take mail-order retail for example. A portable electronic public-address system can be manufactured cheaply but sold for a higher profit and for a higher price than a book. So you would include the PA system in your mail-order catalog when selling to customers outside of the United States. But the cost of shipping books outside of the United States, one or two at a time, is so high that it cannot be absorbed by the lower profit margin and lower price that translate into many fewer dollars. So you would probably restrict a mail-order book catalog to the U.S. market.

Site is the specific location of your business. Such factors as the sunny or going home side of the street, what the neighborhood is like, zoning restrictions, and so forth are critical in choosing location.

Figure 3.4 shows the most favorable locations for small businesses in general, including both reach and site recommendations.

Fig. 3.4   Best Locations for Small Businesses in General in the United States

Reach	Site
New England The Sun Belt The Southwest, especially Arizona Florida Georgia California *A community with* • substantial permanent industry • diversified and stable industries • minimum seasonality (unless you're looking for that)	 • nearness of competition • transportation • parking • nearness of services • "going home" side of the street • sunny side of the street

Business Type   It's usually quite clear what type of business you're in. But sometimes the lines between types can become blurry. Perhaps Colin Ingram captures the distinctions between business types the most succinctly in the following excerpt from *The Small Business Test*:

Retail   Your business is retail if you have a store, shop, mobile vehicle, or any other site from which you sell tangible products directly to consumers who will use the products. Examples of retail businesses are restaurants, video rentals, florists, mobile snack trucks, and vendors at sporting events or fairs. Tangible services such as shoe repairs, TV repairs, or mobile carpet cleaning are also considered retail businesses.

Wholesale   Your business is wholesale if you sell tangible products to retailers. A typical wholesaler buys products from manufacturers; stores them in a warehouse; obtains orders through mail-order catalogs, through a sales team, or from walk-in customers; and sells primarily to retail outlets. Wholesalers include book distributors, parts suppliers to retail stores, and furniture display showrooms that sell to interior decorators, architects, and contractors.

Manufacture   You are a manufacturer if you make original products yourself or if you buy components from other manufacturers and assemble them to form your own products. Manufacturers usually sell to wholesale distributors, to retailers, and to other manufacturers. Examples of manufacturers are candy makers who sell to distributors or to retail outlets, and machine shops that make parts sold both to distributors and to manufacturers using the parts to build their own products.

Service A service business is one that requires a high degree of personal interchange, such as marriage counseling, hairstyling, tax preparation, editing, teaching piano, and fortune-telling. It also includes businesses where the primary product is information, such as information brokers, research services, or consultants of any kind.

Mail-order Mail-order businesses are those that sell to consumers by direct mail (promotional literature mailed directly to individual homes) or through ads in magazines and newspapers.

Mike McKeever, in *How to Write a Business Plan*, describes an additional business type that many one-person businesses specialize in: *project development*. "Developers," McKeever explains, "create and finish a saleable commodity by assembling resources for a one-time project. Normally, the developer knows the market value of the finished product before she begins work. When the project is complete, the developer sells her interest in the project, normally directly to the user or consumer.

"To understand project developers," McKeever continues, "consider a woman building a single-family house on speculation. She buys the lot, secures permits, hires a contractor, gets a loan, builds a house, and sells it. She is then ready to go on to another project. Other examples of project developers include someone who buys, restores, and sells antique cars and someone who purchases dilapidated buildings at a bargain price, fixes them up and sells them."

Personnel In a one-person business, that's you. But in a certain important sense, you might also include your advisors and subcontractors. After all, even though you are a one-person business, you can't survive without the help of others. And a large majority of one-person businesses thrive within a milieu of cross-referrals and mutual support. So when you are thinking about how your business operates and who is involved, be sure to include the key people that make keeping your door open possible. If you use your business plan to raise capital, it will be strengthened by descriptions of the key personnel you work with to accomplish your goals.

Your Market

There are three key steps to understanding your market: (1) identify who your *customers* are, (2) estimate how big your *potential market* is, and (3) determine how to reach your most likely *prospects*. There are several ways to do this, including identifying the demographics of your business area, ascertaining the values and lifestyles of your customers, conducting your own market research surveys, and tracking where your customers or clients come from. There is more to understanding your market than we can adequately describe here, but two good sources of additional help are *Do-It-Yourself Marketing Research* by George Breen and A. B. Blankenship and Chapters 4 and 5 in *Finding Your Niche: Marketing Your Professional Service* by Bart Brodsky and Janet Geis.

Your "Competition"

We put the word competition in quotes to make a point. It is not necessary to think of your competition as "the enemy." A better way to think of them is simply as "others in your field." It is our experience that if we can overcome the cultural standard that encourages us to hate or fear those who are in the same business as ours, we will find that we can actually learn a lot from each other and can offer a level of support not available anywhere else. When psychotherapist Charmian Anderson was first building her counseling practice, she began to invite other therapists to a weekly gathering in her office to discuss their mutual problems and issues. Charmian learned that seldom were two therapists interested in exactly the same kind of clients, and even then they were always from locations far enough apart not to be threatened by sharing their "business secrets." All concerned obtained a level of understanding about building a therapy practice that simply could not have been created in any other way, and many cross-referrals were made once those attending understood how their "competition" might better serve certain prospective clients. This is a perfect example of market research and marketing occurring together, with a big payoff for all concerned.

But, alas, not everyone you meet will be this cooperative. So even though you may wish to be open and mutually supportive, you may not find as much reciprocity as you would like. You can still learn a lot of helpful information about others in your field. Usually your better-known competitors can be identified right away; simply ask people you meet who they use or where they shop. You can casually drive by or visit the competitors you discover to find out what they offer and how it differs from your offerings. Then you will know both how to improve what you are doing and when to send a client or customer to them. Remember to ask the customer to say who sent them or send along a note of introduction. Who knows? In the long run, you might create an ally.

Your Marketing Plan

In general, a marketing plan should contain a complete statement of your overall marketing concept. This means that you must be able to clearly describe your one-person business in a way that makes it easy for most of your customers, suppliers, and subcontractors to remember what you do—what makes you different from others in your field (see Chapter 9). It should be easy to tell what your product or service is and, of course, it should be clear that it is the best that it can be. A clear and complete picture of your pricing is important, too.

Your marketing plan will contain a description of the items listed in figure 3.5, "The Complete One-Person Business Marketing Mix," that seem appropriate for your overall goals.

Your Financing Plan

At what points in the growth of your business will it be necessary to "inject" more capital? How much will you need? Where will you get it? Will it be from family and friends or from outside investors? What types of financing should you use? What can go wrong? What should you watch out for? The answers to these questions will make up your financing plan. In the next few sections we will offer guidelines you can use to answer these questions for your one-person business.

UNDERSTANDING WORKING CAPITAL

Capital is another word for financing your business. Every small business needs a working capital reserve to cover slow periods or to buy inventory in advance of sales. It may also need longer-term capital for the purchase of equipment.

As a one-person business you have a great deal of flexibility. You can keep your personal and business expenses to a minimum, so you can get by on a smaller profit. For example, in many cases you can significantly reduce overhead by working out of your home. To raise the cash you need you can use your personal savings, liquidate personal assets (sell something you own that's valuable), go to friends and family, borrow from your credit cards, or use credit from suppliers. Limited partnerships are another option. Bank loans, credit union loans, and borrowing on the cash value of insurance are other seldom-used options. Often many of these forms of financing are used concurrently.

Even if you are free of debt and launch your one-person business with your own money, it can take several years before the business is able to pay all your personal expenses. And after the first couple of years of running your business you may have no money left. In that case, you will need to find other sources of capital. If you do still have money saved, your business is probably one of the best places to put it.

Both reducing expenses and investing your savings in the business are preferable to borrowing money from someone else. Either strategy keeps the cost of doing business lower because you don't have interest to pay or principal to repay. Moreover, if you haven't borrowed and you decide to give up your business, you can stop whenever you wish. You won't need to consider the effect on people to whom you owe money, because there won't be any.

As much as 80 percent of all the financing that small businesses receive comes from a single category often referred to as *angels*. Angels can be viewed as coming from six basic groups: (1) family and friends, (2) fans and supporters, (3) customers

Fig. 3.5   The Complete One-Person Business Marketing Mix

Marketing Management

• Market Research
    Who are your potential customers?
    How can you best reach them?

• Positioning
    What do you want to be noted for?
    Who are the others in your field?

• Pricing
    What do others charge?
    What will you charge?

Marketing Vehicles

• Advertising
    Newspapers
    Magazines
    Radio
    Billboards & Public Transportation
    Television

• Promotion
    Advertising specialties
    Judgment aids
    Direct-mail letters
    Newsletters or Catalogs
    Directories
    Events
        Direct
        Parallel
    Networking
    Listings
        Newsletters or Catalogs
        Directories (especially Yellow Pages)
        Newspaper & Magazine Classifieds

• Publicity
    Press releases
    Expert articles or profiles

• Public Relations
    Teaching
    Lecturing
    Research reports
    Community service
    Memberships (associations, clubs, etc.)
    Publishing
        Articles/books
        Newsletter
    Benefits/celebrations/awards

• Interpersonal Promotions
    Referral development
    Repeat business development
    Client/contact communications
    Open houses & other indirect Events
    Subcontractors
    Employees

• Firm Identity
    Stationery/card/logo
    Brochure
    Sales literature
    Product catalog
    Advertising art
    Directory copy
    Signage
    Office location and decor
    Annual report
    CV's or résumés
    Publications list
    Media file
    Case-study descriptions
    Testimonials & references

• Management Systems
    Mailing lists (clients, prospects &
        referral sources, suppliers)
    Telephone answering
    Telemarketing
    Marketing results tracking

or clients, (4) suppliers, (5) employees, and (6) private investors new to you. A one-person business has no employees, so that leaves only five categories to consider.

Family and Friends   For most one-person businesses, it is easiest to raise cash from family and friends. Family and friends often expect a smaller return on their investment than strangers because of the emotional investment they have in your success. They seldom expect more than a minority ownership position and are usually flexible about when the investment should mature and be paid back. Family and friends will often overlook the fact that you don't have much of a track record as a self-employed business person or manager, because they know you personally. And finally, family and friends are not usually as eager to see your business grow as are investors not related to you, so you will be able to stay a one-person business if you choose.

Fans and Supporters   Fans and supporters are people who are not related to you and who might not even be your friends but who fall in love with your business idea and want to do something to help you succeed. Everything we have said about family and friends usually applies to fans and supporters as well. Being less emotionally invested in you, however, they may want a larger return or ownership interest.

Customers or Clients   Customers or clients who buy your products or use your services can often become interested enough in your business to want to help out financially. The usual method of customer/client financing is some sort of *prepurchase opportunity*. A prepurchase opportunity is when you sell your products or services in advance of actual delivery in order to raise cash. Coupons that sell for $8, say, but can later be redeemed for $10 worth of goods are an example. Buying a package of ten massages might be another. When the Rainbow General Store in San Francisco wanted to move to a larger space, one of the methods they used to help raise the needed capital was to sell food coupons. Customers paid $8 for each coupon, which they could redeem for $10 when the store opened in the new location. Several thousand dollars were raised this way. The store also raised about $60,000 in direct loans from customers. The move was a success, and everyone was paid back in a matter of a few months.

Suppliers   Suppliers finance your business in a couple of ways. First, consignments of inventory are a form of loan. Although you are using the merchandise owned by the vendor, you don't have to pay for it until you sell it. Second, suppliers lend you money when they extend you credit. In many fields, suppliers will allow you to buy expensive equipment on credit. In some industries, like the book trade, inventory can be purchased with variable-length terms from thirty days to a year or more, and near the end of the period the goods that have not been sold can be returned for a full refund. When you are new in business, suppliers usually start out demanding COD payments and then change to standard credit terms after they gain experience with you.

To make this kind of financing work, use common sense. Always pay your suppliers on time if you can. If you're going to pay late, give them plenty of warning. If you have to negotiate partial payments, be sure to send your suppliers a financial statement, a list of your other payables, a written reason for your payment delays, and a precise schedule of your payment plan. They will appreciate being kept informed and may volunteer to help out in ways that you can't anticipate.

Private Investors New to You This category of angel insists on a high rate of return on their money. They can be as expensive as high-priced credit cards, but they allow you to postpone the repayment of principle (called a *buyout*) until the agreed-upon maturation of their investment. They are not professional venture capital sources, but they do like to use their own money in small amounts, especially for start-ups, for the fun and emotional excitement of being part of an interesting new business. These investors are usually contacted through boutique investment bankers, financial consultants, or financial planners.

TYPES OF FINANCING

There are two basic types financing: *debt financing* and *equity financing* or, more simply, *loans* and *investments*. A loan is money you have to pay back, whether your business does well or not. An investor, on the other hand, is gambling that you will do well in business and be able to pay a dividend on the amount of the investment. If your business does poorly, there is no dividend. If it fails, the investment does not have to be paid back.

The Dos and Don'ts of Raising Cash

Raising cash from friends and relatives is the most typical source of capital for a one-person business. Some businesses need inventory, and many need capital for equipment or fixtures and for leasehold improvements.

We offer three pieces of advice if you have to raise cash for your one-person business. First, put the loan or investment agreement in writing. The key elements of the written agreement are: (1) the purpose of the loan or investment; (2) the terms of repayment; (3) an alternative method of repayment in case there is a problem; and (4) a mediation procedure to handle any disagreements. The inclusion of all these elements in a written agreement is intended to keep your friends as friends and to allow you to go to the next family Thanksgiving dinner without feeling like an outcast.

Second, if yours is a product business with an easily sellable inventory, you can use the inventory as collateral for the loan. To most lenders, a collateralized loan is a lower-risk loan.

Third, make all your loan payments promptly and keep both lenders and investors up to date by providing financial statements on the business. This kind of attention will inspire appreciation for your professionalism. It will give your financial "partners" a feeling of participating in what you are doing, which will stand you in good stead later if you need their help again. If for some reason you must be late or miss a payment, you will have created an atmosphere of clarity and trust.

An excellent source of help on creating a loan agreement is *Simple Contracts for Personal Use* by Stephen Elias and Marcia Stewart. You can use the same sort of structure to make a simple investment agreement. The moment that an agreement, whether for a loan or an investment, becomes so complicated that it starts to make your head spin, you should probably consult a professional for help in making sure everyone is being treated fairly and that the agreement is legally enforceable.

Credit Cards and Credit Lines

Credit cards such as Visa and Mastercard are usually easy sources of credit. However, as great as the temptation may be, it is difficult to justify this kind of borrowing because of the high interest costs. Almost any other source of credit, except loan sharks, is cheaper. The interest on many credit cards runs 18 to 22 percent. If credit cards are a necessary form of financing for you, try to limit your borrowing to the less expensive ones, which charge 13 to 16 percent. We heartily discourage this form of borrowing. If you need to resort to a credit card, it is probably time to rethink your business.

Most one-person businesses are too small for banks to grant them a business line of credit. But many banks are now making it possible to get personal lines of credit at more reasonable interest rates than credit cards. The interest charged for these is usually a few percentage points greater than the prime rate banks charge their favored customers. They operate just like credit cards, except that you get a book of checks instead of a piece of plastic. Chances are if your credit rating is good you can get one of these personal lines of credit to help meet some of your working capital needs.

Limited Partnerships

We know many people who have had difficult, unpleasant, and sometimes nightmarish experiences with partnerships. As a consequence, we do not ordinarily recommend partnerships. Nonetheless, *limited partnerships* can sometimes be used as a form of financing for a one-person business, so we discuss them here. In a limited partnership there are two kinds of partners, the *general* partners and the *limited* partners. In the case of a one-person business, there is only one general partner—you. The general partners make all the business decisions, and the limited partners contribute money, with the expectation of receiving some sort of return. Limited partnerships allow others to put money into your business in a form that generates earnings for them if your business does well.

The advantages of a limited partnership are obvious. The business has less debt, and the limited partners can only lose what they have invested because, unlike the general partners, the limited partners have no liability beyond the amount of their investment. The most likely candidates for a limited partnership are friends or relatives who need a tax write-off. A new business may be perfect for them, because it usually makes little profit and may even report a loss in the beginning, which they can share as a tax deduction. And if the business fails, the limited partners can also deduct the loss that will occur, because the partnership is a form of investment rather than a loan. The disadvantages of a limited partnership are mostly relationship issues. Even though the partnership is "limited," your investors may want to give you advice about how to run the business. If you choose your limited partners carefully, keep them informed, and are clear and firm about the legal and financial responsibilities for running your business that require you to be the ultimate decision-maker, you will certainly minimize the disadvantages.

For help on creating a partnership agreement take a look at *The Partnership Book* by Dennis Clifford and Ralph Warner.

RESOURCES

Blechman, Bruce, and Jay Conrad Levinson. *Guerrilla Financing: Alternative Techniques to Finance Any Small Business.* Boston: Houghton-Mifflin, 1992.

Bond, Cecil J. *Hands-On Financial Controls for Your Small Business.* New York: Tab Books, 1991.

Breen, George, and A. B. Blankenship. *Do-It-Yourself Marketing Research*, 3rd ed. New York: McGraw-Hill, 1992.

Brodsky, Bart, and Janet Geis. *Finding Your Niche: Marketing Your Professional Service.* Berkeley: Community Resource Institute Press, 1992.

Clifford, Dennis, and Ralph Warner. *The Partnership Book*, 4th ed. Berkeley, Nolo Press, 1991.

Elias, Stephen, and Marcia Stewart. *Simple Contracts for Personal Use.* Berkeley: Nolo Press, 1991.

Gill, James O. *Understanding Financial Statements: A Guide for Non-Financial Readers.* Menlo Park, Calif.: Crisp Publications, 1990.

Ingram, Colin. *The Small Business Test.* Berkeley: Ten Speed Press, 1990.

Kamoroff, Bernard. *Small-Time Operator.* Laytonville, Calif.: Bell Springs Publishing, 1992.

McKeever, Mike. *How to Write a Business Plan*, 4th ed. Berkeley: Nolo Press, 1992.

Ray, Norm. *Easy Financials for Your Home-Based Business*. Windsor, Calif.: Rayve Productions, 1993.

Seglin, Jeffrey L. *Financing Your Small Business*. New York: McGraw-Hill, 1990.

Steingold, Fred S. *The Legal Guide for Starting and Running a Small Business*. Berkeley: Nolo Press, 1992.

Steinhoff, Dan and John F. Burgess. *Small Business Management Fundamentals*, 6th ed. New York: McGraw-Hill, 1992.

4

Financial Strategies

Once your financial management and control practices are in place, you can begin to focus on a variety of strategies that will make your business more financially stable. The single most important place to put your energy is in *controlling expenses*. Looking diligently for ways to cut overhead is important, as are the buying practices that you choose, including knowing when to lease and when to buy. Every dollar you do not spend is a dollar in your pocket or one that can go back into the business. After controlling expenses, there are several effective strategies for *maximizing income* and profits, including *pricing* and *customer service*. Focusing on a single business while creating a variety of income streams is also an effective strategy for increasing income, as is choosing your clients to protect against income fluctuations. Finally, good *credit*, effective *collections*, businesslike *estimates* and *proposals*, and *physical layout* are also crucial.

STRATEGIES FOR CONTROLLING EXPENSES

When you start a business, it is hard to estimate how much income you may generate and easy to estimate what your expenses will be. Imagine, for example, setting up a bill-paying service for busy professionals. You might guess that people would pay $15 a month for this service, based on comparable services they buy on a monthly basis. You could estimate the number of people who might sign up if you started by offering the service through CPA friends. There might be two hundred customers the first year, generating about $9,000 total income. So far the key words are *guess*, *estimate*, and *might*.

When it comes to cost, however, you could rehearse the actual operation while paying your own bills. First, you would calculate the time it would take to open the incoming letters, summarize the information on the bills, transfer the figures to a twice-monthly checklist, mail the checklist to the customer for approval, and pay the bills in the form and amount the customer might want. You would add to this a rough guess of supply costs and an estimate of the percentage of overhead that could be charged against this service. If you really started the business, you might find that the income was erratic and unpredictable. Even the pricing might need to be changed to match the demand. But your costs would be tangible, hard facts of life that you could find out ahead of time.

The Two-Thirds Rule for Reducing Expenses

According to this rule of two thirds, the best strategy is always to put two thirds of your energy into reducing expenses and one third into increasing income. The reasoning is that if you do what you can be sure of, you will get a real return on your investment of time and effort. For every dollar that you do not spend, you have a real dollar in your pocket. But the dollars you spend on marketing, promotions, or increasing productivity may or may not increase your income.

Your success at generating income is an unknown in the present. You see the results of your effort as you go along. Because creating income can't be hurried up or known for sure in advance, the potential for loss and disappointment is very great. On the other hand, you can decide not to spend, or to reduce spending, in the present. And when you do, you will see the results immediately.

Insofar as time spent on something can be wasted, you can lose 100 percent of your investment in attempting to generate income, since it might not work. Don't risk your whole business. Put the risk into only one third of your time and effort.

Even after a business has been going for several years, the same strategy applies: When more net income is needed, put two thirds of your effort into reducing costs, because you can be confident of the results. Put the rest of your effort into improving your management and marketing systems.

Most people follow these same practices in their personal lives. They put the bulk of their discretionary income into secure forms of financial investment, especially if their equity in a home is counted. They reserve a much smaller amount for high-return, high-risk investments, thus choosing the known risk over the unknown for the major amount of their effort.

Putting this rule into practice is often easier said than done. Many people who come to us for advice view money and time spent on getting new customers as certain to bring results. "My friend in direct mail assures me that a ten-thousand-piece mailing for $8,000 will get me four hundred new customers worth $35,000 in revenue. How can I pass that up?" argues our typical client.

"Wait a minute!" we reply. "Your friend is assuming a 4 percent response to your mailing. In our experience that would be high. What if you only get a 1 percent response? Then you will only get an increase in revenue of about $8,000. That will just barely pay for mailing. If you work longer hours," we explain, "saving about $4,000 on the costs of a part-time helper, and you also put $3,000 into a machine that will reduce costs by another $4,000 a year, you will have created the same $8,000 increase in profitability with almost no risk at all. You will continue to save $4,000 every year after that, and you'll feel much better spending $1,000 on a well-deserved vacation than in spending $8,000 on the chance that you might bring in that $35,000 fortune."

It is hard for people to see cost cutting as superior to marketing because they get swept up in the enthusiasm generated by the hoped-for future. You can't control your customers' behavior, but you have direct control over your own actions, so anything you do to cut costs is low risk and certain to pay off.

Some Arguments against Bulk Buying

One way to reduce cost that goes against so-called common sense is buying smaller quantities. People often look for quantity discounts and buy far more than they can use in a reasonable amount of time. For example, if you were buying a print run for a book you were self-publishing, you might get estimates of 10,000 copies for $12,000 or 2,000 copies for $4,000, because the unit cost for 10,000 is $1.20 as opposed to $2.00 each for 2,000. Many people would take the larger quantity although they have no idea how well the book might sell.

The problem is, although you could probably sell 2,000 copies of almost any book you published, given a few years, you probably couldn't get rid of 10,000 copies of most books without going to the dump. Aside from being out $8,000, you would also have to store the extra books, probably at additional cost, until you decide to dump them. If the book did sell well, you would have a real number on which to estimate future sales. If, after several smaller print runs, you found that sales continued to be strong, then you might consider ordering a larger quantity.

Most quantity purchases give you a similar problem. Phone numbers and addresses often change before large quantities of letterhead can be used up. Ballpoint pens often dry out faster than people use them.

The simple rule is: *Don't buy in bulk*!

Gift retailer Trish has a sensible approach. "It's not good to buy too much. You can always reorder. A lot of times you get a break when you order large quantities, and it might work out if you know from past experience that you can sell it all. I keep track of the colors that sell the best and when I get down to a certain number of sweatshirts in that color, I reorder. Each supplier has a different shipping rate, so you have to keep that in mind in deciding when to reorder. I'm always watching my inventory."

Ways to Cut Overhead

In a one-person business, almost by definition, the main way to keep overhead down is by doing most of the work yourself. It's probably impossible to do absolutely everything yourself, so you will turn to others from time to time. Occasionally you will use a lawyer or part-time clerical help, or you may subcontract with an accountant or bookkeeper or a graphic artist. Your goal, however, is to streamline all operations so that you can do most of the work with a minimum of effort. After that, you focus on reducing other overhead costs.

As Barbara Johnson points out in her book *Private Consulting*, there are three areas that are prime candidates for cutting overhead: business space, supplies, and hired services. Working from home is one of the most popular strategies for saving on space costs. To cut costs on work space outside the home, try to locate in older or lower-rent parts of town, or arrange to share space with others who do similar kinds of work. Shared space can help lower the costs of phone, copy machine, and other office equipment as well. Office supplies bear watching too: by keeping an eagle eye on wastage of supplies you can realize significant savings. Using only temporary services or subcontractors will help you reduce your hired-services costs even more than using a part-time employee.

Accountant Malcolm Ponder is a perfect example of this kind of cost management. "One of the things that enables me to charge a third of what other accountants do is that I don't pay rent for an outside office and I don't hire anyone other than my secretary, who is seasonal. I have almost no overhead, and overhead is what kills most one-person businesses."

STRATEGIES FOR INCREASING INCOME

How well you follow the two best pieces of advice we can give you about increasing your income can make or break your one-person business: First, *focus on doing just one business.* Second, within that business, *create a variety of income streams.*

Focus on Doing Just One Business

The rule about doing just one business seems obvious but is often ignored. Some people realize that because it is difficult enough to master a single business, it is wise to stay focused. But many one-person business owners, excited by the possibilities their new enterprise offers them or afraid they might not make enough money if they don't take everything that comes their way, often ignore this simple rule.

The Advantages of Leasing

Leasing can sometimes be a good strategy for reducing expenses. There are so many variables, though, that the decision is a complex one. Michael M. Coltman does a good job of explaining the issue in his book *Financial Control for the Small Business* included with kind permission:

A lease is a contractual arrangement where the owner of the asset (the lessor) grants you (the lessee) the right to the asset for a specified period of time in return for periodic lease payments. Leasing of land and/or buildings has always been a common method for an entrepreneur to minimize the investment costs of going into business. In recent years, the leasing of equipment, and similar items, has become more common.

Some suppliers of equipment will lease directly. In other cases, you can lease from a company that specializes in leasing. In other words, the lessor is a company that has bought the equipment from the supplier and has gone into the business of leasing to others.

As a business operator there may be advantages to you to lease rather than to buy equipment and similar assets.

First, you can avoid the obsolescence that you might have if the assets are purchased outright. However, the lessor has probably considered the cost of obsolescence (a form of depreciation) and calculated it into the rental rates. However, a lease contract that allows you to replace obsolete equipment with newer equipment that comes onto the market can give you an advantage over your competitor [who purchases].

Second, leasing allows you to obtain equipment that you might not be able to afford immediately or could afford only with costly financing. In other words, 100% "financing" of leased assets is possible since there is no down payment required and no loan to be repaid with interest.

Even if you have or can borrow the cash to purchase the assets you need, you may prefer to lease. Leasing allows you to use your available cash for investment in longer life assets, such as land or buildings, that over time frequently appreciate in value, whereas equipment generally depreciates.

Third, since lease payments are generally tax deductible, the lease cost is not as demanding on cash flow as it may at first appear. For example, if you lease an item of equipment for $4,000 a year that is tax deductible and your company is in a 50% tax bracket, the net cash cost of leasing is only $2,000.

	Item Leased	Item Not Leased
Profit before lease cost	$10,000	$10,000
Lease expense	$4,000	
Profit before tax	$ 6,000	$10,000
Income tax 50%	$3,000	$5,000
Net profit	$ 3,000	$ 5,000

As you can see by these figures, even though the lease cost is $4,000, the net profit with leasing is only $2,000 less than if the item is not leased. However, this is an oversimplified situation since, if you owned the asset, you would be able to claim depreciation on it, rather than lease expense, as a tax deduction. Also, if you borrow any money to help finance the purchase of an asset, the interest on that borrowed money is also tax deductible.

Finally, even though with a lease the lessor is generally responsible for maintenance of the equipment while you own it, the lessor also owns any residual value in the asset at the end of the lease period. The lease contract may give you the right to purchase the asset at that time, at a specified price, or you may have the option to renew the lease for a further specified period of time. Because of these variables, which mean that each lease arrangement can vary widely, you would be wise to obtain all necessary financial information prior to making the decision whether to buy or lease any item.

A start-up business should spend considerable time defining its product or service focus in a way that is easy for others to understand. And this is the best way to build a stable income flow as the business grows and matures.

All business fields have a body of traditional knowledge, and many have a highly specialized language. Some fields are mastered only after years of experience. Because knowledge based on experience is so important to success, it is a powerful strategy to focus on one field and become good at it. Still, there is a fine line to walk in deciding when different sources of income are related enough to be considered part of the same business.

Our goal in the following discussion is to help you learn when you need to focus your sources of income more and when you can branch out.

Create a Variety of Income Streams

When we talk about creating a variety of income streams, we are talking about three specific things: (1) *having more than one client* or customer, (2) *having* clients or customers that offer *diverse sources of income*, and (3) *protecting against income fluctuations*.

Having More than One Client This makes obvious sense, because it is dangerous for a one-person business to receive too large a proportion of its income from one source. You may start out contracting yourself back to the company you left to start your own firm. It doesn't take a vivid imagination to see what the effects might be of losing a client that brings you a third or more of your income.

Valerie Skonie left a sales-management job to start a service that provides technically specialized salespeople to firms like the one she left. Her former employer became her first and biggest client. She knew she needed more clients, because the person who had chosen her firm might leave and the successor might drop her. Or internal policy could change, canceling the service or bringing it in-house, making Valerie's outside service unnecessary. Clearly, Valerie's immediate priority was to find other clients, which she did, of course.

Less obvious was the case of Arlen, a graphic designer and writer, who did five different newsletters for a large bank for several years. Because he worked for five different department heads, he had a sense of security based on the diversity of income sources within the company. During a financial crisis, however, the bank management introduced a policy against outside contractors, and Arlen had to start his business all over again.

Having Diverse Sources of Income The need for having different sources of income is harder to explain. The purpose of this diversity is twofold: (1) to provide you with good market information and long-term training, and (2) to offer protection against naturally occurring fluctuations in income, to which one-person businesses are especially vulnerable.

While the focus may seem to be on diversity, all your sources of income need to be related within the focused definition of your business. Neil, a photographer, gets income from selling direct services as a photographer, teaching classes in photography, and selling stock photos (stock photos are originals, usually used in textbooks, of "stock" subjects like people, places, and animals or Mt. Rainier, the Lincoln Memorial, and a Flamenco guitarist). Obviously, all of these income streams fit within photography as the focused definition of Neil's business. Besides bringing fun and variety into Neil's life, this approach gives him information on several markets in his field, and it helps him develop new skills. He learns about changing market forces by noticing that more stock requests are coming from England, many of them specifying pets and other animals. This alerts him to a possible future market for his services as an assignment photographer. Or he may find more students in his classes asking about how to photograph pets, alerting him to a new market before most other photographers notice it. Most important, having to keep current in multiple aspects of his field is a form of training that will keep Neil a technically skilled person as long as he is active in this business.

Debra Dadd has a variety of income sources, too. She is a pioneer in the field of education on toxic home and personal environments. Debra writes books, publishes a newsletter, gives speeches, and does consulting, both in person and by telephone—all on the effects of environmental pollutants, at home and work, on our health. From these various income sources, she gains information about new markets. In addition, each part of the business feeds the other parts. Writing books generates publicity tours with radio and TV guest appearances, which in turn sells more books, newsletters, and consulting. On tour she learns about interests in different parts of the country and hears about emerging areas of controversy in which she needs to develop expertise. Her private clients bring up questions, concerns, and experiences that she can use in her newsletter, which in turn provides material for additional books. Debra's is a superb example of how useful variety in income sources can be, since it contributes to the business in so many ways.

Robert Kourik epitomizes the multiple-income-stream approach: "My primary goal is to get enormous satisfaction out of doing the job and to do lots of different things. I don't have any tolerance for repetition. Only when I'm mentally ill do I enjoy repetition. I can't make a living juggling one ball. I have to juggle three to five balls. Sometimes I refer to it as 'You can't make a stable chair with one or two legs, you need three or four.' I do publishing, free-lance writing, consulting, photography, and design work. I also have a product in a gardening catalog that gives me 4 to 6 percent of my yearly income."

Protecting against Income Fluctuations The best protection against fluctuations in income, whether they are seasonal or market driven, is a broad client base. A wide variety of clients will provide the diversity in income sources you need to have a smoother cash flow. To build this base you need to select your customers purposefully, with specific objectives in mind. You must also track your income sources in some detail and frequently review your pricing, your policies, and all other practices you use to attract customers.

In setting objectives for the selection of customers or clients, keep in mind three key problems of one-person businesses: (1) income streams tend to be volatile, (2) there is a constant need to upgrade your skills, and (3) the nature of your business is constantly changing.

As your client base broadens, you should continually monitor it to see if you are attracting the variety of customers necessary to respond to these problems. Build these sources of income into your financial statements by tracking them in your income records. This will amount to a regular audit of your progress in selecting customers with an organized intent.

Clients Who Help Combat Income Volatility

To deal with income volatility, you might focus on three types of clients: *repeat clients*, *appreciative clients*, and *flexible clients*.

Repeat clients are desirable because they have already been sold on what you do and they understand how your work or product meets their needs. Some businesses require repeat customers who visit often (retail stores, for example), others may require repeat clients who only visit one or two times a year (such as orthodontists), and some repeat business is unpredictable (as with morticians and obstetricians). Still, repeat clients are at the core of most businesses (except tourist businesses).

In your search for repeat clients you will want to attract customers who are likely to use you frequently as well as those who will need you at seasonally slack times. For example, a gardener would find desirable a client who would need weekly maintenance all year as well as tree pruning in the winter.

Appreciative clients are those who feel that you do an especially good job and that find your work is just right for them. They therefore refer other clients to you. The more appreciative clients you have, the fewer unappreciative clients you'll have to take. Unappreciative clients are more likely to create conflict, complain about you to others, be slow on their payments, and expect you to fix problems that you didn't cause.

You can develop appreciative clients by educating them about how your work or product might be most beneficial to them. In professional sales parlance this is called "selling the benefits."

Flexible clients are almost a must for many one-person businesses. Small businesses typically find themselves either swamped with jobs and customers or doing and selling nothing. Therefore, a client who will agree to adjust the work schedule or delivery time, to accept work on a smaller scale or shipment of a portion of an order, or to postpone the transaction until another mutually beneficial time is immensely valuable. In many businesses you can find clients who are willing to be flexible if you pay attention to how they react when things go wrong. But taking advantage of clients who are flexible also carries with it the responsibility to be flexible with them, when they need quick turnaround times or a better price, etc.

Clients Who Help You Upgrade Your Skills

In a one-person business it is essential to keep your skills sharpened and up to date so that you are a leader in your field. Two types of clients will make a big difference in this regard: *clients who offer you a challenge and clients who offer you a chance to learn* on the job.

Clients who offer you a challenge: When you take on a client whose needs challenge you to use your best skills and most imaginative approach, the work becomes rewarding in itself. These challenges also encourage you to refine skills that are not called for in every job or product sale.

Clients who offer you a chance to learn are also extremely desirable because they help you grow. Such clients will want you to do something you haven't done before or use a new method to do the same old thing. Each such opportunity gives you a chance to talk to your peers and to ask questions that will keep you in touch with the mainstream of your field.

A chimney sweep who decides to replace some ornamental tiles for the first time might need to meet tile setters and learn about the new uses of tiles in fireplaces. And learning from the tile setter might also bring the chance to be recommended to new clients.

Clients Who Help You Respond to Business Changes

Nearly all businesses are in flux. In fields that change rapidly (medicine, dentistry, nursing, tax law), in-service training is required to maintain a license. Because of these ever-present changes in business you need a way to keep in touch with how your field is changing. We recommend two ways of doing this: building a *broad* client base, and building a *deep* client base.

A *broad client base* means serving a wide variety of clients by offering a range of services that will extend your business into interesting and possibly expanding fields. A *deep client base* means catering to a wide variety of needs expressed by your customers.

The challenge is to balance the demands of these two types of client base, while staying focused on running just one business. Here are some examples of real people we know who have succeeded in building varied client bases that combat income volatility, upgrade their skills, and help them respond to business changes:

- A management consultant to large companies who takes on a few smaller clients and a few nonprofit organizations, teaches classes at a local college, writes a business-software review column, and has several international clients.

- An astrologer with regular office clients who sees a few low-income clients at a local psychic research center, writes magazine columns, and sells a selection of his ten favorite occult books wherever he goes.
- A graphic artist who does a newsletter for one large corporate client, has several dozen small clients, draws her own cartoon strip for a neighborhood newspaper, occasionally designs sets and images for a local TV station, has a low-priced special service for restaurant menus, and is a prominent partner in a local photography gallery.
- An antique dealer who attends only the high-end shows, specializes in Oriental antiques, has a small shop in the "antique ghetto" of a large city, and does on-request searches for one-of-a-kind items.

PRICING PRODUCTS OR SERVICES

Some businesses don't have to worry about pricing because there is a market price for their goods or services that can't be modified, such as the price of developing a role of 35-mm color film at a Fotomat franchise shop. But most businesses have to decide how to price their goods or service and whether it will be lower, the same as, or higher than the market price.

The price you can charge above what is needed to cover overhead is usually not a matter of supply and demand, although traditional economists might try to tell you otherwise. For most businesses, the price charged determines the *type* of client the business will have, not the *number*. Usually, changing the price only changes who your customers will be. A low price will attract few customers if you don't offer what they want, and a high price can bring in many if you do.

The price of your merchandise or service tells the customer a lot about what they can expect from your business. A low price often means that customers must serve themselves and that there will be no refunds or returns. In a service business, it implies amateurism and inexperience or, at best, that you're dealing with a start-up. A high price can often mean the opposite.

Prices that are out of line with those of similar businesses need to be justified to customers through added value. Customers will sort themselves out according to the value they want, and those who choose your business will do so because you meet or exceed their expectations.

For example, a marketing research consultant who charges $1,000 per focus group research session will be expected to show up twenty minutes before the session to discuss it with the client. Afterwards the consultant will deliver an audiotape and a one-page summary of the session. The same consultant charging $2,000 per session will be expected to meet with the client for at least an hour during the week before the session, to hold the session in an interview room with a two-way mirror and a video camera, and to deliver a verbal presentation and a five- to ten-page summary a few weeks later. The pricing determines the client's expectations.

As publisher Bear Kamoroff explains, "Pricing is subjective. You have to charge enough to make it a job worth doing—so that it pays for itself. And you can't charge so much that people are put off by the price.

"I based my pricing of *Small-Time Operator* on what the book cost me to make and on the level of discount I have to give to the people I usually sell to. I also experimented a little. If the book sells for $10 and I have to give a 60 percent discount to my wholesaler, I receive $4. Printing costs $1.50 a book. So I have $2.50 left to cover my incidental expenses and overhead. Does this price earn me enough to make me happy? If it is worth doing, is $10 a fair price for the book? Will people pay that price?

"I did market research at bookstores to see what other books were selling for and I talked to people in and out of the book trade. I didn't want anybody to turn the book down because of the price and I didn't want anybody to buy it in spite of the price.

"Pricing is not that important to a lot of people, particularly with small businesses. People are more interested in quality than price. If you're a good auto mechanic, customers will happily pay you $35 an hour, rather than risk leaving their car with someone they don't know who charges $20 an hour. Unless it gets outrageous, price will not scare people away."

There are three basic rules to follow when you are determining the price for any product or service: (1) pricing should be easy to understand, (2) the price should be complete, and (3) the customer should have a reasonable number of pricing options.

Pricing Should Be Easy to Understand When you make pricing difficult, you are asking your customer to do business with someone else.

The Price Should Be Complete Not only should the customer understand how you arrived at your price, but it should also be clear to them that there aren't any surprises. Just recall for a moment the kind of pricing that charges you for every little part. "On sale now! This computer only $599 (keyboard and monitor not included)." What good is a computer without a way to put in data (keyboard) and a way to see what you're doing (monitor)? This is a form of deception, and not a very subtle one. Most of us would much rather see "This computer is only $999 (keyboard and monitor included)." It instills a much higher level of trust.

The Customer Should Have Pricing Options On the one hand, we've just implied that you should lump the components together and tell the truth about the minimum combination that is actually usable. On the other hand, one way to give customers a reasonable number of pricing options is to break the system down into interchangeable parts. The solution to this apparent conflict? We would recommend pricing all the components as components and adding a slightly reduced price as an incentive for buying a whole system. So, language becomes critical here. Instead of "This computer $599" you would say "CPU $599, keyboard $129, monitor $299—buy all three together for $999." Thus you have given the customer all the options he or she needs to make an intelligent choice. The customer who can find better component prices elsewhere or who doesn't really need more than one of the components knows what to expect, as does the customer who wants to save money by buying a whole system.

Pricing Factors

There are several factors to consider in setting your price, whether you are a service- or project-oriented business or a more traditional manufacturer, distributor, or retailer. We will describe the nine most critical factors in some detail. They are: (1) return on investment, (2) pricing policies of others in the field, (3) marketing strategy, (4) desired customers, (5) seasonal nature of sales, (6) type of product or service, (7) fair trade laws, (8) manufacturer's suggested price, and (9) nationally advertised price.

Return on Investment Sometimes you may simply base your price on the amount of profit you want to make. This is especially likely if you are a manufacturer or distributor and you expect to sell several thousand of a particular product in a given period of time. Suppose you are a fireplace accessory distributor. You have kept good books, so you know what your fixed expenses usually are and you can estimate with some confidence your variable expenses. In a typical winter season, from September through January, your fixed expenses run $1,000 per month and your variable expenses total around $6,000. You expect to sell 3,000 fireplace tool sets during the five-month period. The sets cost you $11 each, or $33,000 for the lot. You would like to earn at least a 10 percent profit. To find out how much you must charge, add $5,000 fixed expenses, $6,000 variable expenses, and $33,000 cost of goods sold, which totals $44,000. Multiply $44,000 by 1.11 (see figure 4.2) to get the total, including a 10 percent profit: $48,840. Now divide by 3,000, the number of tool sets. You get $16.29, the price you must charge per set if you want to cover all costs and make a 10 percent profit. But there are many other factors that might affect the price.

Pricing Policies of Others in the Field If other businesses carry products of a similar quality or type, you must be aware of their prices and be prepared to explain to your customers why you charge a different price, whether it is higher or lower.

Marketing Strategy If you clearly tell your customers what makes your products different, and that difference includes price, you can sometimes create a market niche with the price you charge. You may choose to do this as a part of an overall market strategy. The simplest example is of a business that sets prices and offers quality in a range not served by others in the field. Again, this niche can offer products at either a higher or a lower price.

Desired Customers All other factors being accounted for, you will attract more affluent customers if you charge a higher price. A lower price will attract more price-conscious shoppers.

Seasonal Nature of Sales If you typically have good and bad times during the year, you might set your prices higher during the up times to compensate for the fact that you must lower your prices during the down times, to stimulate sales.

Type of Product or Service The type of product you sell can also influence pricing. Convenience stores, such as neighborhood grocers or national chains like 7-Eleven, can charge more for the items you might otherwise buy in a supermarket, simply because they are open late at night or are located nearby. Special-interest stores generally charge more for a given item than does a department store. Many of the services or products that a one-person business might offer could easily be priced by the convenience or special-interest value that they offer.

Fair Trade Laws Many states have fair trade laws, which allow the manufacturer of a product to make agreements with retailers and distributors about how to price the product. If you live in one of these states, you may have to price your products with that in mind.

Manufacturer's Suggested Prices This is a little different from fair trade laws. The manufacturer tries to protect the quality image of its product, or the profit margins of its retailers, without the aid of fair trade laws. So you may have to price your product according to a schedule suggested by the manufacturer.

Nationally Advertised Prices As a retailer or distributor, you can often get away with undercutting the prices that manufacturers advertise in national media. It is very difficult to charge more than that, however, regardless of how well you can justify it from an expense point of view.

The Five Elements of Price

There are five basic elements that must be considered in setting every price: (1) cost of goods sold, (2) selling costs, (3) operating expenses, (4) profit, and (5) shrinkage, markdowns, discounts, redemptions, and trades.

Pricing Professional Services When pricing professional services there is no "cost of goods sold" to consider, but it is important to remember the nonbillable costs you incur on every job, like supplies, and sometimes postage, phone, or travel, if you have not included them in your terms and conditions. A service business definitely incurs selling costs. These are made up of every expenditure that can be directly attributed to getting clients and jobs. Advertising, entertainment, and travel related to selling are examples. Operating expenses are just that: rent, utilities, general phone, general postage, and so on. For a service business, these are often thought of as administration and overhead costs. You will definitely want to make a profit, unless you are a true nonprofit corporation. And finally, you must take into consideration whether you will ever offer discounts of any kind, such as to members of your trade organization or club, or if you are going to barter any amount of your services. There are three key questions in pricing a service business: (1) How much money do you want to take home? (2) How many hours do you want to work? and (3) How much money do you want above your living and business expenses? If yours is a service business, the exercise in figure 4.1 is an opportunity for you to use these questions and the above considerations in calculating your own fees.

The money you take home will determine the lifestyle you can afford. The number of hours you work will help determine your schedule. The money you want above your expenses will be the amount you can put away for vacations, old age, spontaneous adventures, and so forth.

Calculating how much to charge isn't difficult; just be sure you understand the difference between productive and administrative time, also called billable and nonbillable time (see Chapter 6). Understanding this difference is crucial to deciding how much you want to work. Work includes all the hours you pay bills, do bookkeeping, and tend to filing and marketing activities, as well as the things you do that you can charge a fee for, or the time you spend selling a product. First figure out how many hours of administrative time you must spend for each hour of productive time. Then use the accompanying exercise to calculate your rate. Another way you might price your service is to ask others in your field how they do it.

Pricing a New Product Few people ever have the need to price a new product, but if you do, remember to ask these four questions: (1) What other product is it like? (2) What niche will it occupy? (3) Who will buy it? and (4) What would they expect to pay for it?

Customers will evaluate the reasonableness of your price by finding something to compare your product to. Even Sony's Walkman, which was a completely new concept, was priced at $300 when it was introduced in Japan, because it was compared by customers to similar portable objects such as cameras and walkie-talkies, which were also in the $300 price range at that time. It was first sold in fancy camera shops, with a case like that for a camera. In setting your price,

---

Fig. 4.1 Pricing Your Professional Services

This exercise will help you figure out the minimum fee to charge your clients. The calculations are based on how much income you want to earn, how many days you wish to work, your anticipated expenses, and how much profit you would like to set aside in addition to "salary" and business expenses.

Each line of the worksheet is numbered to correspond to the instructions below. Following these instructions will make it easier to complete the form. The blank form explains all the entries and calculations you should make. We have also included an example that is filled in.

The **first step** is to fill in the blanks for:

- *Yearly Earnings* (1) (this could be the monthly total from the personal budget exercise in Chapter 3)
- *Days worked a month* (2a)
- *Days worked a year* (2b)
- *Desired Profit Percentage* (3)

There is no magic formula for answering these questions. They are simply personal choices that you must make. How much money do you need to spend on your personal lifestyle? (The exercise on calculating a personal budget in Chapter 3 should be helpful in

answering this question.) How hard and how often do you want to work? How much of each dollar you bring in would you like to set aside for the future?

The **second step** is to calculate your *EXPENSES* (4).

The blanks on the form may or may not represent some or all of your expense items. They are provided to stimulate your thinking. Be sure to include any additional items that may apply to your business.

The **third step** is to add up the columns to get *TOTAL EXPENSES* (5).

The **fourth step** is to make a few calculations and fill in the blanks for:

- *Daily Overhead* (6)
- *Daily Salary* (7)
- *Minimum Income Requirement* (8)
- *Daily Profit* (9)

The **fifth step** is to fill in the *Required Billing Rate* (10) by adding the amounts in spaces 8 and 9. This is your "day rate," or what you should try to make per day.

If you want to know your *Equivalent Hourly Rate* (11), divide the Required Billing Rate (10) by the number of billable hours worked per day. (In the example, it is six hours.)

---

therefore, try to figure out the products that will compare with yours, and take those prices into account.

The wholesale price of products is often about half the retail price. So if you can discover how much knowledgeable buyers of your product would pay at wholesale, you can double this to get your retail price. If you discover that your industry uses a different pricing standard, then consider using that.

Often products and services that are new to consumers have been known by professionals in the field for some time. Such was the case with automatic coffee-brewing machines and automobile-buying services. So asking the professionals in your industry what they think the price should be can often be helpful.

EXAMPLE WORKSHEET FOR PRICING PROFESSIONAL SERVICES

1. Yearly Earnings	$24,000	(Enter the amount you wish to earn.)
2a. Days worked a month	22	(Enter the number of days a month you are willing to work.)
2b. Days worked a year	264	(Multiply 2a by 12 months.)
3. Desired Profit Percentage	15	(Enter the percent profit you want.)

4. EXPENSES (Fill in the lines below for your expenses.)

Rent	$200.00	$2,400.00
Office Help	50.00	600.00
Postage	29.00	348.00
Telephone	100.00	1,200.00
Utilities	50.00	600.00
Supplies	50.00	600.00
Insurance	83.33	999.96
Marketing	75.00	900.00
Legal & Accounting	30.00	360.00
Promotion	83.33	999.96
Other	40.00	480.00
Automobile	225.00	2,700.00
Entertainment	100.00	1,200.00
Taxes	50.00	600.00
Travel	100.00	1,200.00
Vacation	166.67	2,000.04
Miscellaneous	100.00	1,200.00
		0.00
		0.00
		0.00
		0.00
		0.00

5. TOTAL EXPENSES (Add the expense figures and put total here.)	$1,532.33	$18,387.96

6. Daily Overhead	$69.65	Divide 5-Total Expenses-by 2b-Days worked a year.
7. Daily Earnings	90.91	Divide 1-Yearly Earnings-by 2b-Number of days worked a year.
8. Minimum Income Requirement	160.56	Add 6-Daily Overhead-to 7-Daily Salary.
9. Daily Profit	24.08	Multiply 8-Minimum Income Requirement-by decimal form of 3-Desired Profit Percentage (160.56 × .15).
10. Required Billing Rate	184.64	Add 8-Minimum Income Requirement-and 9-Daily Profit.
11. Equivalent Hourly Rate	30.77	Divide 10-Required Billing Rate-by the number of BILLABLE hours you plan to work each day.

WORKSHEET FOR PRICING PROFESSIONAL SERVICES

1. Yearly Earnings		(Enter the amount you wish to earn.)
2a. Days worked a month		(Enter the number of days a month you are willing to work.)
2b. Days worked a year		(Multiply 2a by 12 months.)
3. Desired Profit Percentage		(Enter the percent profit you want.)

4. EXPENSES (Fill in the lines below for your expenses.)		
Rent		
Office Help		
Postage		
Telephone		
Utilities		
Supplies		
Insurance		
Marketing		
Legal & Accounting		
Promotion		
Other		
Automobile		
Entertainment		
Taxes		
Travel		
Vacation		
Miscellaneous		

5. TOTAL EXPENSES (Add the expense figures and put total here.)			
6. Daily Overhead	$69.65	Divide 5-Total Expenses-by 2b-Days worked a year.	
7. Daily Earnings	90.91	Divide 1-Yearly Earnings-by 2b-Number of days worked a year.	
8. Minimum Income Requirement	160.56	Add 6-Daily Overhead-to 7-Daily Salary.	
9. Daily Profit	24.08	Multiply 8-Minimum Income Requirement-by decimal form of 3-Desired Profit Percentage.	
10. Required Billing Rate	184.64	Add 8-Minimum Income Requirement-and 9-Daily Profit.	
11. Equivalent Hourly Rate	30.77	Divide 10-Required Billing Rate-by the number of BILLABLE hours you plan to work each day.	

Pricing Retail and Wholesale Goods Returning to our five elements of price, when you are pricing retail or wholesale goods, "cost of goods sold" is often called "cost of merchandise" and is made up of the cost of your inventory and the cost of transportation from your suppliers to your place of business. Selling costs, operating expenses, and profit are defined the same as for any other business, but in retail, shrinkage, markdowns, discounts, and redemptions take on special importance.

A key concept to understand in both retail and wholesale pricing is the difference between "margin" and "markup." Margin is the selling price less the cost of merchandise, while markup is cost of the merchandise multiplied by your markup percentage. To make this easier to understand we are including a table in figure 4.2 that clearly shows the difference between margin and markup.

Pricing Manufactured Goods The five elements of price for manufactured goods also take on a unique flavor. Cost of goods sold is calculated by adding the inventory and transportation costs, as in retail, but the direct labor applied to the manufacturing process is also included. Selling costs, operating expenses, and profit are defined the same as for any other business.

A key concept to understand in manufacturing is something called "contribution." This is manufacturing's way of describing the fact that price must include an overhead contribution from both general operating costs and from the costs of the

Fig. 4.2   Table of True Markups

Margin (as a percentage of retail price)	True Markup Percentage	Markup Factor*
10	11.1	1.11
13	15	1.15
15	17.7	1.177
20	25	1.25
25	33.3	1.333
30	42.9	1.429
33.3	50	1.50
35	53.9	1.539
40	66.7	1.667
50	100	2.00

* To calculate *retail price*, multiply the *cost of merchandise* by the *markup factor* (the decimal equivalent of true markup percentage plus 100). For example, if the cost of merchandise for a particular product is $6 and the *margin* is 40 percent, multiply $6 by 1.667. This will result in a $10 retail price.

actual manufacturing. It is important not to blur these two. For example, your electrical bill for manufacturing certain products can be a significant part of your total electrical bill. It would be a mistake to post 100 percent of your electrical costs into a general utilities overhead account.

How to Do Estimates or Quotes

Project and service businesses are often asked to submit an estimate or quote of how much it will cost to complete a project. Should you charge by the hour or the day? Or can you make a close enough guess as to the true costs of completing the project that you can give your potential client a fixed-price estimate?

Corporate clients are used to paying by the day or half day, but small businesses and individuals often prefer paying by the hour. Many clients—such as those seeking home improvements—prefer to contract for services on a fixed-price basis. For you, the major advantage of a fixed-price contract is that it gives you the opportunity to make an extra profit by working efficiently enough to do better than your estimate. For the client, the major benefit is the assurance that you will not go over budget, because you will have to absorb any extra costs.

Making a fixed-price contract work depends on your accuracy in estimating direct labor costs and direct expenses. To these you add a figure for overhead (the cost to keep your office open) and the profit you would like to make. Overhead is usually calculated as a percentage of direct labor. To figure out your overhead rate, add up the total amount you must spend each year to keep your office open and divide it by the number of days you expect to be billing clients. The result will be your daily overhead expense. Overhead expenses include rent, utilities, phone, and so forth, as illustrated in the "Pricing Professional Services" exercise above. Once you know this figure, you can calculate the average percentage for overhead by dividing yearly overhead by yearly income. Figure 4.3 is a sample worksheet that shows how to estimate a fixed-price contract for a hypothetical computer programming project (and it would look a lot like this for any service business, but project-oriented businesses, like contractors, would also have a materials cost). In figure 4.3 we have used the overhead percentage and the percent profit from the "Pricing Professional Services" example.

Computer and training consultant Bill Dale thinks that the biggest problem in pricing service work is failing to estimate accurately the work effort required for a given project. "As a consultant I have only one resource, my time. If I have to put more time into a project, I have lost a part of my fee income." Bill breaks projects down into small steps that are easier to cost out. The typical steps he might use for estimating a training project are:

- Information gathering
- Research
- Development of outline

Fig. 4.3   Estimating Worksheet for a Fixed-Price Contract

Direct Labor		
Systems Analyst	20 days x $350 =	$ 7,000
Programmer/Analyst	60 days x $275 =	16,500
Clerical/Data Entry	15 days x $100 =	1,500
	TOTAL DIRECT LABOR =	$25,000
Overhead (50% of direct labor, from "Pricing Professional Services" example)		$12,500
Direct Expense		
Air fare		$1,500
Rental Car		500
Meals		500
Hotel		1,000
Modem connect charges		300
Printing (documentation)		400
Postage (express deliveries)		75
	TOTAL DIRECT EXPENSE	$4,275
DIRECT LABOR + OVERHEAD + DIRECT EXPENSE		$41,775
PROFIT (15% Margin, 17.7% Markup)		$ 7,394
TOTAL FIXED PRICE		$49,169

- Client review(s)
- Revision of outline
- Client review(s)
- Development of material
- Client review(s)
- Revision of material
- Proofing of production
- Proofing of reproduction
- Presentation of materials in training session
- Follow-up immediately after the session: debriefing and summary of course evaluations
- Follow-up in the medium term: effectiveness of training, future needs

As Bill explains further, "I add a 15 percent contingency to development and then stick to the figure, provided there are no major changes. This is good for the client because he knows what he'll have to pay, and good for me because if I can work quicker or smarter, I will make more money. I don't agree to on-the-spot quotes. I think them through first. In my experience, quoting on the spot always leads to underquoting because I forget a few steps."

How to Do Proposals

There are three common types of proposal that you can offer your clients: the *handshake agreement*, the *fill-in-the-blanks proposal*, and the *letter of agreement*.

The Handshake Agreement is a simple verbal agreement that comes from a discussion of what needs to be done, how long it will take, and how much will be charged, including which expenses will be covered. This is the most common form of proposal, and the most risky. Handshake agreements feel good, but it is easy to forget to include key items such as due dates and budget limits. Even if you cover all the bases, no one is infallible. People forget details as time passes, and disagreements about terms can easily arise later. If a client insists on a verbal agreement, your best bet is to take good notes and follow up with a letter that outlines what you think was agreed to. This will give the client a chance to clarify his or her understanding, and in many states such a letter is considered to be a form of contract that can be used later to collect a past-due bill. Without a written agreement it is much harder to collect from a disgruntled client.

The Fill-in-the-Blanks Proposal is most often used when dealing with the government or big corporations. The client usually supplies a set of forms that are very detailed as to the specifications of the project. You are required to complete the forms and submit them along with any supplementary materials you feel are necessary.

The Letter of Agreement Proposal is the most common sort of written proposal. You write a letter to the client that addresses at least these three points: (1) When will the project begin, what will the deadlines for each step of the project be, and when will it be completed? (2) What work will be done, and what will the expenses be? and (3) What will the total charge to the client be? A letter of agreement differs from the follow-up letter to the verbal proposal only in its degree of formality. A letter of agreement usually has signature blanks at the end for both the client and the contractor to sign. Copies are retained by each and, as we noted above, the letter is almost sure to be considered a formal contract under the law in most states. This is the type of agreement illustrated in Chapter 11.

Although proposals are most often thought of in relation to consulting or other service work, they are also a useful tool in the product arena. In this case, you are submitting the proposal to a potential buyer of your goods. A proposal to sell goods should contain clauses describing the type of product, quantity, unit prices, delivery schedules, terms of payment, and any other relevant terms and conditions.

Whether you are in a product or a service business, the use of a written proposal can save you a lot of worry and time by making your agreements clear from the beginning. After a proposal has been accepted, you should follow up with a contract of some sort. In many cases, the proposal itself can serve as the contract. The topic of contracts with clients is covered in more detail in Chapter 11.

CREDIT AND COLLECTIONS

Whether you offer credit is often a function of trade practices for your field or product. Manufacturers and distributors almost always have credit programs, and some kinds of retailers offer charge accounts as well. Service businesses, too, frequently offer billing arrangements so that clients can pay for the service after it is delivered.

Billing and Terms

The two most-asked questions are "When should I bill?" and "What kinds of terms should I offer?" The terms of billing arrangements vary by trade or type of product. Terms are specified in the little "terms" box on the invoice that says something like "2% 10, Net 30," or "COD," or, as in the letter of agreement discussed in Chapter 11, "Payment will be made one half on commencement of the work and one half on completion." Terms are a function of trade practice and cash-flow needs. Whenever you offer credit, it costs you something. You may have to borrow working capital to keep going while you wait for payments to come in.

A flat-weave-tapestry manufacturing enterprise, Loom Designs, was made up of two one-person businesses. Robert lived in Mexico and handled the supervision of native weavers. Alice lived in San Francisco, California, and handled marketing and selling. When they got a $30,000 order from a large department store, Alice and Robert thought it was wonderful. The terms were "Net 60 days," and they had enough capital between them to carry their businesses for at least ninety days. Little did they know that the department store was in the habit of paying slowly, and the check didn't arrive for over one hundred days. Because they couldn't be sure when the store would pay, they were each forced to borrow to keep going beyond the ninety days. Naturally they had to pay interest on the borrowed money, even though they used it for only ten days.

Had they known that the large department store habitually paid late, they could have increased the price of the product to compensate for the cost of borrowing the money. Or they might have negotiated a shorter term, maybe "Net 45 days," so that there was a better chance of getting paid within sixty days.

Credit and Collections

Once you offer credit, it is almost inevitable that you will encounter the problem of collections. Not everyone who pays late is a deadbeat, but the challenges of today's economy make it almost unavoidable that more and more people will find themselves in financial difficulty. If you've had the luck of open, honest relationships with your customers then you will usually know whether they are simply behind in their cash flow or about to close their doors. But if you don't know, then you too may be caught off guard by those who cannot pay.

If you offer credit, you also offer terms. Once those terms have been exceeded, it is important to contact the customer right away. But this is not to be taken too literally. In many trades it is standard practice to stretch the terms by a short amount of time. Once you are beyond the generally accepted limit, however, you really must start the collection process.

There is a relatively simple acceleration in collection reminders that you can use as an account becomes further and further behind. Be sure to make a written record of the steps as you take them and save copies of all documents. You will need these should it prove necessary to take your collection to small claims court.

1. When the account is beyond the acceptable late period for your industry it is time to send your first collection letter. Each subsequent letter should be sent one billing cycle after its predecessor.

   The letters should be personalized and addressed to your client with a copy to the person who writes the checks for your client, if possible. The words *First Notice*, *Second Notice*, and *Final Notice* should be prominently displayed on each letter. The first letter should be polite and friendly, suggesting that perhaps the bill has been overlooked and that payment should be sent now so that the customer can maintain a good credit rating. The second letter should explain that the bill is seriously overdue, that the customer's patronage is valued, and that payment will bring them up to date. The third letter should state that the bill must be paid by a certain date, after which it will be turned over for collection, with a reminder about how that might damage the customer's credit rating.
2. A week to ten days after sending the first letter make a friendly telephone call to the person for whom you did the work. If they are surprised by your call, ask them if they would like you to call the person who writes the checks. They will either offer to take care of it for you or they will give you that person's name. Or they may inform you that "the check is in the mail."
3. After an additional week has passed it is time to call again. Friendly and polite are still the order of the day. This time be sure to find out the name of the person who writes the checks because you will need it later.
4. If another week passes with no payment, then call the person who writes the checks directly. Once again either they will tell you when they are going to take care of it or that "the check is in the mail."
5. Once an entire billing cycle has passed it is time to send the second collection letter. Then start Steps 2 to 4 over again.

6. Once the third letter has been sent, you have only small claims court left as your recourse. While going to small claims court is time-consuming, the procedure is relatively simple. If you have documented your phone conversations and saved copies of the original invoice and the collection letters you will almost certainly win a judgment against your client when you present your case. A good source of help is *Everybody's Guide to Small Claims Court.*

7. Finally, you have to collect your judgment. The amount you can win in small claims court varies from state to state, but the minimum in many states is well worth the effort. A good source of help is *Collect Your Court Judgment.* While this book is written for California laws, it will give you good ideas that you can check with your local municipality to verify before using.

Needless to say, your personal relationship with the client and the amount you are owed on any given bill are important factors in whether you choose to follow a collection procedure to its conclusion or simply to write off the amount owed as a bad debt. One of the best ways to avoid collection problems is to have your customers fill out a credit application, then run a credit check before you extend credit. Another policy that is widely used is to offer cash-only terms for the first few payments and then let your customers open a credit account with a limit. The limit can gradually be increased as the customer proves their credit worthiness.

Good help on setting up a credit and collections system can be found in *The Legal Guide for Starting and Running a Small Business.*

CUSTOMER SERVICE

Customer service means being present, willing, and able to provide what your customers or clients need, to fix what goes wrong, or to refer them to those who can serve them better. One of the cardinal principles of good customer service is to get the employees involved. If the employees believe in it, it will happen. That makes it relatively easy, then, for a one-person business to create good customer service. After all, you are not just the owner, you are sole employee.

To create the best possible customer service, you need to ask yourself five basic questions: (1) Why are you in business? (2) What are your products or services? (3) Who are your customers or clients? (4) Who else is doing what you're doing? and (5) How do you rate yourself right now? We offer some good help with question 1 in Chapter 6. Question 4 is covered in Chapter 3, where questions 2 and 3 are also touched on. Questions 2 and 3 are at the heart of Chapter 9, and question 5 is covered there as well.

Probably the key element, though, of good customer service is attitude. The difficulties that can sometimes occur in your personal life and the challenges of the day-to-day management of your one-person business can cause a lot of emotional stress. If you allow this to be reflected by a bad attitude, the inevitable result will be to drive your customers and clients away. So, be sure to take a close look at Chapter 10 as well.

It is important to combine your client/customer-centered attitude with your management systems and support strategies to help you weather even the most difficult of times. When you serve each and every client or customer in the best way you know how, you will create a kind of loyalty that will keep them coming back for years. This may be one of the most powerful strategies you can use to increase income in the long run.

PHYSICAL LAYOUT

The smarter you are about the layout of your physical premises, the more reductions in cost you can create. We discuss the details of setting up your small or home office in Chapter 7, but we want to point out some of the expense-reducing and income-increasing factors of retail, wholesale, and manufacturing layouts here.

Retail Layout

The guiding rules for retail layout are what we like to call the four Cs: Clear, Calm, Clean, and Comfortable. It must be clear what it is your store is trying to be. Don't use upscale shelving and neatly lettered signage if you're trying to run a used bookstore. Overstuffed chairs, odd shelving, and hand-lettered signage would tell more clearly what you are. *Calm* is important, too, to most businesses. Occasionally you

Fig. 4.4   The Relative Value of Floor Space in a Typical Retail Store

Sixth	Fifth	Sixth
Fourth	Third	Second
Third	Second	First
Windows	Door	Windows

From Steinhoff, Dan, and Burgess, John. *Small Business Management Fundamentals.*
Reproduced by kind permission

may choose to create a cacophonic, chaotic environment because that somehow goes with the product you are selling, such as a rock-and-roll nightclub, but frankly we think that in most instances "calm" will sell better and build a better relationship with your customers. *Clean* is important because it helps people trust you and it makes them feel *comfortable* about spending time in your store. After the four Cs your attention should turn to product merchandising and in-store traffic patterns.

Product Merchandising is made up of three key elements: (1) customer access, (2) view of the store, and (3) information/service. *Customer access* means that products are displayed in a way that makes them easy for customers to get to without help from your staff. *View of the store* means remembering the simple principles that draw your customers into your space. For example, fixtures should gradually increase in height from the front of the store to the back of the store. Not only does this invite customers in, it also makes it easier for you to notice who in the store might need help and it discourages shoplifters. Providing maximum *information and customer service* means better-informed customers who will take less sales time in the future and who will probably return more often.

In-Store Traffic Patterns can best be explained by the drawing in figure 4.4, which rank the relative values of floor space in a typical retail store: (1) Your window space is your first and best chance to tell your story. Attractive, educational, frequently changing displays draw renewed interest from walk-by traffic. (2) Goods that people shop for (to compare features and price) should be located at the rear of the store, or upstairs if you have more than one floor. This allows you to show the customer everything you've got as they pass through the store on the way to what brought them in. (3) Service, gift-wrapping, or shipping departments should be in the rear, for the same reason. (4) Convenience items and/or items that define your store should be in the front of the store. (5) But such items can also sell well when placed next to goods that customers seek out the most. (6) Wide aisles are preferable to narrow ones. They provide an ease of passage and subjective feeling of comfort and hospitality. Thirty-six inches is a good minimum. (7) Occasional displays that interrupt the traffic flow are a good way to get customers to stop and learn about what you have to offer.

Wholesale Layout

The guiding rule in wholesale layout is *Store goods so that orders can be filled fast and cheap*. There are five steps to use in implementing this rule: (1) monitor work flow for speed and safety; (2) use the equipment and storage necessary to facilitate this speed and safety; (3) know what sells most frequently and in the largest quantity; (4) keep the things that sell well in easy reach and in sufficient quantity to meet reasonable demand; and (5) use shelving and material-handling equipment to take advantage of vertical space.

Fig. 4.5   Basics of Manufacturing Layout

PRODUCT LAYOUT
- Single product or one product at a time.
- Every product follows same flow route.
- Raw materials are placed where needed in the process.
- Machines are placed to minimize movement of raw materials or products during assembly.
- Lower manufacturing costs.

Example: Auto plant

PROCESS LAYOUT
- Many products or customized orders.
- Each product moves differently through the plant.
- Raw materials are centralized until needed.
- Machines are placed according to frequency of use.
- Higher manufacturing costs.

Example: Job printer

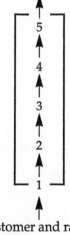

Finished products exit here.

Customer and raw materials enter here.

Raw materials or sub-assemblies may enter here. ⟶

Finished products exit here.

Customer enters here.

Remember that wholesaling is labor-intensive. You are receiving, unpacking, storing, picking, packing, and shipping. More than 60 percent of your time will be spent in your "warehouse." Yes, it is possible to run a one-person wholesale business. Claude had a wood-stove and energy-saving household-products company that he ran entirely by himself, with only occasional temporary help during peak seasons. If you do decide to take on employees, remember that they are key to the success of your wholesale business and treat them right.

Manufacturing Layout

The guiding rule for manufacturing layout is *Don't move it any further than you have to*. Steinhoff and Burgess, in their *Small Business Management Fundamentals*, make an important distinction between process layout and product layout. *Product layout*, or *continuous-production layout*, is for factories that make only one product at a time. "All operations," they explain, "follow the same path through the manufacturing process. Materials are received where needed in the assembly or manufacturing process, all machines are placed at the point where needed without unnecessary moving of materials or products in process, and all product comes from the assembly line at one point."

Process layout, or *intermittent manufacturing layout*, as it is sometimes called, is for factories that product different kinds of products or custom-made products that take different routes through the process depending on their design. These differences are illustrated in figure 4.5.

The primary focus of manufacturing layout is to minimize the movement of work in process that does not add value to the final product. Having people move half-finished products on lift trucks from one machine to another adds no real value to the product but does add costs. So put special effort into minimizing movement.

RESOURCES

Coltman, Michael M. *Financial Controls for the Small Business*. Vancouver, B.C.: Self-Counsel Press, 1986.

Davidson, Jeffrey P. *Avoiding The Pitfalls of Starting Your Own Business*. New York: Shapolsky Publishers, 1990.

Gibson, Bill. *Boost Your Business in Any Economy*. Berkeley: Ten Speed Press, 1993.

Johnson, Barbara. *Private Consulting*. Englewood Cliffs, N.J.: Prentice-Hall, 1982; out of print.

Kamoroff, Bernard. *Small-Time Operator*. Laytonville, Calif.: Bell Springs Publishing, 1992.

Parson, Mary Jean. *Financially Managing the One-Person Business*. New York: Putnam, 1991; out of print.

Ray, Norm. *Easy Financials for Your Home-Based Business*. Windsor, Calif.: Rayve Productions, 1993.

Scott, Gini Graham, Stephen Elias, and Lisa Goldoftas. *Collect Your Court Judgment*. Berkeley: Nolo Press, 1991.

Steingold, Fred S. *The Legal Guide for Starting and Running a Small Business*. Berkeley: Nolo Press, 1992.

Steinhoff, Dan, and John F. Burgess. *Small Business Management Fundamentals*, 6th ed. New York: McGraw-Hill, 1992.

Tuller, Lawrence W. *Recession Proof Your Business*. Holbrook, Mass.: Bob Adams, 1991; out of print.

Warner, Ralph. *Everybody's Guide to Small Claims Court*, 5th national ed. Berkeley: Nolo Press, 1991.

5

Information Management

One of our objectives in this book is to reduce the amount of time you spend handling and storing information, and to make the actual work of dealing with information more fun. Of course you will not be satisfied if you have lots of information but much of it is trivial. Your goal is to handle all of the information coming into your business with the greatest effectiveness and the least effort.

WHAT IS INFORMATION?

In the dictionary, *information* is defined as "the communication or reception of knowledge." But knowledge is actually the *result* of information. Information consists of details, facts, figures, measurements, notes, reports, statistics, impressions, concepts, speculations, evaluations, analyses—bits of intelligence that can be used to increase our comprehension and act as a foundation for taking action. Millions of bits of information flow past us every day, but we only notice those that we find relevant to our immediate concerns. When we look at information with some expectation or pattern in mind, we tend to connect certain bits of it together into a "pattern that connects"—that makes sense or takes on meaning. Otherwise information is just so much noise.

This means, among other things, that the way we organize information becomes critically important to how well we run our enterprise. The better you can capture, store, retrieve, share, and manage information, the better able you will be to manage a successful one-person business.

In this chapter we will look at how to handle the information that flows into your business from phone calls and mail, and we will describe effective systems for keeping track of this information daily and for filing and retrieving it as efficiently as possible.

TELEPHONE

For the majority of one-person businesses, the telephone is the main source of information. In fact, most one-person businesses simply could not exist without the telephone. And the rapid growth in the number of one-person businesses parallels the advent of the telephone answering machine.

Timing

It is wise to apply some control over the timing of calls coming into your business, but how much may be more a matter of personal taste and style than necessity. In the United States, until very recently it has been common practice not to accept calls between 9 P.M. and 8 A.M. Because of the differences in time zones, some businesses on the West Coast start at 6 A.M. in order to match the East Coast opening-time of 9 A.M. And businesses that have overseas customers sometimes work late at night. Customs also differ by trade. For example, politicians call each other until midnight, and farmers start early in the morning. And it is becoming a more common practice among all professions to call about work on the weekend. As we speed along, trying to keep up with the rapid pace of change in the society around us, the boundaries between work and the rest of our lives are becoming weaker. But there are steps you can take to regain a balanced life.

For example, you can control the timing of incoming phone calls by the creative use of telephone technology. The following examples show different ways of using a phone to good advantage.

- Doug, a theater director, has one tape that takes messages but that also refers callers to two other tapes that answer the two most common phone questions.
- Sara, a graphic artist, has two separate phone lines. One she always answers because it is for current clients; the other has a tape for inquiries and return calls.
- Carol, a production weaver, wants diversions, so she has a headset on her phone and answers the phone whenever it rings. She talks as she works, with both hands free. At night or when she is away, she turns on the answering machine.

- Tom, a tile setter, is often out in the field, so he uses a beeper for urgent calls and phones his machine twice a day when he needs a break.

Claude does a lot of his work on the phone. He makes a special effort to track all of his phone calls and to respond to them as efficiently as possible. To do this he starts by separating phone calls into the following categories:

1. *Calls that must be returned right away.* Most of these are from current clients.
2. *Calls he can answer with less urgency, but within at least forty-eight hours or so.* Most of these are from potential clients.
3. *Inquiries he can handle with a form-letter response.* Most of these are from individuals requesting information but who are not clients or immediate prospects.
4. *Friends or social calls.* These are calls that must be returned if Claude wants to keep his community of support intact, but this can be done at various times when he wants a pleasant diversion.
5. *All other calls.* These he answers once a week. Many of these involve inappropriate or mistaken queries. Over the years he has developed a list of resources and people he can refer such callers to. As a result he has slowly developed a reputation for being helpful and supportive, which has led to referrals he might not otherwise have gotten.

Phone Features

The phone companies in major metropolitan areas offer three useful features that you can add to your phone service: call forwarding, three-way calling, and call waiting.

When you are going to be away from your normal place of business, you can use *call forwarding* to send your calls to any phone you choose. *Three-way calling* allows you to add a third person to any phone conversation without the help of the operator. *Call waiting* gives a signal when you are on the line and another caller is trying to reach you. It enables you to put the first caller on hold, answer the second call, and then return to your original call. You can shift back an forth between the two calls as often as you wish.

Without question, call forwarding and three-way calling will make your life easier, but call waiting is controversial. Its advocates argue that it keeps them from missing important calls. Its critics argue that it is rude—like telling someone who is meeting with you that the person waiting is more important.

If you choose to have call waiting, you might make some rules for yourself to avoid offending your callers. First, train yourself never to give the second caller priority, no matter how strong the temptation may be. When you hear the interrupt signal, gracefully ask the current party to hold for a moment. Pick up the incoming call and tell the caller that you are on another call and that you will call them right back. Go back immediately to the first party. Aim at no more than thirty seconds from putting the first party on hold to coming back to them. Be sure to call the second party back as you promised. Paul Rosenblum, a fund-raising consultant for nonprofit organizations, uses this approach, and word of his courtesy has spread. Most of the reactions are favorable because of his consistent use of this approach.

You may also want to consider two other ways to replace the need for call waiting: First, you may want to install a second phone line with the cheapest possible service. Most phone companies refer to this as POTS, or "plain old telephone service." Then hook up an inexpensive phone machine to that line with short outgoing message such as, "I'm on the other line. Leave your name and number and I'll call you right back." Then use your call-forwarding service to put your regular line on call forwarding to your second line. You can still call out on your first line, even when it is in the call-forwarding mode. The second solution is similar but uses a voice-mail service instead of an answering machine.

The main difference between these solutions and our suggested rules for using call waiting is that the people who call you will never experience being put on hold. The drawbacks are that they are more expensive, and if someone calls you right after you have hung up from a call but before you have taken the first line off call forwarding, you cannot answer.

A few telephone companies also offer a service called *delayed call forwarding*, which can handle this second drawback. Delayed call forwarding allows the phone to ring two to four times before the forwarding feature activates, giving you time to pick up the phone if you wish to.

Ultimately, the decision to have call waiting or not is yours. As with all the systems you use, pay constant attention to the feedback you get from your clients, customers, suppliers, or prospects. If you get any negative reactions, change what you're doing.

Answering Machine, Voice Mail, or Answering Service?

Another controversial question for one-person businesses is whether to use a voice-mail system, an answering machine, or an answering service. You will definitely need one of them to stay in business, because you cannot always answer the phone when it should be answered. Even if you are at the phone all day, it's a good idea to be psychologically available to your customers at night as well by having a machine or service answer your phone. Customers will appreciate being able to call and find out your hours and location, place an order, or leave a question. A phone that rings and rings, no matter what the hour, does not instill confidence.

Answering services have been readily available for over thirty years, and as they became more affordable, they helped support the growth of one-person businesses. More recently, inexpensive answering machines and voice mail have contributed to a regular boom in one-person businesses. There is little an answering service can do that an answering machine or voice mail service cannot. A major plus of answering machines and voice mail is that they are cheaper than a service. A typical machine with all the features needed sells for less than $100. Voice mail can often be purchased for as little as $5 to $10 a month. A typical answering service costs $10 to $15 per month at a minimum and more if you want twenty-four-hour service or computer-controlled message-taking.

Another point in favor of an answering machine is that you can retrieve your messages or change your outgoing message at any time of day or night. With answering services, you are constrained by the working hours of the service or by your willingness to pay for extended hours.

A major drawback to answering services is that you do not directly control the manner in which your phone is answered. You and your clients might be treated rudely or put abruptly on hold, and all you can do is complain about it afterwards. If you decide on an answering service, choose carefully and be prepared to pay more to get prompt, courteous handling of your customer calls.

In the final analysis, the life of an answering machine is at least two to three years. You can do the arithmetic, but the conclusion has to be that an answering machine is more cost-effective than either voice mail or an answering service. But one thing an answering service can do that an answering machine or voice mail cannot is make appointments. This ability can be very important to some one-person businesses. If you can find a service willing to do it, you can have the service hold a master calendar for you and book appointments when you are unable to answer the phone.

Salli's massage professional has an answering service that schedules all her appointments. The service is so good at answering calls and handling the bookings that many people assume she has a secretary. Many professionals such as lawyers, heath practitioners, and psychotherapists offer a similar courtesy through their answering services. If you call when no one is in the office, the answering service will make an appointment for you so that you don't have to call back.

For many years, free-lance market researcher Michael Stein used both an answering service and an answering machine. His machine was a two-line model with all the key features, plus an automatic roll-over feature so that if the phone rang when someone was recording a message, the machine would redirect the second caller to the message tape for the second line. Mike found that it confused some of his clients if the outgoing message on the second line was different from the message on the first line, but there were always enough calls on both lines. Mike used the answering service if he wanted to leave a personalized message for a client. Then no one else had to listen to the personal message, as they would if it were on the machine. The system worked this way: The answering machine was set to answer on the second line only. At the same time, the answering service was instructed to pick up all calls. When people for whom there were special messages called, the service gave them the messages. Anyone else was given the choice of leaving a message with the answering service or being forwarded to the answering machine set to pick up calls on the second line. The outgoing message on the machine was simply, "This is voice mail. Leave your message after the beep." There was no need for any identification or explanation because the answering service operator had already done that. This system allowed callers to choose whether they wanted to speak to a person or a machine, effectively handling the machine-versus-service controversy without offending anyone. This same sort of solution could easily be duplicated using a voice-mail system in conjunction with an answering service.

Quality of Service   If you have an answering service, call it occasionally to make sure that the operators are doing a good job. Imagine that you are a potential customer, someone who does not know your business. Remember that in many cases the phone is the only way a customer has of judging your business. Try to get to know your regular operators, their supervisors, and the owner of the business on a first-name basis. Send holiday cards, thank-you notes, or flowers once in a while, especially if you have noticed an operator going the extra distance for you.

If you have an answering machine or voice mail, call your own number periodically to make sure the system is working properly and the message is coming out the way you expect. Be sure to keep messages up to date.

Most Frequently Asked Questions

You can cut down on telephone time by preparing a list of the questions that are asked most frequently and the answers to them. Then, when these questions arise, you will not have to handle them as if they were being asked for the first time. Such a list is also useful if you are sick or on vacation or have someone helping in your office.

If you have lots of inquiries, get a second answering machine or a more sophisticated voice-mail system that will allow variable-length outgoing messages, and use either of them to provide answers to frequently asked questions. You may need a second phone line, but it can be basic service at the lowest possible rate.

If you choose the answering-machine solution, time how long it takes to answer the questions you have chosen to automate, and buy an outgoing message tape long enough to record those answers. Put the answers on the tape, and you are in business. With voice mail you will have to record the answers one at a time as you program the codes for each question. And don't forget to mention in the outgoing message on your primary line that it's possible to get answers to frequently asked questions by calling the second number. Also tell your answering service, if you have one, to pass this information along. Then no matter when people call you, even at three in the morning, they can get some answers.

800 Numbers

Although one-person businesses rarely have an 800 number, it can be useful in a few cases—for example, a mail-order business that wants to encourage phone orders, a software publisher offering a support service for its programs, or any business specializing in selling information. The 800 service can expand your trading arena by allowing customers outside your local calling area to call your business at no charge to them. Whether to get an 800 number is a question of costs and benefits and must be calculated on a case-by-case basis.

In California, for instance, Pacific Bell charges about $40 or $50 a month plus long-distance tolls, which are lower with the 800 number than if the customer called collect. For handling customer requests, feedback, and customer service, this can be an inexpensive way to improve public perception of your product or service and to increase your ability to deliver satisfaction. And once you get your 800 number you are automatically listed with 800 information (800-555-1212), giving you additional nationwide exposure.

Telephone Courtesy

Many people don't know how to talk courteously on the telephone. This sad fact is probably a consequence of phones being a relatively new technology, one for which we have yet to develop widely accepted rules of etiquette. A few pointers will help you establish your reputation as a one-person business that cares about its customers.

First, consider carefully how you answer the phone. Do you pick it up within three or four rings? Do you merely say hello when you pick it up? Somehow, from movies or our parents, we have grown up with the idea that "hello" is all that's required. For business purposes, however, "hello" is a waste of time. Callers need to know they have reached the right person and most won't recognize your voice. Always answer with at least your name and, if you have a company name, give that too.

Second, if you have a hold button don't use it for more than thirty seconds without coming back on the line to let the caller know you have not forgotten him or her. Noting irritates a caller more than to be kept waiting with no explanation. Even with an explanation, don't make anyone wait for very long. Arrange to call back with the information, if necessary.

When giving someone a phone number or address over the phone, speak slowly. Separate phone numbers into three parts, the area code, the prefix, and the four-digit number. Say them slowly and clearly into the mouthpiece: four one five (pause) six seven six (pause) eight eight one nine. Let the pauses be long enough so that untrained callers can repeat what you have said without stepping all over your attempt at speaking the whole number.

On the other hand, now that you know some basic phone courtesy, when you are receiving a number, wait to hear the whole number before you start repeating it back. Otherwise you may find yourself repeating the first part of the number as your caller is beginning to give the second part. Neither of you will hear what the other said.

The same is true for addresses. Break them down into small parts that are easy to repeat and remember and speak them slowly. You will greatly reduce the number of times you have to repeat what you say. If you are receiving an address, listen carefully and wait until the whole address is given before repeating it back. You should be writing as fast as you can. But you will have plenty of time to make corrections at the end without having to ask the other person to start over.

John Parry of Solar Works makes himself available to customers by having a cellular phone, a message service, and an answering machine, all of which have helped his business flourish. "My main phone number, the one listed in the Yellow Pages, rings into my message service and is answered 'Good afternoon! May I help you?' The service can then call me on my cellular phone if they think it's necessary. If it's not an emergency, they take the message and at the end of the day they forward all my messages to my answering machine. When I get home I listen to the messages and can either deal with them that evening or call them the next morning."

Accountant Malcolm Ponder tries to return calls the same day as they are received. "When it's not the peak tax time, I'll return calls a couple of times a day. I feel it's especially important for someone like me who's not in the office all the time. It's important that your clients feel like you are paying attention to them."

Book agent Patti Breitman has figured out a terrific substitute for call waiting: "I have busy call forwarding. I have one business line and one home line in my office. But if the business line is busy it will roll over and ring on the home line. I have two answering machines in my office and two phones. Basically all my outgoing calls are on my business phone. And half of my incoming calls are. I hate call waiting. It's very rude. If I'm on my business phone and the phone rings it will roll over onto the home machine. And that machine says you've reached the right number for Patti, Stan, Vegetarians in Marin." People know if they get that message that I'm on the other phone and I'll call them back quickly. If they get my normal business message they know I'm out of the office.

"This is something else clients love: When I'm on one phone and the other one rings, they'll often say 'Do you have to get that?' and I'll say 'No. The machine will get it.' Which is true. And they're flattered that I don't interrupt to see who it is. People love when you pay attention to them. The person I'm talking to takes priority. Now occasionally I'll listen with one ear to hear if it's my mother calling or if it's Stan. Sometimes I have to take that call, or if it's an editor I've been trying to get for two days and she's finally on the phone I'll say 'I have to talk to this person. Let me call you right back.'"

MAIL

The traditional advice is still good: Open the mail near a trash can, and never touch a piece of paper twice. You can handle any piece of mail either immediately or later. Most mail can be handled immediately; you can either throw it away or put it in a file. It is not an immediate response, though, if the file you put it in is labeled *To Do Later*.

Some mail requires thought over time, but that's rare. The main reason for any delay in an immediate response is lack of time. Sometimes you may need more information in order to give a proper response. Another good reason to delay is that answering mail in a batch may be more efficient.

The most efficient way of handling mail in a one-person business is to assign a time to do it and not open the mail until then. Sit next to a trash can and near the appropriate files. Label these files with descriptors that make sense to you. For instance, you might put mail that needs more information before it can be answered into a file called *More Info*. Mail that can go straight into a file for later reference could go into a folder marked *File*. And mail that can be handled during slow times or all at once on one particular day in the week could be put into a file labeled *Batch*. Mail that needs immediate attention can go into *Answer Now*.

Next, at the appointed hour, be sure to pull the Answer Now folder out and get to work on it. Much of the mail, in this folder can be handled by writing directly on the original letter and keeping a photocopy. This is a quick, efficient way to handle mail, and in many situations it is perfectly acceptable and appropriate. Trade standards and good judgment will help you decide when and if to use this method. It is much like the stock two-way letter form you can buy in any office-supply store. But some people feel even these are rude, so think twice before using this time-saving trick.

Jack, who makes and sells handmade rocking chairs, sorts his mail into *New Orders*, *Information Requests*, and *Customer Mail*. The new orders get an immediate reply, plus a work order with a time estimate that goes back with the confirmation. The information requests go into a pile near the coffeepot, where they are kept in the order received and handled randomly during phone conversations and idle moments. The customer mail is taken home for thoughtful, caring replies, which Jack does with his wife during evenings and weekends.

Patti Breitman opens her mail the minute it comes in. "When I open my mail I make sure I deal with it right then and there. If I have a stack of forty pieces of mail, I don't go to piece number two until I have dealt with piece number one. So if it involves making a copy of it I will get up and make a copy right then and there and send it to whoever I have to send it to, file the original, and say okay, next piece of mail. If it involves answering, I'll write right on the letter. If someone sends me a note with three questions, I'll answer the questions right on the note, put it in the envelope, and send it back. And I'll address that envelope and stamp it and do all that before I open piece number three. My mail is tedious. There are a lot of rejection letters. If I get submissions for totally inappropriate books I put them in a pile and then first thing every morning I send out rejection letters. I respond quickly. I used to have stacks and stacks of mail and it became something I dreaded. Now I deal with it as it happens and it's much more efficient."

Unwanted Mail

When you are in business for yourself, and you have reached a stage of development marked by moderate success and regular work or sales, you will probably begin to notice the phenomenon of unwanted mail. This is mail that you receive because someone you don't know, from somewhere you never heard of, has heard about you or your product and decides to write. Unwanted mail is generally from well-meaning people who have written to you because of an affinity they feel for what you are doing or selling. It is unwanted because their query doesn't really pertain to what you are doing, or it would be better answered by some other person or business.

Early on in your business you don't think much about these letters, and you just answer them when and in the best way you can. But later, as you become more successful or better known, the volume can begin to be greater than you can justifiably handle without taking away from the effective operation of your business. What to do about it is not easy to decide. One solution is to create standard replies that are preprinted or photocopied when needed. This allows you to batch the unwanted mail and answer it at your convenience. Your stock reply could contain some suggestions about where the inquirer might look for answers.

After you have handled a few batches, you will know what the most frequently asked questions are, and you can create a form letter with all of the answers on one page and boxes next to them. Then just check the right answers before mailing the form letters out.

Old Mail

Both ordinary and unwanted mail can sometimes stack up. When you are too busy to answer because of the pressures of current work demands, the stacks may begin to age. How old is too old? This will vary a lot, depending on the contents of individual letters. You will have to make careful judgments about every piece. Generally, though, with requests for information that are more than two months old and that have not been repeated, the chances are good that your answer is no longer needed. You may want to apologize, or you may judge that it isn't really important, in which case there is nothing to do. If you are like us, just reading this paragraph will make you uneasy. The best prevention is to avoid letting your mail fall behind. The best solution is to develop the attitude that its alright to toss some of it in the first place.

DAILY RECORDS

Of particular importance to good information management are the *phone log, activity record*, and *meeting record*. These three systems help you monitor how you spend your time, and they keep you from letting important tasks and agreements go undone, which is a danger if you have them logged only in your head.

Phone Log

A phone log allows you to keep track of who is calling you, why they called, and whether you have gotten back to them. It can also help you track any toll or long distance calls so that you can get reimbursed, if appropriate. Here is an example of a phone log that works.

Activity Record

An activity record allows you to track how you spend your time. Any one-person business can benefit from a diary of this sort because it can be used as the basis for making decisions about time management. To businesses that bill for their time it is of particular importance. It also serves as what the IRS calls a "contemporaneous record," which can be used to document the validity of your travel mileage, meals, entertainment, and other business expenses at tax time. The minimum information includes date, purpose, who was present, and the number of miles traveled or dollars spent. If you use a pocket calendar for your diary, the date is there already, so you have less to write. Also, many pocket calendars have a small table printed in a corner of each page, already set up for expenses so that all you have to do is fill in the blanks.

Meeting Record

Recording your meetings is important for much the same reason as recording your other activities. However, recording meeting information may require more room than a pocket calendar allows, so always have extra paper available. Write down the *date, purpose*, and *who was present*. In addition, it's a good idea to record the *agenda*, or list of what was discussed at the meeting; topics to be discussed at any follow-up meetings; when and where these meetings will take place; and what the various attendees have agreed to do as a result of the current meeting, or in preparation for the next. Here is an example of a form that you could use to save writing time.

Fig. 5. 1   Phone Log

Phone Log					
Date	Time	They Said	I Said	Type	Status

Type: B = Billable • O = Outgoing • I = Incoming • M = Meeting
Disposition: √ = Done • Msg = Message Left • ↓ = Dropped • → = Delegated

Figure 5. 2   Activity Record

Activity Record					
Project or Client:					
Type: 1. Mail 4. Visit 2. Phone 5. Other _____ 3. Computer 6. Other _____			**Contact Persons:** A: B: C:		
		Time			
Date	Notes	Start	Stop	Elapsed	Type

FILES

A good filing system helps you organize two kinds of information: the kind you use daily and the kind you refer to only once in a while. If you use it daily you want to get your hands on it quickly. Information you use less often might be stored away, and take a little longer to retrieve but it still should be organized in a sensible fashion. It's also important to keep the sheer volume of files manageable by systematically discarding records that are no longer essential to your business.

For ongoing business activities, you need an effective system for keeping track of all the paper each project generates. Your system should organize activities and projects, clients or customers, prospects, and general management information. Obviously, the faster you can retrieve information from your files, the more efficient you will be.

The Fat-File System

Most people have at least a minimal filing system for their business records, which very often consists primarily of manila file folders stuck in a file drawer. Although it looks neat and tidy on the outside, chaos often reigns within.

If this describes your filing system, we may have just the system for you. It's called the fat-file system. It is very easy, especially in the beginning, because you start with just one file folder and put everything into it. You can create your fat-file system using any of the many kinds of folders that are available today from office supply stores and mail-order companies: a manila folder, a hanging folder, or even an expandable accordion type, letter or legal size. The important thing is that the look and feel match your aesthetic sense and make it fun to use. Color helps, and file folders come in a wide variety of colors today.

As soon as your first folder becomes so full that it takes more than five minutes to find what you are looking for, create a second folder. It now becomes necessary to label both folders so that you know what each contains. You could simply divide them up alphabetically, with A–L in one folder and M–Z in another. Or you could use a numbering system, or file by date received, and so forth. Label them in whatever way is personally meaningful to you.

After many years of trying out different systems, Claude has come up with a simple one that groups all information about ongoing activities into four categories: clients, accounting and fiscal, promotion and future work, and mailing and phone lists. The fattest files are in the category of accounting and fiscal, where all the bookkeeping and tax records are kept.

The client files are pretty fat too, containing documents, notes, and materials on every project for every client in the past two years. Records on clients for whom no work has been done in the past two years are kept filed away in a box in the storage closet.

Fig. 5. 3   Meeting Record

Meeting Record	
Reference: Date: Hour: Place:	
Participants:	Agenda:
Decisions, Conclusions, Actions Taken or Advised:	
Agenda for Next Meeting (Date, Location, Items):	
Notes:	

The file for promotion and future work contains such marketing information as ideas for newsletters, testimonials from happy clients, and thoughts and plans about future work. It also contains copies of all the marketing and promotional materials that have been used over the years.

The file for mailing and phone lists contains business cards, change of address notices that need to be entered into the Rolodex, copies of mailing lists, and the telephone numbers of all clients, prospects, suppliers, and referral sources for new business. These four files cover 80 percent of Claude's storage of ongoing information, and have grown into a couple of drawers-full of records over the past several years, necessitating the creation of subcategories within each. But because the fat-file principle has been maintained, it still never takes longer than five minutes to find an old piece of information when it is needed.

Reference Files

Reference files contain information that you may want occasionally but for which you have no regular need. If you find that you are retrieving something less than once or twice a month, it probably belongs in a reference file. You might start such a file, for example, to hold a wish list of books or magazine subscriptions that you want to buy when your cash flow allows. Or to keep clippings of ideas and information on a topic or field that interests you. Other items, such as maps and recreation or travel information, photos, slides, video- and audiotapes, as well as software and data disks, also fit in the category of reference material.

The simplest storage solution is to buy a few sturdy cardboard boxes such as the archive boxes manufactured by Bankers Box and used by attorneys for storing records. These are just the right dimensions to hold either letter- or legal-sized files, and they are strong enough to stack three or four high. Just be sure to label them clearly on the outside so that you can quickly find the box you need.

Plans and Dreams

Another important part of information organization is to keep your plans and dreams fresh and accessible. Filing them away in the back of a file drawer is like filing them in the back of your mind: They can easily be forgotten.

We recommend reserving wall space for them, where you can pin up a planning calendar, vacation ideas, or notes and drawings about long-range projects. In this way your plans and dreams will be right in front of you. Another idea is to put a notebook right next to your bed, so it is easy to review your long-range goals just before falling asleep.

Actively cultivating long-range plans and dreams creates a "big picture" context and a higher level of motivation to do the day-to-day tasks necessary for your long-term success as a businessperson.

Labeling for Keeps—Or Is It?

What was life like before 3M Post-it Notes? They come in numerous sizes, colors, and formats, and they have countless uses. But a note of caution from personal experience: don't use Post-its if you want a permanent label. As labels for boxes slated for long-term record storage, Post-its just won't work. You'll discover, as we did, that when you go into your storage closet a couple of months later to retrieve a record, what you'll find is a pile of Post-it Notes lying on the floor in front of your boxes.

Post-its were designed for temporary labeling. They use a low-tack adhesive, and it weakens with time. For long-lasting labels that cannot be easily removed, write directly on the box or use a permanent label, available from most stationery stores.

Discarding

Discarding is an important and often-overlooked record-keeping task. It consists of systematically putting into the recycling bin everything that you no longer need to run your business. It is easy to throw away junk mail or information that has outlived its usefulness, such as old magazines or letters. You must be careful, however, in deciding what financial information to discard and when. You may need your financial documents if you have to defend your tax returns against a federal or state audit. Other records may be needed if you are ever sued. Some records must be kept up to seven years. Capital gains records need to be held for the period of the gain.

To know how long to keep your various records, check with your accountant or lawyer if you use one. Or, you might get a "discarding booklet" prepared by a company that manufactures filing supplies or shredders. These booklets contain tables of recommended retention periods. They are available at many office supply stores or from the manufacturer (see Resources, at the end of this chapter).

INFORMATION OVERLOAD

As we noted previously, today's world is filled with information. Even when you organize and choose what you will pay attention to, it is still terribly easy to be overwhelmed with information. There are no simple answers, but we have a couple of suggestions that have worked for others.

First, discriminate between the information you really need and the information that is merely interesting. The information you require to efficiently run your business is a small subset of all that is available. But people can be buried by their interests. Don't assume that just because you find something interesting you have to collect and store it. Look around in your own support circles and make note of those friends and associates whose central focus overlaps with an interest of yours. Once you have identified these people you can often forward to them the information about your peripheral interests. Since they are the expert on that subject, you will be able to contact them later when you really need the information again. And they will be able to provide you with far more information on the subject than you could ever have saved on your own.

Another way to reduce information overload is to continually work on clarifying your central purpose. The clearer you are about your goals, the easier it is to let go of information that does not directly serve those goals.

Finally, when in doubt, use intuition to make judgments about what to pay attention to. If you have a hunch or strong feeling that something is important, then pay attention to it. If it is just mildly attractive, you can probably let it go.

Organizing how information flows through your business might seem unimportant when you have so many other things to do, but the more organized you are the less time you will need to spend tracking and retrieving the information needed to manage your business. It's well worth your effort to develop office systems that smoothly and efficiently separate the wheat from the chaff, and we hope this chapter gives you a good head start.

RESOURCES

Akers, Susan Grey. *Simple Library Cataloging*, 4th. ed. Chicago: American Library Association, 1954; out of print.

Aschner, Katherine. *Taking Control of Your Office Records: A Manager's Guide*. New York: Macmillan, 1986.

Records Control and Storage Handbook, with Retention Schedules. Franklin Park, Ill.: Bankers Box. Describes in detail not only when to throw your records out, but also how to keep them in storage until the retention period is over. May be ordered from Bankers Box, 2607 North 25th Avenue, Franklin Park, IL 60131.

Stibic, V. *Personal Documentation for Professionals: Means and Methods*. New York: El Sevier Science Publishing Company, 1980. Basic systems for filing books, reports, journals, photocopies, slides and photos, letters, and so on. ·

Thomas, Violet S., Dexter R. Schubert, and Jo Ann Lee. *Records Management: Systems and Administration*. New York: John Wiley, 1983.

Winston, Stephanie. *Getting Organized: The Easy Way to Put Your Life in Order*. New York: Warner Books, 1991. Covers maximizing storage space, reducing shopping time, increasing efficiency, and so on.

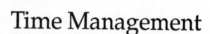

6

Time Management

Time and timing are critical to the success of your one-person business. Poor timing and poor use of time are among the most frequently reported causes of small-business failure. We often talk about controlling time through good time management without understanding what the word *manage* means. *Manage* comes from *manus*, the Latin word for hand. Time management, then, is the art and science of handling time.

Small-business advisor Paul Terry says that most people manage their time one of three ways: "We squeeze . . . we stretch . . . or we juggle. So we either squeeze it in, stay up late and stretch it out, or we do it all at once and hope we won't get hit on the head by the things we're juggling in the air. That's the strategy that most people use. One of the things about one-person businesses is that you'll never have as much time to apply to the planning and development of your business as you have in the start-up and early years. That's the only time you're really going to have to pay attention to planning, because the actual running and managing of your business will take up most of your time. So you never have time, it seems, to stand back and do planning. There are all kinds of books on time management, all kinds of techniques to check out your time. Use them to keep track of how much time you spend on a daily basis or a week and see where it all goes, if you can. But I have found that no matter how good the system is, we can sabotage it and we often do. I think the most effective thing to know is that you probably will sabotage it and that's okay, as long as you re-create a system that works for you again. Because we'll have a to do list and we can put it in front of our mirror and a week later we don't see it. It disappears into the background. We might have to put it in different places so that we continue to see it. It can be something that simple. I think a lot of people buy these time-management books and they carry them around and some of them are very religiously used. At other times they get left somewhere and then after a while they're not used anymore and you go back to writing things on slips of paper.

"What happens with time in a one-person business is that you actually manage your business better as you go along because you've obviously become more efficient in how you handle clients, how you enter data, how you get the product out the door. But you don't notice that you become more efficient because you become larger, you have more transactions during the day, and so you don't give yourself credit for managing your time better because you don't recognize that you are managing more complexity. It's that delicate balance between the complexity issues in our business and the fact that we can manage it well or not well based on how efficient we become. I don't know if I have found the solution to managing my time. I'm certainly guilty of stretching, squeezing, and juggling. Sometimes I do them simultaneously.

"If I'm forgetting to bill for my time even though it's right in front of me I'll get a bigger clipboard that will be more obvious so that I will keep banging into it until I remember. Or I'll look at the fact that I may need to computerize a process for tracking time or a manual system that's not working anymore. Or I'll see that I need to have someone else come in and help me and say, "Okay, look. This is an area where I have a weakness. I need to have you support me or I need to hire you to teach me this new skill. And then I get better for a while and then I may slip back. I think it's not something we're always in control of or that we manage well. I think we go through fits and starts of feeling in control of our time. I think the other thing about developing our business and time is the impression that we have that it all has to be done at once and that there is a period of time that must pass until you have all the pieces together. You cannot possibly incorporate your business, get all the legalities in place, order all your products, design your own mail-order catalog, write your business plan, write contracts with your vendors, and set up a billing system, all within the first month.

"But there's a tendency to think that we must do this or we're going to lose the opportunity or someone else is going to take over our idea. So we feel obsessed with working as quickly as possible, and I think all that does, like any machine that's built too quickly, is assure that when you try starting it, it crashes and burns. I think the same thing about the business. The business is an entity. The business itself is a product and it needs to be cared for and nurtured in different ways. It cannot grow too fast, anymore than you can fast-forward a flower. If you give it too much sun and water it will die on you. And a business will die on you too, if you move too quickly.

"We have to look at time as a finite issue. You may be able to stay up all night long for a couple days, but after that you will crash and burn for two days and you will not be effective and efficient."

In this chapter we will introduce some important ways of viewing, organizing, and using time to your best advantage. The importance of clarifying your personal vision, purpose, and goals in life will be described. Making what you have to do explicit, prioritizing, and scheduling will also be covered. The difference between billable and nonbillable time and why it is important to focus on both will be explained. We will also take a look at basic time-management methods and tools including short-, mid-, and long-range planning, to-do lists, calendars, office hours, and how to make meetings work.

WHY MANAGE TIME?

For most of us, an important reason for starting a one-person business is the opportunity to create meaningful, fulfilling work. Whatever your reasons, the only way you can succeed with your one-person business is by taking action. There are two primary paths of action you can take: (1) you can change your external situation and (2) you can change your internal situation.

For anyone interested in a one-person business, changing the external situation means actually launching their business. Or, if you already have a one-person business, it means improving your work environment, enhancing your management systems, and increasing the quality and number of your customers. Changing the internal situation means finding ways to better use your talent and skills, improving old skills or acquiring new ones and working on your character or your attitude.

You may focus for a while on either the internal or the external path of action, but our experience is that eventually you will follow them both. Many people report that the major reason they have chosen the one-person business form is for the chance it offers them to *take action that is true to who they are*. But being true to who you are requires finding out who you are.

Over the years, we have tried most of the time-management systems available and found them roughly equal in their ability to provide real time-management help. If you already know who you are and what you want to do, than almost any time-management system will get you organized enough to make truly productive progress. Where most of them fall short, however, is in the area of helping you look at yourself and identify what your goals really are.

To surmount this shortcoming, we have devised a six-step method of our own. The steps are: (1) Open up to your *vision* of life; (2) clarify your personal *purpose* and values; (3) identify the *goals* implied by your vision and purpose; 4) turn your goals into measurable *objectives*; (5) break the objectives down into *actions steps*; (6) break the action steps down into *daily tasks*.

VISION, PURPOSE, AND GOALS

Because you make all the decisions about how you spend your time and because you only have to answer to yourself, running the one-person business provides the perfect opportunity to build self-reflection and self-development into what you do to make a living.

Self-reflection and self-development start with the process of clarifying your personal vision and values and, not surprisingly, this has a direct benefit to your business. Our experience has shown us that one-person-business owners who make a point of continually clarifying their personal visions and values are the ones whose use of time is by far the most productive. We're not sure why this is, but it seems likely that your interest and perseverance are greater when you pursue goals you believe in—goals you feel passionate about—goals that come from clear vision and values. Once you embark on the road to self-knowledge, it will be much easier to pick a new one-person business or refine an existing one so that you are truly doing what you love and what you are really good at.

Open Up to Your Life Vision

What do you really believe about life? What is your overall "life vision"—the big idea, main desire, the "real" purpose, the reason for existing? What is the life context for your one-person business? What beliefs or values have motivated you to choose the one-person business form?

These are very large questions and not easy ones to answer. Sometimes it helps to break these questions down into smaller ones. Here is a list of suggested questions that might help you begin to see *your* life vision.

What do you value most in life? Name your five most-important life values: what you would pay the most for, sacrifice the most for, take a stand for?

What are the three most important goals in your life right now? Answer this question quickly—write down what comes up in the first thirty seconds. What pops up first will most likely be what you really want. Further consideration will allow your mind to list all the reasons why these goals won't work or censor them from fear that they are unacceptable to others or unreachable by you. So write down the first things that come to your mind. They are probably the most important, even if they are scary or challenging.

What would you do if money were not an issue? This might mean that you don't need money to do what you really want. Or perhaps you will win a million dollars in the lottery tomorrow? What kind of work would you do if you didn't need to worry about money? Would it still be your one-person business?

How would you spend your time if you had only six months to live? How does the prospect of dying soon change the way you would spend your time? What would you do differently if you knew you had only a short time left? Would you still deliver some form of the products or services of your one-person business?

What have you always wanted to do but been afraid to attempt? What fantasies or dreams have you had that you haven't acted on because you thought they were too difficult or might lead to suffering? List as many as you can now before fear stops you from even looking at them. Is your one-person business in this list, or have you talked yourself into starting it because you thought you had to make money or prove yourself before you could have what you want?

In looking back over all the things you've done in your life, what activities or circumstances gave you the greatest feelings of fulfillment? mental well-being? self-esteem and self-worth? The further back in your life you can go the better. Activities you enjoyed when you were a child can be especially enlightening. The answers to this question can be key indicators of where your personal niche might be found today. Does your one-person business allow you to do some of these activities or be in circumstances like those you found fulfilling?

Imagine that you could have one wish that would allow you to realize anything you wanted. What would it be? What would you dare to dream if you knew you could not fail? This can be one of the most important indicators of your true vision of life. Is your one-person business part of this dream?

For the best results, put this book down and take the time now to answer these questions, or at least to make an appointment with yourself to do so. If you can write down the answers to these questions, you will have taken the first step on the road to realizing your life vision. In our experience, you can have whatever you write down—as long as it stays within the simple limits of physical realty. You cannot, for example, become taller or learn to jump from towering buildings without a parachute. But any physically real vision you have can be made to happen with perseverance. And the clearer you get about your vision the more likely it will happen.

Clarify Your Personal Purpose

The path to a fulfilling life begins when you take the first step of clarifying your life vision. Your vision can be large—larger even than you can remember without a written description. But you must begin to narrow that vision by bringing a certain amount of focus to it. Trying to accomplish too much ends up in dispersing and weakening your energies. A fulfilling life begins when you focus on a central organizing purpose that is most important to you right now. When you become clear about your personal purpose, then pursuing the goals it implies will lead to a richer, fuller life. Hopefully, one of those goals will be the successful management of your one-person business. But if it isn't, at least you will have the opportunity to choose something else before you waste years of your life on the wrong goal.

Your personal purpose can change as you learn more about how life works, who you are, and what you want from life, but you can begin now with the purpose you currently see. To help you better see your personal purpose, we have devised four steps to determining your personal purpose.

The Four Steps to Determining Your Personal Purpose

1. *Limitless Visioning.* Limitless visioning is the context in which you answer the seven questions listed above. Limitless visioning is an attitude of openness and faith that *you can have what you want* if you can simply envision it as the first step on the path of action to acquiring it. Limitless visioning is grand and abstract and sets the stage for the next step: active imagination.

2. *Active Imagination.* Active imagination builds on limitless vision by making what you want more concrete. In active imagination you create a sensory-rich image of what your life, including your work, will be like when you are doing the right thing. *Sensory rich* means creating details of the environment and your activities in it. Are you indoors or outdoors? What is the light like? What are the smells, colors, textures, and sounds? Are you working with people, things, data, or animals? and so forth.

3. *Creative Eulogy.* Creative eulogy further enriches the image of your future life by adding a sense of how you will be remembered when you are gone. When you write your own eulogy from the point of view of the people you leave behind, you help to solidify both your limitless vision and your active, sensory-rich image of the future.

4. *Personal Statement of Purpose.* Finally, you must boil down what you learn from these first three steps into a personal statement of purpose: a statement of what your life is going to be about from today forward. It will include the substance of your overall vision, the sensory-rich images of your future life, and a glimpse of how you will be remembered after you die. Once you have written your personal statement of purpose, you can begin to work on identifying the major *personal goals* implied by that purpose.

Identify Your Personal Goals

A goal is a place you intend to end up: an expected outcome; an anticipated result. A goal doesn't tell you how to get there, how to have a particular outcome, or how to achieve a specific result. And it doesn't tell you when. A goal is usually stated as a big picture, which unless you break it down into smaller parts will be almost impossible to achieve. But if you do break your goals down then you can attain them in stages, step by step.

The Nine Steps to Accomplishing Personal Goals

1. *Develop Passion.* The first step in changing any part of your life is to develop or uncover an intense, personal passion to change the way things are and to live life to its fullest.

2. *Practice Faith.* You need faith that life will present you with meaningful opportunities, and you must believe beyond a shadow of a doubt that you have the ability to recognize and fulfill them. The more you can develop faith in your ability to achieve your goals, the more rapidly you will move towards their attainment.

3. *Develop Tradeskills.* Hands-on learning, facing the facts, minimizing risks, and persistence are especially important. Never give up. There are bound to be setbacks and disappointments. You must "pick yourself up, dust yourself off, and start all over again." Your persistence is the measure of the belief in yourself. If you persevere, nothing can stop you.

4. *Choose Goals That Help You Grow.* Make sure your goals are challenging. Choose goals that make you stretch your present level of knowledge and skill. Move out of your comfort zone and try to ride the edge of what you are capable of.

5. *Write Down Your Goals.* This is vitally important; it is the most effective way to enlist the help of your own inner wisdom. This is a critical step in attaining any goal. Until your goals are written down they are not goals, they are just so many fantasies.

6. *Make a List of Benefits.* List what you stand to gain or experience by attaining your goals. The longer your list of benefits, the easier it will be for you to attain each goal.

7. *Make a List of Obstacles and Barriers.* There are always obstacles to overcome and barriers to get around. When you write them down you objectify them and make it easier to overcome them. Once you have objectified them they will not seem nearly so important or threatening.

8. *Create a Clear Mental Image of Your Goals and Objectives as Already Accomplished.* Play this image back at every opportunity. What does it feel like to have double your current annual income? How will you act differently? Who will you interact with? What will you say? Will you spend the additional income? Save it? Will you invest it in marketing, furniture, a computer? What will your business look like if it generates twice the income? What will it be like to interact with more customers or clients? What kind of customers or clients will they be? Will you be known as an

expert in some part of your field? What part? Will you attend trade shows? Give speeches? Teach workshops about your success? And so forth.

9. *Manage Your Time Wisely.* Make appointments with yourself to accomplish the steps toward your goals. Always ask yourself the question "What is the best use of my time right now?" Review your calendar daily, weekly, and monthly, quarterly, annually; or however often makes sense for you.

Robert Kourik—writer, publisher, photographer, consultant, and landscape designer—likes to define goals in expansive, vague terms to allow for flexibility. "My goal is to provide modern, busy people with nondogmatic environmental advice and a full range of practical techniques. I believe your work will define the business as much as, or more than, your intellectual anticipation. Remember, your business will probably be like one of a zillion, tiny plankton, not one of the few glorious whales—unless you're lucky. The goal is to be a really good plankton."

OBJECTIVES, ACTION STEPS, AND DAILY TASKS

Once you have identified the goals implied by your vision and values, you must also determine priorities at each step of the process. First, you need to take your most important goals and turn them into measurable objectives. Then do the same thing with those objectives: Begin with your most important objectives and turn them into action steps. Then turn your most important action steps into daily tasks and put them into your calendar. And you do the most important daily tasks first. At every step of the way you are doing what is most important first.

What this tells us is that making the most of your time always involves three important components: making what you have to do explicit, setting priorities, and scheduling what needs to be done. Then if a friend who you would like to visit with drops by when you have to get two more boxes ready for the afternoon mail, you know what your priorities are. You don't wish you had more time; you know you have to get the work done. So you explain this to your friend and invite him or her to watch or to help, or you set another time to get together.

Making Things Explicit   The primary tool for making things explicit is the *to-do list*. It can be written on anything: on paper (in a notebook or on the wall), on a blackboard, or in a computer. Most people find it easy to come up with a sizable to-do list in, say, ten or fifteen minutes. But many people make the mistake of putting goals and objectives down on their to-do lists. Goals are too abstract and objectives are too big. A to-do list should contain only those things that you can actually accomplish in a given day. When an objective, or even an action step, takes more than a single day it needs to be broken down into a smaller steps. These smallest steps are your *daily tasks* and they make up your to-do list.

Your to-do list will be doubly helpful if you reserve some space on the left side of your paper or blackboard to write the disposition of each item: the answer to the question "What have I done with this item?" One method, shown in figure 6.1, uses a set of symbols for the three most common dispositions: done (a check mark), dropped (a down arrow), and delegated (a right-curving arrow). Any symbols can be used that make sense to you. Experts in time management offer this tip: Instead of the negative act of crossing out an item, reward yourself with a few kind words, written next to each item as you complete it. Positive, reinforcing words like *good work*, *well done*, and *great* are fine. It may seem silly at first, but like the grade-school star system, it still feels good, and many people find it more motivating than simply crossing out a completed item.

John Parry of Solar Works spends a lot of time in the field, so it makes sense for him to keep an ongoing list in a file that he carries with him. "Everyone that I deal with gets onto a form with their name and address on it. If I do the work, there is also a job form. There's space for the hours I work, the materials I use, costs, and so forth. Then the form goes to different places. When they're active, they go to the active file which is with me all the time. And there's a list that I keep with me that has all the repair jobs I need to do. All the installations, estimates, all the 'when I have times.' So if I'm out, I schedule the work. If I get done with a job at three and I still have a couple hours, I can look at my list and call someone up and say, 'I've got some time, can we get together and do this?'"

Prioritizing We recommend two effective methods of prioritizing and suggest you try both to see which one suits you best. The first is Alan Lakein's ABC method. Alan suggests that you sort all to-do's into three categories: (*A*) for "critical, goal-related, must be done today, true emergencies"; (*B*) for "important, goal-related, must be done soon but not today, might be delegated"; and (*C*) for "can wait, may or may not be goal-related, no significant time, should do when can." You do the As, put the Bs in a drawer until you can get to them, and throw the Cs

---

FINDING YOUR PERSONAL NICHE

To maximize your chance of success as a one-person business, it is important to find your *personal one-person business niche*: the service or product that allows you to be who you are and show excellence in what you do.

Self-esteem is a major determinant in how difficult or fulfilling you will find your one-person-business-to-be and therefore how successful you will become. But it is hard to like yourself if you are only mediocre at everything you do. The superior strategy, then, becomes one of finding what you are really good at—what you feel passionate about—what you find immensely satisfying.

A good way to start is by looking at what interests you. What attracts your attention? What would you do, even if you weren't paid to do it? What would you do if you had no constraints of time, money, or abilities?

away. Later you check the drawer to see if any of the Bs have turned into As or Cs and handle them appropriately.

Another method we have tried (but can't remember where we found it) is the priority/stress level method illustrated in figure 6.1. With this method, you classify all your to-dos into As, Bs, and Cs, as with Lakein's method. But you go one step farther and also classify them into 1s, 2s, and 3s, according to how stressful they are. A will be the most important, and 3 will be the most stressful. The method works by completing your to-do's in the order of most important, least stressful. In other words, do the A1s first, then the A2s, A3s, B1s, etc. The theory is that by doing the important things that you feel the most comfortable with first (A1s), you will be more productive and will feel more of a sense of accomplishment. The things you are best at will offer you the least stress. When you do important, but not-so-stressful tasks, you will not only accomplish a lot, you will also get more done than if you wrestled with the things you're not good at, no matter how important they are.

Scheduling   After making tasks explicit and prioritizing them, it is necessary to set aside the time to actually get them done. This is critical because when you are busy, it is easy to forget to set aside the hour a week it might take to do the book-keeping, or the thirty minutes a day needed for making marketing calls, and so forth. The most powerful scheduling tool available to you is a calendar, which we will describe in some detail in the next section.

Eliminating Time-Wasters   In *The Time Trap* (New York: McGraw-Hill, 1972), sociologist Alec MacKenzie reported on his research into the problems and solutions of the time-management crisis. He conducted a study with a wide variety of executives, including forty Canadian army colonels, thirty American university presidents, twenty-five Mexican company managers, and a number of insurance brokers, black clergymen, and German managers. What he found was a list of nearly thirty critical "time thieves." Further research on the top time-wasters for women (reported in MacKenzie and Waldo, *About Time! A Woman's Guide to Time Management* (New York: McGraw-Hill, 1981) found more than twenty time thieves in common with the worldwide list. The economic pressures in today's world, however, make it increasingly obvious that it is naive to include household-management tasks in a list of time-wasters. Things such as chauffeuring children; maintenance and repairs of cars, washing machines, lawn mowers, and so on; doctor's appointments, music lessons, or sports events for the children; housework, errands, and cooking; interruptions by one's children or one's parents, and other personal or family business are essential responsibilities of both members of a primary household couple. For this reason we do not include them in the list, even though

Fig. 6.1   To-Do List

To-Do List			
Disposition	*Stress*	*Priority*	*Description*
Disposition: ✓ = Done • ↓ = Dropped • ⌁ = Delegated			

MacKenzie and Waldo did. Here is their complete list in order of severity, from most to least:

> Telephone interruptions
> Crisis management, shifting priorities
> Lack of objectives, priorities, planning
> Drop-in visitors
> Ineffective delegation
> Attempting too much at once
> Meetings
> Personal disorganization, cluttered desk
> Inability to say no
> Lack of self-discipline
> Procrastination, indecision
> Untrained, inadequate staff
> Incomplete delayed information
> Paperwork, red tape, reading
> Leaving tasks unfinished
> Unclear communication and instructions
> Understaffed
> Confused responsibility and authority
> Socializing (see telephone and visitors)
> Interruptions by boss
> Disorganized boss

Looking closely at this list it becomes obvious that almost all of these time-wasters are symptomatic of two essential issues: (1) *the inability to say no*, which permits telephone interruptions, drop-in visitors, unnecessary meetings, excessive socializing, and interruptions all of which result in tasks left undone, and (2) *unclear priorities*, which shows up as a lack of objectives, priorities, and planning, and leads to crisis management and shifting priorities, ineffective delegation, attempts to do too much at once, personal disorganization, procrastination and indecision, unclear communication and instructions, and confused responsibility and authority, all of which contribute to leaving tasks unfinished, unnecessary meetings, and the inability to say no.

The inability to say no seems to stem from four primary sources: (1) (not surprisingly) a lack of clarity about ones own priorities, (2) a desire to please others, (3) fear of offending, or (4) a genuine humanitarian impulse to help others. The first three can be overcome with some effort, but you'll have to be discriminating about the last one.

If someone comes to you with a true humanitarian need that you can fill, you'll probably be better able to help if you ask him or her to return at a time when you can give your undivided attention. Emergencies are a valid exception, but in most people's lives there are very few real emergencies.

To clarify your priorities, use the approach we offered in the section above on "vision, purpose, and goals." Overcoming a desire to please others or a fear of offending is a different matter. The most effective way we know of doing this is to grit your teeth and "just say no." Use the following active-listening exercise to make saying no easier:

1. *Listen actively.* Repeat back what the requester is saying using the same words they use, but modified to reflect your position. If he or she says something like "I need you to help me finish up the McDonough project," you say something like, "You need help with the McDonough project."
2. *Say no right away.* As soon as the requester asks for your help, tell him or her that you are not available. This way no false hopes are generated. You may say something like, "I'm sorry, but I am fully committed already."
3. *Explain your reasons.* It is important that the requester understand why you are not helping at this time. You do not want him or her to think you don't care, only that you cannot help at this time. Say something like, "Given my own commitments to the Johnson and Alabaster projects, I just don't have any time left to help you with McDonough." If you don't have a clear reason to refuse helping, then say something like, "Let me get back to you on that. I need to look at my schedule."
4. *Offer alternatives.* Show your good faith and willingness to help. Say something like, "Have you checked with Bob or Sharon? Can they help you?" or, "Can you wait until Friday when I'll have more time?"

TIME PLANNING

Planning is not usually thought of as a time-management activity, but it should be. It is useful to divide planning into three primary periods: short-range, mid-range, and long-range. Short-range planning covers from the present to six months from now. Mid-range is from six months to two years. Long-range is from two to ten years, and sometimes longer. Although the process of planning for these three periods is roughly identical, naturally the degree of detail and abstraction changes.

Short-Range Planning

Short-range planning is easy when you use the three steps we talked about above: making things explicit, prioritizing, and scheduling. First, write a list of the things you need to get done. Next, rank them so that the most important items will get done first. Finally, using a calendar, schedule when you will do them.

Calendars Calendars are indispensable tools for short-range planning. There are basically two kinds: those that go in a notebook and those that go on the wall. Use only one calendar to keep track of the immediate future. With two, it becomes difficult to reconcile the information. A large wall calendar has the advantage of keeping your schedule, larger than life, right before your eyes. This is the best choice if most of your work is done in your office and you seldom need to visit clients or customers. The few times you need to jot down an appointment and happen to be away from your calendar, a small pocket notebook or a piece of paper should suffice until you can transfer it to the wall calendar. If, however, you are on the road or in clients' offices most of the time, a good notebook calendar is essential.

Month-at-a-Glance Calendars

Notebook calendars come in a variety of sizes and layouts, from pocket size to 8½ by 11 inches, and from one or two days on a page to a week or month. Although any of these is suitable for noting your day-to-day commitments and appointments, the month-at-a-glance is the most helpful. It provides a perspective on the near future that will help you stay in touch with your work load. Because you can accurately see what is going on, you can more easily spread the work load across a reasonable period of time. This will help you avoid becoming overloaded.

Custom-satchel designer Teri Joe Wheeler agrees. "One of my biggest breakthroughs this year is that I decided to carry around a regular calendar. It's just the ordinary kind that hangs on everyone's wall. But it folds in half, and I can slip it into my bag. Those engagement calendars that show you a week at a time don't work for me. I need to see the whole month at once."

Notebook Calendars

Since the mid-eighties, the availability of good pocket calendars has grown phenomenally. This is directly related to the growth of one-person and other small businesses, and it has created a boom in the office-supplies industry.

Almost any office supply store will have some kind of notebook calendar that will meet your personal needs. Of the brands available in office supply stores, Day Runner and Record Plate have a wider-than-usual choice of pages, permitting you to customize your system. Quo Vadis also has a good variety of hard-bound book calendars that are especially designed for clergy, doctors, or other professionals, and Rolodex has entered the market with a choice of pages similar to Record Plate. Day-Timers, available through mail order, offer a wide choice of pages and binders and is reasonably priced. You may be able to adapt one of these to your needs.

Three- to Four-Month Calendars

Another helpful time-management tool is a chart you make yourself, covering three or four months at a time, that serves to remind you of future promises and plans. You can post your regular monthly meetings, holiday and vacation schedule, other planned time off, and so forth. It is especially important to have this kind of calendar if your business is seasonal, if you are a manufacturer, or if you give lectures, workshops, and seminars. In these types of business you must promise performance well before the delivery date, and without this chart you run the risk of overcommitting yourself or of making promises without taking your longer-range goals into consideration. This tool is also helpful in planning your marketing schedule, because you can see when you can comfortably take the time to hold your events.

Using Your Calendar

Whichever calendar you choose, review it frequently—especially the last thing Sunday night or first thing Monday morning. It's important to take a good look at the coming week. While you're at it, you can review how the last week went and move forward anything you didn't get done. This is also an excellent time to look at your goals and check whether you are still on track.

It's also good to do a mini-review each morning and evening. Note your accomplishments and take a few minutes to consider how the day is going to shape up. Examine your week or month-at-a-glance calendar and your daily to-do list. At the end of the day, think over your accomplishments, reward your work, and fall asleep after reviewing your plans and dreams for the future.

For watercolorist Pam Glasscock, taking this mental time-out is important. "It really helps to take time the night before to think out what I'm going to try to accomplish the next day. This looking ahead had become a mental routine for me. When I don't do this, it always takes me longer to get started in the morning."

Computer and training consultant Bill Dale agrees, but he likes to work with a bigger chunk of time. "I plan the next week every weekend, usually Sunday morning. I also use quarterly planning meetings to review my goals for the next year, and I review these with my accountant about every six months. A wall calendar would be useless to me because I travel so much. I use a planning diary. The key in all time management is to avoid having to copy from one place to another. So I write commitments (in pencil) straight into my diary."

Robert Kourik warns about becoming a victim of all these new time management systems: "I feel it's important not to be brainwashed into using all those linear business forms and day planners, unless they match your personality. Many creative people can't keep notes or fill out a calendar on lined paper to save their life. I believe in scribbling any way you want—big letters, pictures, color, doodles, sketches—whatever it takes to make the information stick in your brain. The only linear forms that really have to count are spreadsheets and tax forms."

Mid-Range Planning

Mid-range planning involves a time span of six months to two years. The primary planning tool for this period is the cash-flow projection, which is described in Chapter 3, "Financial Management and Control." This kind of projection is ideal for time management. When you begin to see the pattern of work and money flowing into and out of your business, you can better plan how to organize your mid-range time. A cash-flow projection is laid out very much like an income statement, but the numbers you plugged in are your best guesses about the income you expect or would like to make, and your calculations of the expenses required to keep the business open and to generate that income.

All one-person businesses should use a cash-flow projection as a time-management tool. With it you will spot problems before they might otherwise have received your attention, and you will see how you are doing over time and whether you need to change your behavior in the future. You will also discover things like the seasonal pattern of your business, which would not be apparent to you if you viewed your business only in a shorter time frame.

Additional mid-range planning tools include wall charts that show major holidays, special events, or commitments you have made that are further in the future than your short-range calendar covers.

Long-Range Planning

Long-range plans are bigger and more abstract than short- or mid-range plans. They are the maps of your efforts to clarify your vision, values, and goals and are not meant to be set in concrete. When you get lost in the day-to-day operation of the business, your long-range plans remind you of the reasons you went into business in the first place. As you grow and gain more experience, your long-range vision will probably change, and that is fine. You will find it easier to run a successful business if you make regular appointments with yourself to go over long-range plans and update them to match who you are becoming and where you want to go—probably at least once a year.

As we said in Chapter 5, "Information Management," actively clarifying your vision and values, and developing the long-range plans that go with that clarification, creates a "big picture" context and a higher level of motivation to complete the day-to-day tasks necessary for your long-term success as a businessperson.

Writing down the goals that are implied by your vision and values is an important part of successful long-range planning. If you write your goals down and do nothing else but review them in a year or two or even five, you will be surprised at how many of them you have accomplished.

Dress designer Kate Bishop confirms this approach. "About every six months I write down my short-term goals. I put them in front of my appointment book, alongside my long-term goals. I look at them every once in a while. When my short-term goals are accomplished, I make new ones. When I write down my goals, they always get accomplished. It's helpful to see how accomplishing my short-term goals furthers my long-range plans."

In her book *Wishcraft*, Barbara Sher developed an excellent way to help realize long-term goals. She recommends creating a "planning wall" on which to put pictures of your heroes and charts of your plans. These charts include (1) a flow chart, which serves as the master plan to coordinate everything else; (2) a Tomorrow section with drawings or pictures representing your long-range goals and a target date for their completion; and (3) a Next Five Years section for completion of specific concrete goals. You then coordinate this wall chart with a calendar system so that you can break your long-term goals into steps that can be accomplished day by day.

Another idea for keeping your long-range goals accessible and fresh in your mind is to put them in a notebook next to your bed so that you can review them just before falling asleep.

BILLABLE AND NONBILLABLE TIME

The running of any small business can be divided into three basic categories of time: (1) time that is spent making the products or performing the services that the business offers; (2) time spent selling those products or services; and (3) time that must be spent on general tasks that "keep the doors open."

We often think of the "real business" as the making of the products and the performing of the services. But a business cannot succeed if we do not also spend time selling what we make or do, as well as performing administrative tasks like paying the bills, making the deposits, keeping the books, sweeping the floor, answering the mail, and so forth. The productive work you do—what you can bill for—may often seem subsidiary to the administrative responsibilities you must perform, leading to feelings of frustration. This feeling is very common among people who are newly self-employed, and rare among those who have been in business for some time. To the old-timers, the distinction between work and interruption is no longer clear. Either the trivia has come to be appreciated for its value or it has been discarded. In fact, most of what people call trivia is actually the basic administrative work that keeps a business going. In a one-person business this can represent a very high percentage of time.

"Interruptions" turn out to be fundamental to your business. Answering the telephone, sending the mail, buying supplies, and having planning meetings with clients are all important aspects of your work. Experienced people know this, and work with certainty, confidence, and efficiency: the result of blending all the elements of their work.

In a one-person business, more than in any other form of business, owners find that they have to make better use of their administrative and selling time and be more fruitful during their periods of peak productivity.

All businesses, large or small, have to deal with nonbillable administrative and selling time, but in bigger businesses part of the administrative work is handled by others, and there are often people devoted exclusively to selling. In a one-person business you must do it all: make the products, deliver the services, sell what you make or do, and sweep the floor.

A photographer like Neil Putnam puts in a large amount of administrative time (sometimes as much as 80 percent) to productive time (20 percent). The administrative time consists of meeting with clients and prospects, talking on the phone, handling mail (including requests for samples of work), getting supplies, doing bookkeeping and other paperwork, and lots of cataloging and filing of past work. The productive time consists of shooting the photos and developing the film. If Neil resented this ratio he would never succeed in his business.

By contrast, a therapist might spend 40 percent of administrative time to 60 percent of productive time. In this case, the administrative time would include making appointments, keeping records of sessions, bookkeeping and other paperwork, interviewing potential clients, and meeting with other professionals. The productive time would be the actual therapy sessions with clients.

Administrative and productive times differ for each type of business. For free-lance writers, public speakers, and consultants, two hours of administrative time for every hour of productive time is not unusual. For gardeners, goldsmiths, and truck drivers, the opposite might be true: one hour of administrative for every two hours of productive time.

When you accept the reality of administrative time and its inherent relationship to productive time, you will find yourself taking a different approach to your business. You can begin by patterning your approach after people who have been in business for many years. Experienced businesses have consciously designed their administrative time to be as supportive and efficient as possible and to be a rewarding, enjoyable part of their business.

Property manager Ted Rabinowitsh probably speaks for a lot of experienced businesspeople when he says, "I'm not comfortable unless I have both time and money elements worked out so that they are clear and under control. What I like is the balance. I enjoy doing the paperwork and I enjoy doing the physical work, but I wouldn't want to have to do either of them exclusively."

OFFICE HOURS

A one-person business has its own tempo and rhythm. Setting hours is easy for some businesses and hard for others. The best way to maintain control over your business time is to set hours of operation and make sure everyone knows what they are. Many small businesses have office or store hours on Monday through Friday, from 9 A.M. to 5 P.M. Clearly, they are encouraging people to call and come by during these hours, and people will. To allow time to attend to anything that takes you away from the office, or for uninterrupted time to get work done that requires concentration, as a one-person business you may find it necessary to set shorter hours such as noon to 5 P.M., or by appointment only. You cannot simply shut your door and tell your secretary to hold all calls, so it's crucial that you make some workable policy and stick to it.

Before any visitor ever reaches your business—whether client, customer, friend, or relative—you should make clear what your expectations are about when it is okay to drop by or call your business. Your outgoing phone message and your business cards can contain this information.

Inevitably, though, you will still get occasional surprise visitors who drop by at other times. The best way to handle a surprise visitor is to decide immediately whether you welcome the interruption. Sometimes you might be ready to take a break anyway. If you do not want to visit, the best way to handle the situation is by quickly making it known that you are in the middle of some work that requires your full attention and that you cannot stop at the moment. Then ask the visitor if he or she might be available when you are planning to take a break, or during normal business hours.

If you can handle surprise visits quickly and inoffensively, you will display a professional attitude and will be able to give higher-quality attention to the visitor at a better time.

MEETINGS

In most one-person businesses, meetings consume a lot of time, so it is important to make them as effective as possible. Both one-on-one meetings and group meetings can be set up in ways that make them run more efficiently, take less time, and produce the decisions you need.

One on One

Most of your meetings will probably be with just one other person such as a customer, a supplier, or someone with whom you are doing a joint project. These meetings will take place on the phone, in your business location, or at your customer's or supplier's place.

Regardless of location, if you take a few minutes before the meeting to prepare, you will profit greatly from it. Make a few notes about the topics you want to cover, the order in which you want to cover them, how long you expect to take, and what you would like the outcomes to be. This kind of preparation will keep the meeting or phone call from deteriorating into a bull session, or ending without your having covered all the reasons the meeting was called in the first place. Then, at the beginning of the meeting, let the other person know what you would like to talk about, how long it might take, and what you would like the outcome to be. Once you have his or her agreement, you can proceed on a much surer footing. Unlike the random discussions that so many meetings seem to consist of, your meeting should yield practical results arrived at in a direct fashion. Don't forget, however, to provide for a little time in the beginning and at the end of the meeting for personal exchanges. This helps to maintain friendly relations in addition to getting business done.

Group Meetings

Exactly the same procedure can be followed for a meeting attended by three or more people. Many people run meetings according to the old authoritarian model in *Robert's Rules of Order*, if they impose any kind of structure at all. A more effective approach was introduced to the business world in 1976 by Michael Doyle and David Straus in *How to Make Meetings Work*. They describe the various roles that participants can play and the processes that can be used to keep meetings short but have them result in actionable outcomes. The basic elements are the same as for one-on-one meetings. The difference is that all members of the group are encouraged to make the advance preparation of a list of the topics to cover, the order in which to cover them, the time it should take, and the expected outcomes. Then when the meeting is convened, the group agrees on one person to be the *facilitator* and one person to be the *recorder*.

The facilitator starts the meeting by helping to build an agenda from the topics, priorities, and time limits the participants agree on. During the meeting, the facilitator makes sure that everyone gets a chance to speak, the topics get covered, and the time agreements are kept. The recorder uses a flip chart or large pieces of paper on the wall to record what people are saying throughout the meeting, starting with the selection of the agenda.

These roles are only superficially like the old roles of chairperson and secretary. Unlike the chairperson, the facilitator is not in charge of the meeting. In fact, it is recommended that the facilitator not participate in the meeting. In this way he or she can be regarded by the group as being focused on the process of the meeting, while participants focus on the content. To accomplish this job, the facilitator makes a verbal contract with the group:

1. I won't contribute my own ideas.
2. I will try to remain neutral.
3. I will focus the group energy on the agenda.
4. I will defend group members from personal attack.
5. I will be the meeting chauffeur.
6. I will make process suggestions, but basically, it's your meeting. You decide.

The recorder attempts to build a "group memory" that is a reflection of the consensus of the group rather than the recorder's interpretation of what was said.

The recorder does this by using a large chart pad or paper on the wall and by following these seven simple rules:

1. Be brief.
2. Alternate the use of different colored pens.
3. Catch the phrase (noun, verb, object), not the whole sentence.
4. Use bullets to set off key points.
5. Use big margins so the notes are easy to read and points can be added later.
6. Number the pages.
7. Keep checking in with the group to confirm that you have correctly recorded what was said.

In rare instances, the facilitator or recorder might participate briefly in the meeting, but only if they explicitly and clearly step out of their roles. "Joe, will you take the facilitation for a moment? I think I have something important to say on this topic." "Sally, could you take over the Magic Markers for a minute? I want to say a few words about what Bob just brought up." This option should be exercised rarely and only if the group has agreed ahead of time that it is acceptable. So that no one feels left out, the group should pick different people to be the facilitator and recorder each time.

We have encountered some interesting dynamics related to the number of people in a group. When there are fewer than six people, you seldom need a facilitator. In a group this size, something happens to lead all the participants to act as facilitators, making sure that everyone is heard from, no one is attacked, and that the agenda is followed. But the moment you add a seventh person, a facilitator seems

---

Tools for Group-Process Decision Making

BEFORE MEETING

- Choose facilitator.
- Gather agenda items.
- Delegate responsibility for each item.
- Divide items into reports, decisions, and announcements.
- Bring material and supplies needed.

AT MEETING

- Connect, check in, and share excitement.
- Review agenda items:
  Prioritize.
  Set times.

- Contract for roles:
  Facilitator.
  Recorder.
- Go through agenda:
  Take an easy item first (for example, reports before decisions).
  Break large issues into small parts for discussion.
- Take breaks if meeting is long.
- Make announcements.
- Set next meeting time.
- Evaluate this meeting.
- Close.

to be essential. With twelve or more people in a group, it sometimes helps to break up into smaller groups from time to time, in order to work on a particular agenda item. The groups might go off into different rooms, or to different corners of the same room, for ten or fifteen minutes. After they arrive at a consensus using the facilitative group process, they come back and report to the larger group. The meeting of the whole twelve can then proceed. This approach works remarkably well to move things along when issues arise that the whole group doesn't seem able to resolve.

RESOURCES

Books

Covey, Stephen R. *The Seven Habits of Highly Effective People*. New York: Simon & Schuster, 1990. A time-management system built around seven habits: (1) be proactive; (2) begin with the end in mind; (3) put first things first; (4) think win/win; (5) seek first to understand, then to be understood; (6) synergize; (7) create balanced self-renewal.

Doyle, Michael, and David Straus. *How to Make Meetings Work*. New York: Jove Publications, 1986. A detailed description of a new collaborative meeting style. Superior results and time savings over *Robert's Rules of Order* or other authoritarian styles.

Fanning, Tony, and Robbie Fanning. *Get It All Done and Still Be Human*. Menlo Park, Calif.: Open Chain Publishing, 1990. Provides focused methods for overcoming the false split of work time versus free time.

Grudin, Robert. *Time and the Art of Living*. New York: Ticknor & Fields, 1988. Inspirational essays offering penetrating insights and observations about time and its elusive bounties.

Hunt, Diana, and Pam Hait. *The Tao of Time*. New York: Simon & Schuster, 1991. Describes the problems of information overload and how to overcome them. Introduces the Taoist concepts of nonresistance, individual power, balance, and harmony with the environment as a method for living better with time.

McCay, James T. *The Management of Time*. New York: Prentice Hall, 1986. Introduces methods for increasing alertness and storing energy for future difficulties, identifying and shielding against energy losses, knowing when to stop, and investing in personal growth.

Servan-Schreiber, Jean-Louis. *The Art of Time*. Redding, Mass.: Addison Wesley, 1988. Discusses the five elements of art according to the Greeks (order, balance, contrast, unity, harmony) and explains how to apply them to time management.

Sher, Barbara, with Annie Gottleib. *Wishcraft: How to Get What You Really Want*. New York: Ballantine Books, 1986. The classic manual for self-organizing and getting what you want, once you know what your goals are.

Calendars

Two good sources for notebook calendars and supplies are:

Day-Timers, Inc.
One Day-Timer Plaza
Allentown, PA 18195-1551
215-395-5884

Day Runner
Harper House
3562 Eastham Drive
Culver City, CA 90232
213-837-6900

Setting Up Shop

If you are just starting your own business, or if you are moving to a new or bigger location, you will have a million little details to work out. All businesses need headquarters, but for a one-person business having the best possible office environment is critical. Your workplace must be conducive to getting the job done efficiently and, depending on your type of business, it must be pleasant enough to spend a lot of time there and neat enough for clients to visit. Different businesses need different accommodations, so in this chapter we will talk generally about concerns that people have in opening an office and about ways that we and other one-person-business owners have responded to them.

THE CHOICE—TO WORK AT HOME OR
AWAY FROM HOME

At some point you may face the question of whether to have your business in your home or to find a suitable location away from home. There are several common reasons for working from home: You save the expense of an outside location. You have a short commute. You can get up from bed in the middle of the night or walk from the living room to your office whenever you have a good idea or just an urge to work.

The arguments against working from home include local zoning restrictions that prohibit it and weak psychological boundaries. That same convenience of being able to work whenever you want can also lead to the sense that you are always at work: that you can't seem to get away from it. To combat this feeling you might reorganize your work space so that the aesthetic boundaries reinforce stronger psychological boundaries. Sue, a travel agent, visits her wealthy clients at their home or office to assist them in planning for their "adventure" vacation. Back at home, Sue has created an office environment that sets the stage for total concentration. Once inside her office she draws the curtains, turns on the lights, closes the door, and settles down to work. When she is finished for the day, she reverses the process and leaves her work behind. If you cannot actually close the door to your work space, perhaps you can create a screen of some sort or, if necessary, move your office out of your home.

Working in a regular business location can often give you an image of professionalism that is just not possible in your home, no matter how nice it is. Also, some clients or customers might expect you to be in an outside location and be hesitant to do business with someone who works out of the home. Maintaining an outside office is almost always more costly than running your business from home, and it is sometimes not as convenient. But offsetting these disadvantages are clearer boundaries and a more professional image.

OFFICE AT HOME, WITH FAMILY—
SPECIAL CONSIDERATIONS

I wanted to spend more time with my family.
I didn't want to miss watching my kids grow up.
Just once I wish I could be the one who bakes the brownies and helps with the school play.

We often hear statements such as these and, in fact, being home and available to children is one of the leading reasons for the rapid growth of one-person businesses. In addition to wanting to be there for their children, many people are aware that running their business from home allows their children to develop the attributes of tradeskill we discussed in the opening chapter. By living with a business, children absorb a sense of what business is about and why it can be rewarding. They will have more options when the time comes to choose between seeking employment and creating a business of their own.

Being your own boss and working from home gives you flexibility. You can join an aerobics class, make the time to attend an important track meet at school, or get to know your children's friends. And with the time that would otherwise go to commuting and dealing with office politics, you can also become more active in your community. All of this sounds, and is, wonderful, but it doesn't happen magically. To make it work requires planning on your part, especially when it comes to what we've termed *spillover*.

Spillover

Spillover occurs when your small child races to answer the door for a client or picks up the phone to answer an important overseas call. Spillover is having the dog answer the door. It is two cats racing around your office during an intense moment in a client meeting. It is your husband politely knocking to inquire whether you want to go next door for dinner tonight. In general, spillover is having your personal or home life intrude upon your work: a major nuisance that requires a lot of thought and some experience to avoid. Solving this problem is tricky because the whole idea in creating a family is to be open and available to each other. But an office in the home makes it necessary to create some boundaries.

Eliminating spillover involves four main considerations: reducing noise, avoiding interruptions, providing adequate child care, and maintaining good communication with family members, particularly children. If clients come to your home, your space should fit their expectations of professionalism. They must feel that you are offering them the best of service, including your undivided attention. Homelike noises always seem intrusive in a professional setting, so do whatever is necessary to keep your office separate from family affairs. You may need to set up shop in an outside building or in the basement or attic, or to soundproof your office space.

Reducing Noise   Noise is a very important consideration in setting up your workspace. Paul and Sarah Edwards have done a good job explaining why in their book *Working from Home*:

> Noise was the number-one environmental concern identified by office workers in the Lou Harris poll for Steelcase, a leading office furniture manufacturer. This is not surprising, because even moderately high noise levels cause increased blood pressure, faster heartbeat, and other symptoms of stress, while excessive noise causes fatigue, distraction, and errors in work.
>
> While too much noise certainly interferes with work, a total absence of sound is also stressful. As one person who moved his office home says, "The first thing I noticed was the silence. I never realized how much I appreciated the sounds of the office."
>
> Just how much sound do you need to stay mentally alert? Probably not more than thirty decibels, about the sound of normal air-conditioning. Even better would be twenty decibels of sound, about equivalent to leaves rustling in the breeze.
>
> The average office has a noise level of about fifty decibels. The sound of an average conversation is about sixty decibels, while the vacuum cleaner in your home runs at about eighty decibels. Prolonged exposure to over seventy decibels may result in hearing impairment.

Here are several sound-control techniques that the Edwardses recommend:

1. Draperies over windows. For maximum effectiveness, these need to be lined and floor length.
2. Ceiling treatments such as acoustical tile or commercially applied sound-absorbent material.
3. A thick pile carpet with an underpad to absorb noise in the room.
4. Heavily padded furniture.
5. Weatherstripping on doors and windows.
6. Indoor barriers such as room dividers or screens; outdoor barriers such as a concrete block wall over five feet high.
7. Solid-core doors in place of hollow-core doors.
8. Double-glazed windows.
9. Wall coverings such as fabric or cork.
10. Acoustical drywall with thick insulation placed between the studs of the new wall, or paneling on top of your existing walls.

Before you spend a lot of money or time on any of these sound control measures, however, find out if the noise is coming through a heat or air vent. If it is, using one of the sound "masking" techniques described below will be more effective.

To produce enough sound to keep yourself alert when working at home alone, you can create your own background noise. Consider using sounds like these while you work.

1. A stereo playing low.
2. A gurgling fish tank with a water filter and air pump.
3. A cage of songbirds such as canaries.
4. A "white noise" generator.
5. One of the commercially available records or endless-loop tape cassettes that play sounds from nature such as the sea and the wind.

Because these sounds are rhythmical, they will also help mask noise you can't screen out by other measures.

Avoiding Interruptions   It is also essential to establish uninterrupted working hours with your family and to develop rules dealing with clients coming to your home. To avoid interruptions, try to have a door that you can close, which family members are permitted to open only in an emergency. The idea of an emergency varies from person to person and, to a child, losing a ball may be considered an emergency. So everyone must clearly understand what is meant by the word.

Adequate Child Care   Child care is perhaps the most difficult issue to deal with when working at home. After all, if you chose to work at home in order to be near your children, what have you accomplished if you send them away to be taken care of? Our rule is this: If your children are in school full time, then you can work around their schedule. Hire someone to come in for the few hours after school, involve them in part of your work, and so on. If they are not in school for a full day, you will have to hire someone to look after them. This probably means sending them away from home—unless you have a huge house with a live-in unflappable grandparent who enjoys spending an entire day with the grandchildren. To attempt to make very young children conform to your business requirements can be downright cruel; it is also probably impossible.

Good Communication Communication is crucial and especially so if having a business in the home is new for your family. Suddenly the rules are different. Rooms are off-limits. You are home but not home. A child with something to share has to wait until a certain time. In *Working from Home*, Paul and Sarah Edwards give in-depth coverage to all of these issues and many more. Regarding communicating with your children, they emphasize giving them as much information as possible about when and where you will be working, when you will and won't be available, who will be available when you can't be, and exactly what is expected from them. As the Edwardses explain in their book:

> Some questions children may be troubled with in connection with your working at home include:
>
> Am I still important?
> How much can I get away with?
> Are you still available to me when I need you?
> Who is going to be in charge?

When you work from home, you must provide your own structure and make up your own rules about space, privacy, and accessibility, all of which is challenging at first. With perseverance and a lot of support from your family, however, you may wonder how you ever did it any other way.

Business advisor Tom Perry, who seems to have an ideal office-home arrangement, smiles with satisfaction when he explains how he managed to make it work so well. "I've found lately that I am much more effective in my business. I no longer work on weekends, for instance, and I have a much higher income than I did a couple of years ago. Two years ago my children's schedules were very disruptive. They went to two different schools and had different hours, and I was involved in carpooling and being available to them when they came home. Now they attend the same school and both leave at 7:30 in the morning, and they return at 2:30 in the afternoon. We have a housekeeper who takes care of them until 5:30. This is an ideal arrangement for everyone, and it's made all the difference to me. I can get an early start, which allows me to take a two-hour lunch with a friend or colleague and still put in an eight-hour day and have the weekends free to be with my family."

OFFICE LAYOUT

A useful metaphor for the best-possible working environment for a one-person business is the cockpit of an airplane. All the controls necessary to get the vehicle off the ground, fly from point to point, and land safely, are within easy reach. The dials and meters that give ongoing read-outs on how fast the plane is moving; how high it is; whether it is level, climbing, or falling; if there are other planes in the vicinity and if we are headed for a collision with them; and so forth, are also easily read from the pilot's seat. The pilot never has to leave that seat and go to some other part of the aircraft to move a control or read a gauge.

The same compactness should be true of your working environment. Both the physical plant (your office or store) and your information environment (your books, mailing lists, filing systems, and so on) can be organized with efficiency in mind.

"Most everything I need is within three feet of me, so I can access data very quickly," explains Paul Terry. "The files on current clients are in the left-hand drawer of my desk, and the phone log is kept on top of the desk. When a new client calls in I pull out a blank inquiry form and get the basic information I need in order to work with them. Then I send out whatever they need along with a note. I keep a memo of what I have sent them in an inquiry file that I keep on my desk. If they become a client, I open up a file folder for them, with the basic information on the first page. Any subsequent meetings are also filed there. As long as a client is current, their file stays in the file drawer in my desk. If they become non-current, they go into a nearby file cabinet."

Maxine, a job-development researcher, has two basic work areas. "I have a table where I keep intake forms. When I get a referral I put the filled-out forms there. This is work I need to look at and organize. The other table is where I've got my printed forms and notes about phone calls I have to make and reports I have to write. Every time I walk into the office I look at both tables and can see what I need to do. I can easily see if things are piling up over here and nearly cleared out over there. If there's a pile I know I have to work late that day. Everything is right there close at hand."

Neil, a photographer, uses a color-coded filing system. "I keep one file for each company, each individual, or each division of each company. These are right next to my typewriter. My green files are for projects that are going smoothly; the yellow ones are for projects that need special attention. In the closet are the projects I don't need to have access to as much, the ones that are either historical or void. Then I have two milk crates with hanging files full of potential client information. I keep them near the desk, but not in immediate reach."

RULES FOR ORGANIZING YOUR SPACE

Several basic principles can be applied to the physical organization of your work space:

1. Make it easy to tell where to replace an object or tool after you have moved it. For tools, a good method is to hang a pegboard on the wall, figure out where each tool should be hung for maximum efficiency, and then draw an outline around the tool when it is in place. If the pegboard is dark, draw a white or light-colored outline; if it is light, draw a black or dark outline. Then whenever you take down several tools at a time, it will be easy to hang them back up where they are supposed to go. Your original decision about where they should go will be maintained.

2. Keep the most frequently used objects, tools, and supplies closest at hand. This rule takes precedence over logical structures such as alphabetizing. The opposite of this rule applies to storage of old documents and seldom-used tools.

3. Avoid built-in desks or other fixtures. Use adjustable shelving. Buy a pair of two-drawer file cabinets rather than a four-drawer unit. You can put a board across the pair to make a desk, or you can stack them, like a four-drawer cabinet, to take up less floor space. A modular approach allows you to change your office arrangement when your needs or aesthetics change. Lightness and flexibility are desirable because you are always learning how to be more efficient. Avoid furniture or equipment that is difficult to change or adjust.

4. Never put something heavy above you where it could fall and injure you. Heavy objects should be lifted up, not down, so store them underneath or below other fixtures, or in the bottom of shelves or cabinets.

5. It is easier to look down than up. Most desks stand 24 to 29 inches high, so that when you sit in a normal chair, you naturally look down at the desk top and at any work or equipment on it. If you are using a computer, always position it so that the center of your monitor is about 17 inches in front and about 6 inches lower than your eye level, or square with your chin, when you are sitting in your normal work chair. One caution, however: Looking down for long periods of time places a strain on the natural curve of your neck that can lead to such symptoms as neck aches and headaches. To prevent this, you should take regular breaks to stretch and relax your neck. You can also help your neck by sitting up straight, back supported, with your ears aligned with your shoulders and your chin tucked slightly under.

6. When using a telephone, try to find a way to keep your hands free. There are good telephone headsets on the market, but don't get the kind that stick the headphone speaker into the channel of your ear. This can cause trouble

with wax buildup. Also, watch out for the cheap Asian imitations. We have had the best experience with Plantronics brand headsets. They are more expensive than most, running in the $50 to $125 range, but they are much more reliable and comfortable, as well as having much better speaker quality and mouthpiece microphones.

7. Be health-conscious. Avoid the coffee-to-get-up, alcohol-to-come-down syndrome. Good health requires that you stand up and move often. Sitting for long hours isn't good for your body. Good chairs and posture are important, as are fresh air, visual diversion, and control of noise level.

FURNITURE AND FIXTURES

Because a one-person business must be very efficient and cost-conscious, we have gathered together a sizable amount of information about what works the best to promote health and to provide a maximum of efficiency at a minimum cost. Here are some specific points to be aware of when choosing the furniture and fixtures that will go into your working environment.

Lights

With lights, placement and quality are the main concerns. Place your light sources so that light comes from behind your head whenever possible. For close-up work that requires direct lighting of the work surface, such as pasting up a newsletter, you would either need two separate lights, or a light that can be adjusted. Many lighting systems are easily adjustable. The most widely known is the swing-arm lamp, available in most hardware, office supply, and furniture stores, which has two spring-loaded arms that allow you to move the light toward or away from the work surface and in a 360-degree arc. This makes it possible to point the light almost anywhere you need it. Lamps like this can be easily moved. The lighting in Claude's home and office consists almost entirely of swing-arm lamps, which work equally well in the kitchen, living room, bedroom, or office. He has purchased several different kinds of mounting brackets, including a couple of floor stands, some lead-weighted desk stands, and the normal screw brackets that allow these lamps to be mounted to a desktop or wall. Luxo is the most well-known brand of swing-arm lamps, but there are less-expensive brands of equal quality.

Quality of light, the other major lighting concern, involves choosing between natural, incandescent, or fluorescent light. Many people feel that indirect natural light is the best. Some people just like the looks of it and others think it is healthier. Ultraviolet light, or UV, is the source of vitamin D from the sun. Getting forty-five minutes or more of outdoor light each day is essential for maintaining normal health, and the UV part of the light is the most important. However, even if your workplace has windows or skylights and you can control the light coming in with shutters or shades, most of the ultraviolet light is screened out by the glass or plastic, if not by the shutters or shades.

You can replace some needed daylight with the kind of fluorescent lighting known as *full-spectrum*. In addition to providing some missing UV, this light allows you to see things in their true colors, instead of in the yellowish color of incandescent lighting, the blue of "cool" fluorescents, or the reddish yellow of "warm" fluorescents. Studies conducted for over a decade have indicated that people who work under full-spectrum lights experience improvement in visual acuity, more energy, and fewer colds or illnesses than people who don't. The best-known brand of full-spectrum tubes is manufactured by DuraTest and sold under the brand name Vita Lite.

The only drawback to full-spectrum lighting is expense. The light tubes themselves are two to four times more expensive than regular fluorescent tubes. But if you take into account the health issues and that they are 5 to 10 percent less expensive to operate than the equivalent incandescent lights, you may be able to justify the investment. If not, then you will have to choose between incandescent and regular fluorescent.

Fluorescent lights provoke a lot of debate, with the number of vocal critics on the rise. The electricity coming into our homes and offices cycles on and off at the rate of sixty times a second. This is a function of how it is manufactured and transmitted across distance, and we need not understand the technicalities of this process in order to discuss the problem it causes. Many people who work under fluorescent lights have seen them flicker, either subliminally or out of the corner of their eyes, and it makes them uncomfortable, tense, irritable, or worse. Although fluorescent lights do flicker, research has shown that usually less than 10 percent of the population will notice it if the power modulators, or ballasts, used to run fluorescent lights are in good condition. All too often, however, the ballasts are ignored until the lights are flickering so badly that everyone can see it, or they start to hum so loudly that no one can miss it. This ballast problem affects full-spectrum tubes also. The solution is to maintain your lights by changing the ballasts when they start to wear out.

Regardless of whether you choose incandescent or fluorescent lighting, make certain you spend forty-five minutes or more outdoors each day to get your daily dose of Vitamin D. You cannot completely replace your need for natural sunlight with full-spectrum lighting. But if you are using fluorescent fixtures, it is a good idea to replace all the tubes with full-spectrum tubes as a supplement. Those of you who want full-spectrum lighting but already have incandescent fixtures should look for the incandescent full-spectrum lights known as "daylight bulbs." Lightbulb-shaped fluorescents that can be used in incandescent fixtures and that operate at a much lower cost than incandescent bulbs are also widely available.

Chairs

Your chair is the single most important piece of office furniture that you will buy. The right chair will help prevent the potential ailments that can arise from the unnatural behavior of sitting. As a one-person-business manager you may spend a minimum of 20 to 30 percent of your life sitting in a chair. The human body was not meant to sit for hours at a time, so aside from moving about periodically, you should give your body as much support as possible by sitting in a good chair at the right height.

Many different kinds of chairs are available, but the so-called "ergonomic" ones are the best if you shop for some of the following simple features. Your chair should encourage you to sit with proper posture. The back of the chair should fit firmly into the lumbar, or lower, region of your back. The chair should be high enough from the floor that when you sit in it, your feet rest flat on the floor. Coordinate the height of your chair with the height of your desk. Sit upright in your chair and let your arms drop relaxed at your side, then bend your arms at the elbow. Your hands should be resting on the surface of your desk as you hold your lower arms, from the elbow to your hands, straight out from your body. At most, there should be only a slight upward bend. For most people, this makes the desk surface from 24 to 29 inches from the floor. You can always adjust your chair height so that your arms are in the correct position, then put your feet on a stool or footrest if they do not reach the floor, or buy a chair with a built-in footrest. Chairs that are easily adjustable usually cost more, but they are worth it.

If you have more than one working surface, each a different height from the floor, you may want a chair with hydraulic adjusters. These will allow you to quickly readjust your seat height for whichever work surface you are using. Another important feature is casters. A chair with large, smooth-rolling casters can glide across carpet or bare floors with ease. This can be of particular help if you have an L-shaped desk or a small office with two or more desks close together. With a rolling chair you can move quickly from one working surface to another, and you won't need to take up space with a second chair.

If you are stuck with older, nonergonomic chairs, you can lessen the negative effects of sitting in them for hours at a time by using foam wedges and lumbar cushions. These are widely available now, even appearing in auto parts stores for use while driving. If you have trouble finding them, ask your doctor or a local chiropractor.

Desks and Working Surfaces

Desktops tend to be loaded down from time to time and should therefore be able to carry the load. Most decent-quality desk furniture meets this requirement, but be sure to keep it in mind when you are shopping around.

With working surfaces, flexibility means that you can easily move a unit from one place to another, and you can use it for more than one purpose. A $20 door, set on two file cabinets, is much more flexible than a $500 rolltop oak desk. If decor plays a part in your decision, you will have to be creative. Charmian Anderson, a therapist, created a flexible desk using an oval piece of glass spanning two beautiful brass table stands. The principle is the same as for a door and two file cabinets, but this variation fits better into the decor of her elegant office. It meets her need for flexibility, too, because she can move it easily. And with dimensions of 3 by 6 feet, it could serve as a meeting-room table in the future if necessary.

Storage Systems

When you only need occasional access to files, cardboard archive boxes are a good safe choice. If stored in a dry place, cardboard is all you really need. If you want to protect some of your records from fire, then you will need a fireproof file cabinet or a bank safety-deposit box. For fast, easy access, filing cabinets are best, but—depending on the setup of your work space—you might find such alternatives as Crate-A-File useful. Crate-A-Files are plastic boxes, similar to milk crates, that can be stacked one on top of another; they include metal or plastic runners for holding letter-sized hanging folders. Both crate-type files and regular filing cabinets are available with casters. This added flexibility allows you to move them easily from one location to another, eliminating the need to cross the room to pull files out and put them back. It also makes a small space seem bigger, as you can roll the files out of the way when they are not in use.

What doesn't fit into a filing drawer or box will probably go on a shelf. Most hardware and furniture stores sell modular shelving. It comes in two basic forms: on-the-wall bracket systems and knock-down cubical systems. On-the-wall systems are fully adjustable but require you to put holes in the wall and are therefore semi-permanent. Cubical systems are stackable and simply need to be assembled and put into place; they can serve as moving boxes if you change offices.

RESOURCES

Alvarez, Mark. *The Home Office Book: How to Set up and Use an Efficient, Personal Workspace in the Computer Age.* Woodbury, Conn.: Goodwood Press, 1990. An excellent discussion of the issues of setting up a home office that is equally applicable to an outside office.

Edwards, Paul, and Sarah Edwards. *Working from Home.* Los Angeles, Calif.: J.P. Tarcher, 1990. The best book available on all aspects of working at home.

Home Office Computing. A monthly magazine on the issues of working at home, with emphasis on office equipment, especially computers. 730 Broadway, New York, NY 10003; 800-288-7812.

National Home Business Report. A quarterly now in its sixth year of publication, providing access to other small business networks, individuals, and businesses. National Home Business Network, Box 2137-P, Naperville, IL 60567.

Working Mother. A monthly magazine focusing on the concerns of working mothers, including those who work at home. 230 Park Avenue, New York, NY 10169; 800-525-0643.

8

Choosing Office Equipment—
High Tech or Low?

Many one-person businesses run with little or no technology. But for most, office equipment is central to their success. Numerous machines and devices are available to help you run your one-person business more effectively. Three of them—the answering machine, the typewriter, and the facsimile (fax) machine—are outstanding efficiency boosters. They are almost essential pieces of office equipment. In fact, if it weren't for the typewriter and the answering machine, most one-person businesses simply could not exist. And since the early 1980s, the fax machine and the personal computer have begun to play major roles in defining not only how you run a one-person business but in many cases the businesses themselves. Many one-person businesses are now based on computers; that is, they provide information or services that could not be provided without the use of a computer, and often a fax machine. Two other pieces of office equipment experiencing a growing role in one-person businesses are the photocopy machine and the cellular phone.

This chapter will give you a set of criteria and a selection process for evaluating any office equipment, from answering machines and typewriters to photocopiers and fax machines to cellular phones and computers. First, we will examine typewriters, answering machines, and fax machines to illustrate the tradeoff between features and cost. Then we will demonstrate how our selection process works in evaluating photocopiers and computers. When we are through you should be able to adapt the selection process to your own needs; it can help you decide whether to add any piece of office technology to your equipment inventory.

EVALUATING TECHNOLOGY—FEATURES VERSUS COST

"He who dies with the most toys wins!" is a popular and seductive notion of the day. But an effectively run one-person business will absolutely avoid this game. If you have plenty of discretionary income and want to take pleasure in playing with the latest electronic and mechanical toys, then have at it. Otherwise, be sure that keeping your toy box full of the newest and neatest technology can be comfortably justified as a wise business decision.

The best way to avoid high-tech consumeritis is to resist the impulse to buy something just because it is new. Develop an approach, like the one described in this chapter, and use it consistently to help you decide whether buying any new machine makes economic sense.

The tradeoff between features and cost is the first important consideration in deciding whether to purchase office technology. The manufacturers of most office equipment offer each type of product with a range of features. Sometimes the lower end of this range is perfectly suitable, in both price and capability, for a particular function you would like to perform. Although other criteria can be added to your selection process, the features-versus-cost consideration is a basic one and in many cases will suffice. The telephone answering machine and typewriter are so basic to the running of any business that we will assume every business will want one. With that in mind, let's use them to illustrate the features versus cost analysis.

Telephone-Answering Machines

Of all the equipment you might buy to make running your one-person business easier, the telephone-answering machine tops the list. We have given many reasons why this is so in Chapter 5, "Information Management."

Of the wide variety of telephone-answering machines on the market, our clients have reported the best success with Panasonic models. That is not to say that there aren't other good brands, but, rather, that we have had the most positive experience with this one. Panasonic answering machines seem to be well built and offer more features for the money than many others. Brand name is not the main consideration, however. Shop for features first, price second.

Features   Look for four key features: (1) a voice-activated, unlimited incoming message; (2) remote message retrieval; (3) the ability to change your outgoing message from a remote phone; and (4) time- and date-stamping of incoming messages.

Cost Low-end units cost as little as $50 to $75 but lack voice activation, remote access, or some other feature. In the $75 to $100 range you can almost always get all of these features. If you're willing to pay more than $100 you can get a machine with even more features, most of which you won't really need. Be sure to buy a power-surge protector to go along with your machine, as many of the newer, solid-state models will burn out or lose the outgoing message from sudden brownouts in your local power system.

Typewriters

At a very basic level, the office machine that is second in importance to the answering machine is not the computer but the typewriter. For many one-person businesses the computer represents a level of power that is overkill and a level of learning that is overwhelming. Some very successful one-person businesses don't use computers at all. In any case, it is best to try performing any function manually before you automate it. If you have a manual system that works, you should carefully weigh the costs and benefits of computerizing it. This will help you avoid the many problems that can arise, which we will discuss later in this chapter.

The typewriter makes a one-person business easier to operate in several ways. First, it's easy to use. Second, it's faster than handwriting. Third, it can actually automate many of your simpler writing tasks without the trouble and expense of a computer. Let's evaluate typewriters by comparing features versus cost in some detail.

Features With the new electronic typewriters, even people who type with the hunt-and-peck method can bang out letter-perfect documents, forms, and envelopes. Most of these machines have a small liquid-crystal display (LCD) panel above the keyboard that allows you to preview what you are typing and to make automatic corrections (from one to three lines of text) before you commit it to paper.

For only a bit more you can buy models that will permit you to store information that you use over and over, such as addresses, or phrases or paragraphs like the closing to a letter. This capability can save you a tremendous amount of time. Some models also have spell-checking. At the top end in price and features are typewriters with a disk drive and monitor that give you most of the features of a computer while maintaining the familiarity and ease of use of a typewriter. If letters and short documents constitute the bulk of your written output, such a word-processing typewriter might well be the perfect tool.

Cost In general, the price of most high-tech office machines is cut in half every two years, until a new generation of features and benefits is introduced. For instance, in the mid-1980s an IBM Selectric typewriter that used interchangeable font balls and could correct one character at a time cost $1,200 new. By 1990, several manufacturers sold models that used interchangeable daisywheels and could correct several lines at a time for under $500. You could buy an Asian clone of the original IBM Selectric for under $300. It is, therefore, best to temper the need for increased efficiency or output with patience and to wait until the equipment with the features you want falls into your price range.

By balancing the low cost against the required features, most one-person businesses can easily justify the purchase of an electric typewriter, at least a basic low-end model.

Facsimile Machines

The facsimile, or fax, machine is really a hybrid of the telephone-answering machine and a computer with a modem. In much the same way that you can leave a message on a telephone-answering machine, you can leave a message (document) on someone's fax machine or receive one on yours—at a time convenient to either of you. You do not both have to be available at the same time. And, as with a computer with a modem, the message you send can be many pages long and include pictures or graphics.

Features The basic features to look for if you do decide to buy are ease of setup, CCITT Group 3 compatibility, automatic phone versus fax switch, automatic redial, 16-shade gray scale, halftone receiving, paper cutter, automatic page feeder, thermal versus plain paper, polling, and memory dialing. There are many other features, but these are the ones you won't want to be without.

Cost In the early 1980s fax machines were available at prices ranging from $2,000 to $10,000, depending on the features included. Prices began to fall significantly in the eighties, and today a wide range of low-cost units is available. Even plain-paper fax machines have begun to drop to an affordable cost for one-person businesses.

But don't be seduced by the apparent glamour of fax. Think only about whether you have a real need for one (for example, if you have a lot of overseas clients). Think about what your monthly fax expenses are now, if any. If you are spending 50 to 100 percent of what a monthly lease or purchase payment would be, then having your own machine starts to make sense.

A good rule of thumb is that if you need to fax ten to fifteen pages a month, you might be able to justify your own machine. This is because, as soon as you have your own machine, you will tend to fax at least twice as many pages as you currently do. With fax services charging from one to five dollars per page to send and receive fax documents for you, the arithmetic often shows that your monthly fax bill can equal a lease or purchase payment.

When should you forget about fax machines? If you never even think about it, if nobody ever asks you for your fax number, or if it just doesn't fit in with the way you run your business, then forget fax machines for now.

ON THE LOOKOUT FOR TECHNOLOGY
FOR YOUR BUSINESS

Long before you become a self-made expert on office technology, you may be aware of parts of your business that could benefit from automation. By paying attention to your communications needs and the way in which information flows through your business, you will be ready to evaluate any new technology that looks like an economical and effective way to streamline your business.

In recent years, California's Central Valley has seen the growth of a network of professional agricultural consultants. These people specialize in knowing how to control the pests and diseases that infect farm crops. Because their clients are farmers who live very far apart and because their work requires them to be in the field for most of the day, the consultants needed a special communications system: one that allowed them to respond to their client's urgent calls without going back to the office several times a day.

Answering machines weren't the solution; since the consultants weren't near telephones they had no way of retrieving messages from their machines. Instead, they turned to a citizen's band or short-wave radio with a home base-station. A farmer could contact a consultant's home base by phone or radio knowing that the consultant's spouse or partner could relay the message by radio. The consultant would then get back to the farmer as quickly as possible or drop by if the farmer was nearby.

As you might expect, these agricultural consultants were among the first to use cellular phones when broadcast stations were built in their areas. Because they were already aware of their communications needs, they easily recognized how this new technology could make their system run more smoothly. Also, the cost of a cellular phone dropped rapidly from $3,000, when they were introduced in 1984, to less than $1,000 by 1987, and down to a mere $300 to $500 by 1992—making it an affordable technology in a very short time.

This is a perfect example of one-person-business owners who were ready to take advantage of a new technology when it came along. They knew what they needed and quickly recognized the additional flexibility that cellular phones would provide, as well as the difference in service that they would make possible. Potential opportunities like this will occur to you as you become aware of the needs of your business and of existing technologies that are just now reaching an affordable price range. Cellular phones, fax machines, photocopiers, and computers are among the low-cost technologies that you may want to look at from this perspective.

QUESTIONS TO ASK ABOUT ANY TECHNOLOGY

Regardless of low cost, you should never buy any technology until you absolutely need it. You can determine this by asking the following questions:

- Will it reduce my expenses?
- Will it increase my income?
- Will it save time or increase my output?

In addition, you will need to evaluate the true costs of buying and using any new technology. Ask these basic questions:

- Is it a very new technology, or has it been around for a while?
- How much will supplies and maintenance cost?
- How long will it take me to learn to use it?
- Will I have to continue to use the old manual system too, until I know for sure that the new technology works?
- What will be the additional costs, such as special furniture or accessories?
- What is the real life of the equipment?

With these questions as guidelines, let's take a look at photocopiers and computers. You could use this same process to evaluate any high-technology purchase.

Photocopiers

Will it reduce my expenses? Making photocopies can cost as much as five to ten cents a page if you do your copying at a commercial location. With your own copier you can bring the cost down to from two to six cents a copy. However, when you own a copier you will probably make at least half again as many copies as you did before, because it is so convenient.

Will it increase my income? This is hard to measure, since usually you will not be selling the photocopies themselves. But when you can quickly and easily copy an article or letter and send it to a client or customer, you can expand your communications and create a different kind of relationship with your clients. The result may be an increase in business.

Will it save time or increase my output? You will definitely save time when you have your own copier, even if you make more copies than you used to. Organizing the material to be copied and then going out to a photocopy store is always more time-consuming.

Is this a new technology, or has it been around a while? Photocopiers have been around long enough that it is difficult to buy a bad one. Although certain models or brand names are better than others, they all operate at a more or less standard level of performance. This makes it necessary to look to features other than performance as the criteria for choosing one.

How much will supplies and maintenance cost? This is the trickiest question for photocopiers, because toner cartridges and drums vary greatly in cost. It is important to find out how many copies you get per toner cartridge. If you buy a model that has a separate toner cartridge and drum, you need to know the average life expectancy of the drum. Figured over the time you expect to be using the machine, expensive toner and short-lived drums can make an inexpensive copier cost significantly more than an expensive model that is more economical to operate.

Copiers are usually low-maintenance machines. To keep them trouble-free, have them serviced once a year. You can buy a service contract for under $200 a year, or you can pay $50 to $100 an hour each time you call the service technician out. Ask others who have copy machines about the service record on their machines or check recent reviews in magazines such as *Consumer Reports*.

How long will it take me to learn to use it? For photocopiers this is not a very important question. They are all easy to use and it usually takes only a few minutes to learn how. It's when something goes wrong inside the machine that you might have trouble. All have different instructions for removing jammed paper or replacing the heating element. Ask about fixing these problems before buying to see if you understand the procedures and could do them yourself in an emergency. You don't want to have to pay for a service call just to remove a piece of jammed paper.

Will I have to continue to use the old manual system too? For longer runs and for collating, folding, or binding services, it is still best to go to an offset printer or photocopy store. You can confirm this by checking prices in your area. But remember to include your time as one of the cost factors as well as the wear and tear on your machine (most personal copiers are not designed to do big runs of copies).

What about additional costs? Most personal copy machines are small enough that you won't need any special furniture. Still, you may want to buy one of the small stands that have space for paper and supplies built in. You may also want to buy accessories such as paper trays or automatic collators. Another useful purchase might be a desktop page folder—they cost around $200 to $300, and can fold up to three sheets of regular $8\frac{1}{2} \times 11$-inch paper at a time to fit into a No. 10 envelope. If you mail out a lot of photocopied material in No. 10 envelopes, one of these machines will save enough time to pay for itself in the first year you have it.

What is the real life of the equipment? This is an important question, because it's too easy to equate equipment life with the depreciation schedule that is set up for tax deduction purposes. Most equipment lasts significantly longer than its depreciation life. If you use the true life expectancy of the equipment in your cost calculations, it might change your decision. And true life expectancy can vary widely. *Consumer Reports* is a good place to turn for help in making the calculation.

So, should I buy a photocopier? That depends. If it will truly save time and money, it will probably be a good investment. Relating it to your level of income might be the safest way to make the decision. If you make $50,000 a year, and you want to spend only 1 percent of your income, what kind of a photocopier can you buy for $500? The good news is that you can buy a simple plain-paper copier that will make $8\frac{1}{2} \times 11$-inch copies for under $500. The bad news is that you usually have to load the blank paper one sheet at a time, and there are virtually no additional features, such as different paper sizes or enlargement and reduction.

More good news is that you will find most personal copiers range in price from $700 to $1,700. These machines produce about six to ten copies a minute and are a good choice if you make fewer than a thousand copies a month. Moreover, the copy quality is just as good as that of the most expensive business copiers.

Computers

A computer is better than anything else at sorting numbers and letters at super-fast speeds. This capability may help you do things faster than normal, but it also allows you to make mistakes faster than normal. You can expend a lot of energy and lose a lot of sleep trying to get a computer to do what you want, and mistakes can be devastating. For these reasons alone, deciding to buy a computer is not as simple as choosing a typewriter or a photocopier. Because a computer can do many different things, including get you into trouble very easily, you have to ask yourself a few extra questions. Begin with three simple steps: (1) decide what you want the computer to do; (2) find the software that does that; and (3) buy the hardware that particular software runs on.

Decide What You Want the Computer to Do. This is a bit more difficult than it sounds. There are many software packages available today, but only a few of them are of real use to a one-person business. Computer salespeople will tell you that you can completely change your life by getting a computer. Then they will proceed to sell you the hardware, often with little consideration for what you need. Or they will tell you that all you need is word-processing, database, and spreadsheet or accounting software. Seldom do they take the time to get to know you and your business and to discover what your unique needs might be.

The computer is a fun toy, and the tasks it can help a business with include accounting, list management, sales tracking, inventory, desktop publishing, letter writing, graphic presentations, financial analysis, and much more. When you decide to computerize, however, you should do it a little bit at a time. First, make a list of all the things you want the computer to do for you; be sure to prioritize it. Start computer shopping with the most important function in mind. Don't try to find a computer that will do everything you need right from the start. Computer technology changes rapidly, but computerizing your business should proceed slowly and carefully. By the time you are ready to computerize some of your lower-priority tasks, you may be able to afford an even better system or one better suited for doing that particular task. For example, if you have a limited budget, your primary need is for desktop publishing, and you are a completely naive user, you would probably be better off with software written for the Apple Macintosh. But if fast word processing and spreadsheet analysis is more important to you, an IBM or IBM compatible is not only better but much faster. If money is not an issue and you can buy top-of-the-line hardware, there is no real difference in speed and performance between Apple and IBM.

Find the Software That Does What You Want Unless you are a computer programmer, want to get deeply involved in modifying software, or are willing to hire someone to help, you should concentrate on three types of software that come ready to use without a lot of practice or modifications: telecommunications software, word-processing software, and list-management software.

Telecommunications Software. Most one-person businesses will find using a modem (a device that allows your computer to talk to another computer over the phone) to be fun, but only marginally useful, so telecommunications may not be high on your list. But if your business sells information, you might profit from using one of the many databases and commercial conferencing systems available over the phone using a modem. If you are isolated by geography or circumstances, you can also find emotional and technical support on local, regional, and national conferencing systems like the Working From Home forum on CompuServe. Writers may value the ability to exchange computer files with coauthors or send finished manuscripts to an editor over the phone. But for other than information-oriented businesses, telecommunications will have marginal value.

Word-Processing Software. The advantages of word processing are greatest in a business that creates a lot of reports, letters, or other documents. If your business requires only a few letters or forms, you will probably be better off using a typewriter. Word processing allows you to create a document much faster than you can with a typewriter by allowing you to forget about spelling, punctuation, grammar, or what the finished document will look like. After you have completed the typing you can go back and make all the corrections and modifications you like before you print. This takes much less time than the old way of composing several drafts on your typewriter before getting one just right.

Once you master this way of "processing words," however, you'll find, as with a photocopier, that you start creating many more documents or letters than you used to. So the saved time is partially lost to increased output. This is probably to your long-term advantage. Just as sending out photocopies to clients or associates can be beneficial, using word processing to communicate more frequently can have a subtle positive effect on your volume of business.

List-Management Software. Computerized list management shines in cases where you are doing a lot of mailing to clients, customers, or prospects and you have more than a hundred but less than five hundred names on your list. It shines because you can use it to sort the names at high speed using whatever criteria you select: alphabetical, by zip code, by city, or by any of a number of codes that you can assign to each name as you enter the data. You can print out labels or envelopes much more quickly than you could type them one at a time. You can create repetitive personalized letters, which allow you to send the same letter to more than one person with the computer inserting each person's name and address in the letter for you.

The range of one hundred to five hundred names comes from our experience with dozens of businesses trying to maintain their own mailing lists. If you have less than one hundred names it is usually easier to handle them manually, as we describe in Chapter 9, "Grassroots Marketing." For numbers between one hundred and five hundred, the computer allows you to handle your own list management quite effectively. With more than five hundred names, maintaining the list takes enough time and energy that you can probably justify hiring an outside service to do it.

Other lists you might want to computerize include inventory, books, audio- and videotapes, and—if you are an information or consulting business—the people and businesses that you can refer others to. Except for inventory, these lists are handled pretty much like mailing lists. Software programs have been specifically designed to handle each one of them. For inventory, the applications tend to be specific to a type of business. Check with peers or trade publications to see what is available for your type of business.

What about Accounting Software? One-person businesses are unique; each one has special accounting needs. Therefore, any accounting package you buy will need to be modified to meet those needs. In some cases the modifications may be simple and few, but in others they can be extensive. Some accounting packages are easy to modify and some are not.

Good accounting software costs from $50 to $4,000 for a complete system. The difference is in how complete they are, how easy they are to modify, and how extensive the reports they can generate are. There are too many packages on the market for us to be able to evaluate them here, and by the time this book comes to print, any specific information given would probably be out of date. But it is good to keep a few broad issues in mind when considering accounting software.

First, if your manual accounting system works okay now and doesn't take a lot of time, then forget about computerizing it. With even the simplest package you'll spend more time setting up the software and learning it than it's worth.

Second, think about automating only a part of your system. Perhaps you need just automatic check-writing or checkbook-balancing, time and billing or accounts receivable, accounts payable, payroll, or inventory. There are many good software packages on the market that do only one of these and do it well. Even if you decide to automate all of your accounting, do only one feature or subsystem at a time—but do try to buy all of your software from the same company so that the individual modules can be more easily integrated with each other.

Third, check with others in your field to see if some enterprising company has created a special accounting package specifically for your type of business. These are called *vertical market* packages and they are available for a growing number of businesses. Among the professions you are likely to find such packages for are doctors, lawyers, dentists, chiropractors, and accountants. Other fields for which packages have been developed include retail stores, property management, mail-order fulfillment, direct sales, travel agents, and construction. Check with your peers and your trade organization to see what is being recommended for your particular field.

Buy the Hardware It Runs On. After you have chosen your software, the type of computer you need to buy will be obvious. In the United States the major contenders are the Apple Macintosh and the PC manufactured by IBM and a host of other vendors. Most of the IBM-compatible hardware components manufactured today, whether in the United States or overseas, are of the same relative reliability. An IBM clone manufactured in Korea will in all likelihood be of equal quality, and last just as long, as a computer manufactured in Japan, Taiwan, Hong Kong, Europe, Canada, or the United States. Quality is more a function of brand and model than point of origin. Even the big companies such as IBM or COMPAQ buy components manufactured throughout Asia and South America.

This means that the most important hardware feature is not hardware at all but the service and support that come along with it, especially with an IBM compatible. When you buy your hardware you can expect a warranty on parts and labor that is good for from ninety days to one year. After the warranty period you can purchase a service contract for $200 to $500 a year. This can work out to be relatively high, since computers are pretty reliable. When they do need fixing the hourly fee for service runs from $75 to $100, with most repairs lasting less than two hours. But if you don't want to worry about yours being the exception, the service contract could be your best bet.

The most economical sources of support for your hardware (and your software too) are the computer-users groups or special-interest groups (SIGs) located in your area. You will have to sift through a lot of advice before you find the answer that actually works, but the cost is low (just membership dues) and the people who populate these groups represent a broad base of experience and knowledge that you can draw on. Groups exist that focus on almost every brand of computer and software package.

Printers: Letter Quality or Laser?

One of the most frequently asked hardware questions is "Should I get a laser printer?" This question can best be answered the same way as you would if you were choosing an entire computer system. What do you want to print? How do you want it to look? Buy the software that does that. Buy the printer the software was written for.

If you want fast, legible printouts, but you are not concerned with how fancy they look, you will probably want to get an impact dot-matrix printer. If the typewritten or letter-quality look is important to you, you will choose between an ink-jet or a laser printer. However, some dot-matrix printers come so close to looking like letter quality that many people are choosing them. With these you can switch between a high-quality near-typewriter look and a lower-quality but high-speed output, both on the same printer.

Ink-jet printers are whisper-quiet, generating only a forty-five-decibel noise level, as compared to the seventy-five to eighty-five decibels generated by dot-matrix printers. Ink-jet printers are extremely reliable and have a print quality almost equal to that of a laser printer. They are ideal for most graphics applications and are much faster with graphics than dot matrix printers.

By the late 1980s, laser printers offering a resolution of 300 dots per inch and print speeds of from six to fifteen pages a minute cost from $1,400 to $5,000. Higher-resolution laser printers cost $12,000 or more. Twenty-four-pin printers offering near letter-quality output at print speeds from 45 to 160 characters per second were costing from $500 to $1,500. Ink-jet printers offering resolutions of 150 to 300 dots per inch at speeds from 20 to 200 characters per second cost about $1,000. The differences in price were a function of features and brand name.

By the early 1990s, near-letter-quality dot matrix and ink-jet printers could be purchased for as little as $300, and "personal" laser printers were available for $600. Once again, waiting until you have a real need can save you money. Our best advice is to pay as little as possible for the few features you absolutely need. Then wait two or three years until the prices drop to a point where you can buy additional features at a more affordable price — about the time you may need to buy a new printer anyway.

Evaluating Your Computer Choices

With the foregoing in mind, let's run the computer purchase decision through our selection questions.

Will it reduce my expenses? For a one-person business the answer is usually No!—even though having a computer may enable you to reduce the amount of money you are spending on subcontractors. You won't lower your overall expenses, because you will now use more paper, printer ribbons or toner, envelopes, floppy disks, and miscellaneous supplies related to the computer than you ever thought possible. Contrary to the popular belief, using a computer does not lead to a paperless office. Studies sponsored by the Department of Defense to create the so-called paperless office have been going on since the mid-eighties and still haven't managed to eliminate paper completely. Just the opposite is true: Once you get the hang of word processing, you put out more documents, not fewer. Also, wastage increases because you tend to make more corrections when all you have to do is push a button to print out your document again.

If you want to check whether this holds true for you, just add an expense item labeled Computer to your chart of accounts and in it post all of the items you buy for the computer. The first year that Claude started making full use of his computer, his office supplies account jumped from $1,200 to $2,300—an increase of 48 percent. He has since added a computer account to help him keep costs under control by tracking them more closely.

Will it increase my income? Maybe. At first a computer may have no measurable effect. But if you implement an accounts-receivable program that helps you to stay on top of collecting the money owed to you, your net income may go up. Or, as you master letter writing, promotional mailings, and so forth on the computer you may see an increase in income that is directly traceable to your use of word-processing and list-management software. A mail-order-business that installs one of the good mail-order-fulfillment packages may see a dramatic increase in sales traceable to an increase in good customer service.

Will it save time or increase my output? After you have gotten through the initial learning curve and are properly set up, you will be able to take advantage of the computer's strongest points, saving time and increasing output. Realizing these two benefits is mostly a matter of picking the right combination of software and hardware, and setting them up correctly.

Is this a new technology, or has it been around a while? The computer industry is well known for bringing both hardware and software products to market that have not been fully tested and corrected so that they run error free. For this reason, you should avoid buying the latest and greatest software or hardware. Stick to the three questions listed earlier—"What do I want the computer to do?" "What software does that?" "What hardware does it run on?"—and you should be safe from finding yourself the "beta-test site" for some computer vendor. (When a product is almost ready for the commercial market, its creators get a few companies to volunteer to test it in a real-life situation. This is the "beta test." After all the things that can go wrong are found and fixed, the product can be offered for sale. Often, however, vendors in the computer industry move too quickly through this stage and customers who have actually paid for the product become unwilling beta-test sites.)

How much will supplies and maintenance cost? As we said earlier, supply costs will rise. The most critical supply item in a computer system is ink: printer ribbons, ink-jet or toner cartridges. You can buy long-lasting ribbons, but sometimes the shorter-lasting ones are on sale at a price that works out to be cheaper on a per-character basis. Be diligent in shopping for high quality but low price. You can save money by refilling your own ink-jet cartridges. Using a simple hypodermic-like needle you can inject ink back into spent ink-jet cartridges. And you can also save money by having your laser cartridges refilled if you can locate a service in your area. Otherwise, shop around because prices on laser cartridges are highly variable.

Paper is the next most-critical supply. You can easily use up an entire forest in a very short period of time. So think carefully about your printing habits and buy recycled paper. An average box of three thousand sheets of $8\frac{1}{2} \times 11$-inch paper with tractor-feed edges will run between $15 and $30. If you plan to use your computer a lot, you can expect to go through a box every six to eight weeks. You can make a more precise guess by calculating how many pages of documents, letters, invoices, and other printouts you anticipate making.

As we said earlier, the cost of maintenance should be relatively low because computers are fairly reliable. If, however, you choose to buy a service contract after the warranty expires your costs will go up by $200 to $500 per year.

You will need to think ahead in this way in order to know how much more to allow for supplies and maintenance. Once you know how long supplies will last and what quantity you expect to use, you can easily calculate the increase. A good rule of thumb is to expect your office-supply expense to go up by at least 20 to 30 percent.

How long will it take me to learn to use it? This depends on which applications you are going to try to learn. If you buy a Macintosh and use only MacWrite, you will be happily processing documents within a few days of first turning the machine on. If you buy an IBM and an advanced word-processing program such as WordPerfect, you will spend a few hours at a time, daily, for several weeks or months in order to master more than half of the program's features. Each type of application has its own learning curve, or period of time over which you master it. Accounting software has a long learning curve; it sometimes takes up to a full year before you can use all of the essential features of a very good package. MacWrite has a very short learning curve, as short as one day for some people.

To figure out the potential learning curve for the packages you intend to buy, ask the salesperson what the average learning time is and then multiply that by a factor of at least two. You can also ask to "test drive" the package, which means that the vendor will set it up on a computer for you to play with. Press on to another store if they say no. Most stores will cooperate since the computer industry needs all the customers it can get. Probably the best way to estimate learning time is by taking an introductory workshop, if any are offered in your area. In a few hours, usually for under $50, you can learn a lot about how difficult a package may be and whether it will to do what you need.

Will I have to continue to use the old manual system too? You bet. It is essential to continue using your old way of doing things until you are completely sure that the computer system works. For most applications the trial period will last only a matter of months. But for something like accounting, you don't want to discover at the end of a quarter or a year that the package you bought doesn't calculate your taxes accurately and, moreover, that you don't have any way of figuring them out manually, other than by redoing everything by hand.

What will be the additional costs? If you plan to spend a lot of time at your computer it would be wise to give careful consideration to buying special computer furniture. Units that have a special shelf for the printer as well as adjustable shelves for the keyboard and monitor can make it easier to work long hours. Copy-holders, diskette storage boxes, a printer stand, and other such accessories can help you stay organized and comfortable while working at the computer. And as we stressed in the previous chapter, always give special attention to your chair.

What is the real life of the equipment? Because computers have very few moving parts they can last years beyond the figures given on depreciation tables. A computer may still be chugging away ten years after you have fully depreciated it. Before a computer wears out it is likely that you will find some new, better software package that runs on a newer computer, and you will want to move up.

Printers are another matter. By their very nature, they beat themselves up as you use them, so you may find yourself buying a new printer after only three or four years. If you buy a top-of-the-line model from a reputable company you can expect the unit to last at least twice that long. Laser printers are a different matter again. Because the technology used in a laser printer is basically the same as that used in a photocopier, the life of the photoelectric drum is an issue. The remaining moving parts and solid-state circuitry will last several years. As with the computer, it is more likely that you will buy a new laser printer because the features have been improved or the price has dropped than because it has worn out.

Because computers are so durable, computer users often find themselves with one or more computers that just sit around unused. Claude has at least three old computers that he lends to friends from time to time. Salli, who is usually unimpressed by technological toys, has gone through three computers—the result of upgrading her first Macintosh which she purchased less than a year after buying an Apple II.

You might also decide to buy a new computer system when the price finally drops to a level you can afford. As with most high-tech office equipment, the price of computers is cut in half every two years, until a significant change in the technology comes about. For example, Claude bought a Radio Shack TRS Model 100 lap computer for $900 in 1985. It had its own operating system and could run only a small number of packages written specifically for it. It had a 32,000-character memory, no disk drives, and only a small liquid-crystal display screen that showed eight rows of 40 characters each. In 1988 he spent $900 on a Toshiba 1000 laptop computer that could run thousands of different programs and had a 640,000-character memory, a built-in disk drive storing 800,000 characters on hard-cased floppies, and a large LCD screen that displayed twenty-four lines of 80 characters each. By the early nineties, $900 would buy an IBM compatible laptop computer with a 4 million-character memory and an 80 million–character hard disk.

So, should I buy a computer? The conclusion has to be that you can get more for your money, or pay much less for the same thing, if you can wait a year or two to buy the equipment you want. Again, the simple rule to follow is *Don't buy any technology until you absolutely need it.*

HOW MUCH OF MY INCOME SHOULD I SPEND ON NEW TECHNOLOGY?

In our experience, 1 to 5 percent of your gross income is the most you should spend on the acquisition of new technology in any given year. If your purchase doesn't

Guidelines for Buying a Computer

1. A checklist for deciding: Do I want a computer?
   - ☐ I like gadgets.
   - ☐ I read a lot.
   - ☐ I like to spend hours on simple routines like balancing my checkbook.
   - ☐ I like to watch TV.
   - ☐ I like video games.
   - ☐ I like to tinker with appliances and machines.

   If you checked three or more, you're probably the type of person that wants a computer, whether you need one or not.

2. A checklist for deciding: Do I really need a computer?
   - ☐ I do financial analyses that require many calculations and recalculations.
   - ☐ I write a lot or am planning to write a book.
   - ☐ I manage a one-person business and need to know what's happening more often than the once-a-month report from my accountant.
   - ☐ I am a consultant to middle- or upper-level managers in corporations and make a lot of my recommendations based on information in reports generated by the company's main computer.
   - ☐ I am involved in a computer business.

   Any one of these is reason enough to buy a computer. With the price of computer systems dropping each year, it becomes easier and easier to justify buying a computer. There are many good software packages available to help you with each of these functions. If you are a professional or in the specialized retail trades, you can probably find a package designed especially for your business, though you may have to make a thorough search for it.

3. Rules to shop for a computer by:

   Memorize these two sets of rules before you go out looking for a computer system.

   a. How to buy a computer:
   - Decide what you want it to do.
   - Find the software that does that.
   - Buy the hardware it runs on.

   b. How to test drive the software/ hardware system:

   Go into as many computer stores as you have the patience to endure. For any software you are interested in, ask the salesperson the following:
   - Does it do what I want?
   - Show me.
   - Now let me do it!

   The first set of rules will make it difficult for you to purchase a system that fails to do what you need. It will also restrain you from buying more than is necessary.

   The second set of rules will help you defend yourself against aggressive, commission-conscious salespeople. A slick sales clerk can demonstrate a package so that it appears to do what you want, but when you get it home, you may have a hard time figuring out how to get it to work again.

live up to your expectations about saving time and money, you will have spent an amount small enough not to cause havoc in your business. More than 5 percent begins to be difficult to live with, especially if the equipment doesn't turn out to be as beneficial as you expected. Using the 1 to 5 percent figure, a person with a gross annual income of $50,000 could afford to spend from $500 to $2,500 per year on the acquisition of new equipment. If you have either heavy accounts payable or business loans that you are servicing you should stay at or below the 1 percent level.

RESOURCES

Recommended Accounting Software

There are many good accounting software packages available—so many, in fact, that it is impossible for us to stay current on them. You would be wise to choose your accounting software with the guidance of your accountant. In spite of what we've just said, though, most one-person businesses will find that the suite of accounting packages manufactured by Intuit Software of Palo Alto, California, will meet their needs. They are all single-entry packages, technically, but that is all that a business with a small volume of dollars or transactions really needs. They are available for both Macintosh and IBM or IBM-compatible computers. *Quicken* is Intuit's "personal accounting" package; *Quick Books* is their "business accounting" package. But either one of them will suffice. The real difference is that *Quick Books* includes accounts payable and accounts receivable modules, and *Quicken* does not (although you can fake them if you are clever). *Quicken* integrates investment and retirement accounts into the system, whereas *Quick Books* does not. Both packages are upgraded frequently, so buy the latest version. *Quicken* and *Quick Books* by Intuit, 540 University Avenue, Palo Alto, CA 94301; 415-322-0590.

Office Equipment

Of all the pieces of office equipment we have tried, we've found the desktop letter folder to be one of the most useful and time-saving devices available. There are several good ones available, but we use the Execufold available from ADI Machines for Business, 20505 East Valley Blvd., Suite 112, Walnut, CA 91789; 714-594-0097. It can fold up to three stapled sheets of 8-½-by-11-inch paper at a time.

The automatic stamp dispenser available from most post offices is also a great time-saver. It costs about $15 to $20 and holds a roll of one hundred or five hundred first-class stamps. Each time you press down, it automatically dispenses a single, premoistened stamp and affixes it to the surface of what ever the dispenser is resting on (hopefully an envelope).

Books

Alvarez, Mark. *The Home Office Book: How to Set up and Use an Efficient, Personal Workspace in the Computer Age.* Woodbury, Conn.: Goodwood Press, 1990. This book contains a thirty-five-page section with brand-name information on computers, software, printers, telephones, answering machines, fax machines, and so on. While some of the information is dated, the general overview is useful.

9

Grassroots Marketing

In any business, marketing your goods or services is absolutely crucial to success. Although many businesses have a part-time or even a full-time person who is responsible for getting the word out, in a one-person business there is only you. And because you are busily wearing the many hats you need to keep the business going, you may be tempted to delegate the marketing domain to a professional. Or worse, to place a few ads in the local paper and cross your fingers.

What is marketing? Marketing is letting people know that you have something they want or need. The traditional definition of marketing is "A system of organizational activities designed to plan, price, promote, and distribute something of value (product or service) for the benefit of present and potential customers." We define marketing as *everything* related to how you operate your business. Every action your business takes sends a marketing message. As Padi Selwyn, national speaker and trainer, is fond of saying: "Marketing is a thousand little things done right." (and big things too!)

Often business owners become so engrossed in the day-to-day operation of their businesses that they put off marketing until a "slow" period. We think one of the major reasons so many businesses fail is that they haven't allowed the time and resources necessary to devise a marketing plan and carry it through.

In this chapter we will give you tools to help unravel the mysterious world of marketing and lots of ideas to help you create a marketing plan specifically for your business. After advising hundreds of businesses, we have defined a simple marketing strategy that works. It's a strategy based on personal recommendation and is extremely cost-effective. We call this strategy grassroots marketing. While grassroots marketing works well for larger businesses too, it's especially viable for the one-person-business owner who is often long on creativity and short on cash.

THE CASE AGAINST ADVERTISING

To many people, marketing is synonymous with advertising, where, supposedly, you pay the fee and customers flock to your business. And the business that can't afford the fee is out of luck. The fact is that *advertising is the least successful means of getting the word out about your business*. It is so far down on the list of successful marketing strategies as to be borderline. So spend your limited marketing budget on building personal recommendations first and advertising last.

Advertising has made many consumers cynical because it often amounts to paid-for propaganda that is neither trustworthy nor memorable. Ads are everywhere: On Band-Aids, the bottom of putting-green holes, on buses, the back of restroom doors, on T-shirts, undies, and in our elementary school classrooms. What one-person business could possibly be heard among the hundreds of messages vying each day for customer attention?

For professionals, advertising has traditionally been considered sleazy. Until recently, a lawyer who advertised his or her services as being superior or less expensive could be disbarred. This taboo is based on common sense, for who, after all, would choose a pediatrician, let alone a brain surgeon, based on the claims of an ad? Most people find the businesses that provide the important services in their life through personal referrals. Professionals are quite aware of this and have traditionally relied exclusively on word of mouth to attract new clients.

Unlike in advertising, there is no hyperbole involved in stimulating personal recommendations. People recommend to others only what they have come to know and trust. Although it is a big responsibility to make sure your business is the kind that customers will want to tell their friends about, it also feels good. In fact, positive word-of-mouth commentary is one of those win-win situations. You win because you attract new customers. The new customers win because they are delighted with your excellent service or the high quality of your products. The person who cared enough to share the news about your business wins both your appreciation and that of their friend. All this good feeling is what we mean by *grassroots*.

Mensch Marketing

Mensch is a Yiddish word meaning "a real person." Mensch marketing is letting other people know you appreciate and care about them as human beings, not merely as customers. Patti Breitman, a literary agent who is a strong believer in good manners, says:

> It's very unusual in the business world to find someone who will send you a thank-you note after they go to a party. I worked in publicity for a long time and I know that when we would throw a party and spend hundreds of thousands of dollars promoting a book we would never get a thank-you note from the guests.
>
> I think in terms of people instead of jobs and roles and expectations. So I always send thank-you notes. If I'm invited to speak somewhere I'll send a thank-you note for the opportunity. If I'm invited to a party, even at the American Booksellers Association, I will always send a postcard to the person who is my contact with that company and thank them for having invited me. If there's a story in *Publishers Weekly* about a publisher I work with, even if it has nothing to do with one of my clients or books, I'll congratulate them. If they take out a cover ad, or if there is an ad about one of their books in the *New York Times*, I'll send a note or call up and say "Great coverage," or "Great ad. Congratulations!" And that's remembered.
>
> Now more than ever people are referring people to me. The word of mouth is good and strong and steady because I pay attention and I follow up. If a friend calls and says, "My friend is going to call you," I'm nice to that person. I treat everyone equally. Even someone who writes a hand-written letter on crumpled paper. I'll write them a decent personal rejection letter. I don't want to use a form letter because I care about them. I'll suggest that they type their next submission letter and that they go to the library and use *Literary Marketplace* to find an agent that covers what they write. Marketing is basically just being a decent human being. Being nice to people is the best marketing. It is the bottom line.

When Padi Selwyn was public relations director of a medical center, the center had a program to reach out into the community. She would send congratulatory letters to people who had received promotions, offering them a complimentary tour of the facilities and stating that if they ever needed any information to please call her. Selwyn remembers:

> I had so many people say "Nobody acknowledged my promotion other than you, whom I don't know, and my mother." This was a marketing device; these were not people I had a relationship with, but it expanded the mailing list of the medical center and made me a lot of friends in the community. It took such little time and effort. We are talking a first-class stamp and a couple of note cards.
>
> I have built an incredible network just acknowledging other human beings on the planet. It's so basic and it's so un-high-tech and simple and strategy-less that's it's overlooked. But it's right in front of our faces. It's so much more powerful getting a note of appreciation than it is to receive a newsletter. Being a *mensch* is the best marketing tool I have found.

PERSONAL RECOMMENDATION—THE HEART OF GRASSROOTS MARKETING

People recommend a business that makes them feel good. One where the customer is held in the highest regard. A business in which high quality and excellent service are consistently the norm. We believe the highest award someone can bestow on a business is to give it their recommendation.

Personal recommendation is so familiar to us that we forget how incredibly powerful it is. Most of us patronize businesses that are well run and that consistently offer quality goods and excellent service. For the most part, we have learned about these businesses from the personal recommendations of our friends and family. It makes sense, then, to base our own one-person-business marketing efforts on this same premise.

When you focus on your customers and gain their trust, they will not only recommend you, they will remain loyal to you. And this repeat business is what one-person businesses thrive on.

The three main factors in attracting enough customers to show a profit are providing the product or service customers want, getting new customers, and getting repeat business. Accomplish these three steps at a reasonable cost and your business should prosper. A referred customer clearly comes to you at a lower cost than through any other means. So the least costly and most effective marketing strategy is *people telling other people about your business*. Besides being cost-effective, personal recommendation has unlimited potential.

Why do people go out of their way to recommend certain businesses? Is there a magic formula? What makes someone feel like sticking their neck out to sing the praises of another business? The two things that promote personal recommendations better than anything else are *high-quality goods* and *superior service*.

Theodore Levitt of the Harvard Business School states, "There are no such things as service industries; there are only industries whose service components are greater or less than those of other industries. Everybody is in service."

Custom-satchel designer Teri Joe Wheeler puts it this way: "Since I do custom work, clients appreciate small touches that make my product unique. This tells my customers that they are special. It takes more time but it's worth it in the long run. People want some magic, something personal. They want to know their possessions have quality, because it's part of their statement about who they are. And because I provide that kind of quality, customers recommend me to others."

Don Anderson runs a one-person dental lab and, as he puts it, "I try to beat everybody in town on quality. I do every bit of the work myself. Instead of the product going through a lot of different hands, the most qualified individual in the lab does everything."

Trisha conducts her gift-retail business according to the rule "The customer is number one." "I give all my attention to the customer," she says. "While explaining the taffy-making process, I let them know that my taffy has no preservatives or candy wax, and then I give them a sample. I love having people sample my taffy and other goodies. I give newlyweds special samples, and I think word has spread because I get newlyweds in here all the time. If someone buys something and they are unhappy, I ask them why. If the item is defective I send it back to the manufacturer. If there's any other reason, I refund their money and absorb the loss."

Catherine Campbell, a family-practice lawyer, also provides extra service to her clients. "I keep a three-by-five card on every client I have. When I close their case, I make a note to send them information relating to child support, spousal support, custody, or visitation issues. If a really good article appears in a legal journal or some popular publication, I package it up and send it to every person who has an active card. When I close their file, I send them a letter that says, 'Thank you for hiring me; I hope you are satisfied. I will be sending you articles or information as it becomes available on the following subjects.'"

Noted author and lecturer Dr. Tom Ferguson operates his business on the same principle. "In general, I promote my services and products by being visible and by doing good work. I don't advertise. In the books that I write, there is a section in the back that tells people where they can write in for catalogs or related publications. This is a good marketing tool. Also, when I give seminars I take a more active role than most speakers do by getting involved, when possible, with the basic structure of the conference. I am very willing to plan the whole one-or two-day workshop, so that what I'm offering can take place in a setting that will be more meaningful to the participants. Whenever I'm doing a weekend seminar I like to offer a session where people are encouraged to break up into special-interest groups of their own choosing, without any leaders. I feel that for a lot of health professionals, the best thing that happens at these events is meeting their peers. It's important for people to link up. Equally important is to have representatives of local self-help and self-care agencies come and explain what they're about. Then it's not just someone from the outside coming in dispensing knowledge and just disappearing."

As a one-person business you are always representing your business in one way or another: standing in line at the ATM machine, squeezing the melons at the supermarket, discussing the world situation at a party, or cheering for the kids at the soccer game. You are at the center of your marketing efforts. Paul Terry, advisor to hundreds of small businesses explains: "Everyone that you come in touch with is potentially a client or a referral to another client because they are either impressed with you as a person, impressed with your skill at providing a certain service or product, or they want to just help you because you're a small-business person and they are too."

CREATING A MARKETING PLAN

Assuming you offer a quality product or service, it is actually relatively easy to design and carry out a dynamic marketing plan. Doing so can be one of the most rewarding and fun parts of your business.

To help you develop your own marketing plan based on building the grass-roots relationships that stimulate personal recommendation, we have divided the process into six phases: (1) *Understand the elements of a business transaction*—there is more to it than just price; (2) *Decide what business you're in*—create a clear description of what your business offers, especially what is unique about it; (3) *Discover your clients*—that is, do the homework necessary to understand who will buy your products or services; (4) *Identify your supporters*—the people who can help you and those who can personally recommend you; (5) *Create a marketing calendar* of activities to attract your potential clients; and (6) *Choose your marketing vehicles*.

Understand the Elements of a Business Transaction

There is more to a business transaction than just the price. Price is important, but so are quality and service, recourse and repair, education, packaging and merchandising, public relations and community service, and research.

We have covered price in Chapter 4, but let's discuss the others to give a clearer notion of why it is important to include all the elements of a transaction in your marketing plan.

Quality and Service The quality of your offering, be it product or information, says a lot about the kind of business you are running. If you sell poor quality you will have poor results (unless your business message very clearly states that you are specializing in selling the cheap and slipshod).

In the April 1992 issue of *INC. Magazine*, Paul Hawken wrote about a way of looking at service that fits for many one-person businesses: ". . . in that moment when we contact one another, when a person comes to us for help and for a product, it's not just a service opportunity to sell more. It's a human opportunity. Because both we and the customer know what poets and rabbis and pastors and preachers have been trying to tell us for years: that this life is transient and ephemeral, that success and failure as popularly defined are really impostors, and that we as people find meaning with our hearts and our minds and our hands and our souls when we have the opportunity to serve another human being."

Quality and service are intimately linked. Service is the way you guarantee your quality. If it doesn't meet the customer's needs, take it back.

Recourse and Repair These are the two most critical elements of service. Inherent in providing excellent service is having a superior recourse policy in place. Many customers are shy about telling you if something about your business displeases them. It's up to you to provide a vehicle for your customers to let you know when something goes wrong. Follow-up is one very good way to encourage your customers to let you know how the transaction went from their point of view. If the volume of your business is too large for you to follow up every transaction, such as in some retail businesses, then randomly sample your customers every few months.

Your brochures, invoices, and office literature should include a statement encouraging customers to give you honest feedback about your business. Every time a customer complains to you it's a chance to improve your business. It's the "to you" part that's essential. The Ford Motor Company estimates that a dissatisfied car owner tells twenty-two people about his or her experience, while a satisfied car owner tells eight people that he or she is pleased.

Make sure you have your refund and recourse policy in writing; customers hate surprises. In the event that something out of the ordinary occurs, and you have really goofed with a customer, a recourse policy that's in writing is essential.

Don Anderson owns a high-end dental lab and knows that in his line of work delivering on time is part of providing excellent service. He says, "It's hard to start a business and real easy to blow it. Even if your work is perfect, if you miss a delivery and the patient took time off work and was in the doctor's office and the tooth wasn't there—oh man! You're going to have one angry phone call.

"I have a policy that I've never seen another lab have. First of all I apologize and then I give them the work for half off. The dentist knows I have lost my profit margin and that I covered their lost time. I have this policy so that my clients know I'm serious about getting the work there on time."

Education This refers to all the things you do to make sure that any question your customers might have about your products or service can be easily answered. This does not mean waiting until the question is asked. It is important to be proactive by discovering everything you can about the offerings you make and then passing that information along to your customers in the form of classes, brochures, or a well-informed sales pitch.

Friedman's Microwave stores are a good example of using education as an integral part of marketing. Classes that teach microwave cooking are offered on a regular basis. Customers can sign up and discover everything they need to know, including whether or not microwave cuisine is for them.

Packaging and Merchandising Packaging is what goes around your products. Merchandising is how you display them. How your products or collateral marketing materials look says a lot about the business you are running. You have a tremendous opportunity to include several of the elements in a transaction on your packaging: recourse policies, customer-service phone numbers, educational information, and price, to name a few. Both packaging and merchandising can be effectively used to tell your business story.

Public Relations and Community Service Public relations and community service are all the efforts you make to be a part of the community in which you live and work. Money is not the only way to support your local community. Your labor, time, expertise, products, or services are also valuable. You can be active in local organizations like the chamber of commerce or your child's PTA. You can participate in the sponsorship and work necessary to put on local cultural events. You can donate your product or service to the local social services projects such as homeless shelters, libraries, or the public television station, for their annual fund raising drives. These are just a few of the ways in which you can show gratitude to the community that makes your business possible by giving back to it.

Research   Every transaction contains a small research component. You are always on the lookout for new and better products, better ways of serving your client, and everything you can find out about your customers needs.

It is easy to see from this brief discussion that price is not the only, or the most important, element of a business transaction. Keeping this in mind as you develop your marketing plan will assure that you effectively meet most of the needs that customers might have and keep them coming back.

Decide What Business You're In

Marketing doesn't work well unless you can describe your business clearly. An easy way to organize your thoughts about this description is the four P's of marketing: *product, price, place,* and *promotion.* Each of these components contributes equally to the success of your one-person business. Clearly, marketing is much more than promotion, and it is only by continually refining and improving each of the four P's that you will have a successful business.

Product   Product is simply the business you are in. Even a strictly service-oriented business is still selling a product—less tangible, of course, but a product nonetheless.

Understanding your product is the first step toward describing your business. You should be able to describe this product with ease and clarity in terms of the benefits to your customers. *Benefits* are in the answer to your customer's question, "What's in it for me?" Many businesses make the mistake of describing their business from the point of view of the *features* of their product. Features are product attributes that no one cares about nearly as much as the business owner does. Keep in mind that people buy benefits, not features. Or as the saying goes, "People don't buy manure, they buy green lawns."

For instance, if you sell home-security systems, it's much more powerful to describe your business by saying, "Secure Homes, Inc. helps people protect their most valuable belongings and feel completely safe in their homes at all times," rather than "I sell a twenty-four-hour home-security service from the heart of downtown Cleveland and have been in business for fifty-six years."

Let's look at what it takes to clearly describe your product or service so that people will understand exactly what you have to offer and feel comfortable recommending you.

Your Business Identity in Thirty-Five Words or Less

It's a powerful exercise to describe the benefits of your business in thirty-five words or less. If you can state it as clearly as, "I help your small business—from one to ten employees—with management issues such as personnel, marketing strategies, time management, support services and financial projections," or better yet, "I help small-business owners create management systems, work teams, marketing strategies, and financial controls that work," then your friends and admirers can more readily refer prospects to your consulting business.

For you, too, it's ideal to have a concise, well-thought-out description ready to pull out at parties, social occasions, or in more formal networking situations. Be sure to include the special services, goodies, and extras that you offer, emphasizing the role your business plays in your customer's life.

Take a moment now to write out a description of your one-person business in thirty-five words or less. Be sure to include special services you offer, and keep in mind your typical customer's point of view, stressing the benefits.

Review your description at least once a year and, when your business changes in subtle or not so subtle ways, be sure and bring everybody up to date on your new business identity. You are living your business, and what you offered three years ago might be a lot different than what you offer now.

When we suggest to clients that others might not really understand what they do, they usually give us a look of disbelief accompanied by the statement "Everyone knows what a photographer . . . dog trainer . . . desktop publisher . . . fill in the blank . . . does." Occasionally a client has already worked out an excellent description, including their special market niche, and is ready to use this description to promote word-of-mouth recommendations. But this kind of individual is rare. Even though the majority of clients cannot come up with a description, they scoff when we ask them to carry out the following homework assignment: Ask ten people, including friends and family members, to describe exactly what service or product they think your business offers.

The purpose of this assignment is to find out if those most likely to give referrals have more than a generic idea about what business you're in. Are you just "a photographer" to them, or can they say with assurance, "Pat specializes in candid wedding photos and does a top-notch job of photographing children. You won't have to drag your kids to a studio—he'll come to your home."

Most clients return enlightened from this experience. Usually their friends, and sometimes even their spouses, have only a vague idea of what they do. Friends who wanted to recommend them, for instance, but who knew only that they were a "woodworker," were put in the position of lamely telling others something like, "I know a really nice man who works with wood, but I don't know exactly what he makes. Here's his name and number—you can call him and check." This is obviously not an inviting referral.

Before we interviewed Alexandra Hart for this book, we knew only that she was a desktop publisher. What exactly did that mean? Was our fantasy of desktop publishing applicable to her particular business? What did she actually offer? Who were her clients? We discovered that Alexandra designs business cards, logos, stationery, posters, and books. For no extra charge she will travel to a client's office, thereby providing a much-appreciated extra service. We can now give her name with confidence when someone asks for help creating an image for a business or designing a poster for a jazz festival.

Paul Terry notes, "We have very little time to make a first impression, so if you can get what you do and who you do it for in a very short sentence or paragraph then people are left with some concise, strong words or a clear anecdote of what you do. I have clients practice in small groups. I have them write it and rewrite it, memorize it and put it up over their desk—it becomes part of their initial introduction, it becomes part of what they say on the telephone it becomes part of what they begin and end a talk with."

One of Paul's most telling research projects consisted of writing to thirty business friends asking them the following questions: "What do I do?" "Whom do I serve?" "If you were going to recommend me, what would you tell people that I do?"

"Some people thought that I provided a service I haven't provided for five years," he recalls. "It was really good feedback for me because your business friends and existing clients are, in effect, your marketing reps."

Information and Professional Businesses Once you can clearly state what your business does, the next step is to think about how you can give specific information on aspects of your work that most people won't be familiar with. An ignorant client will often feel uneasy about business transactions. An educated customer, on the other hand, knows how to use your services and feels confident recommending you to others.

It helps if you think of yourself as a facilitator. For example, if you are an experienced realtor, you know that most clients haven't the faintest idea of the services you perform for them. Your thirty-five-word description may explain that you are a realtor who specializes in bare-land sales and are very knowledgeable about the history of each parcel as well as surrounding acreage, but it doesn't answer the question "What's a realtor going to do for me?" Your clients may harbor the notion that you sit at your desk most of the time, reading a good novel while waiting for escrow (whatever that is) to close so that you can hop a cruise ship to the Far East with all your profits. If, for example, you take the time to create a sheet outlining the procedures involved in the sale of land, and another on what is involved in a home purchase or sale, you will create both informed and appreciative clients who will be much happier to pay your fee. More important, this understanding of what you do fosters trust. And from trust come referrals.

People want to be informed, active participants in what they pay for. They are no longer willing to hand over their health, legal, real estate, banking, or accounting problems to an expert who will "take care" of everything. More and more clients seek out businesses that understand the need to be an informed partner working with a service provider, one who explains everything and offers alternatives when appropriate. These consumer demands are difficult for many professionals to deal with, but a one-person business is flexible enough to convert rapidly from the old-fashioned paternalistic-maternalistic mode to the new practice of being open with information.

Information and Retail Businesses   Informing and educating customers is not the exclusive province of the professional. More and more retail businesses are also demystifying their operations, and by doing so are attracting loyal customers. Examples of this trend are photo-processing stores where the curious can observe film being developed, sushi bars where every detail of the meal preparation is performed just a few feet from the diner, and upholstery stores that combine showroom and workroom in order to encourage interested customers to learn a bit about the process of re-covering a couch or chair.

Keith Yates Audio, located in midtown Sacramento, California, is a "kick off your shoes, make yourself comfortable, and enjoy the best sound systems available" business. Yates bases his top-of-the-line audio sales business on multiple sales over the long run, rather than on the traditional one-time sales pitch. He maintains a very low overhead, which enables him to carry the products he believes in. He doesn't discount and he doesn't advertise. He is willing to spend hours with clients, because he feels that the more people know and appreciate music, the more loyal customers he will have.

Rainbow General Store, a sixteen-year-old collective located in San Francisco's Mission District, is an excellent model of how a retail store can build trust through providing information. To help expand customer awareness, the store posts signs in the produce section explaining the origin of all fruits and vegetables. If the produce is organic, they say so; if they are unsure of the origin, they pass on that information as well. Customers to whom the purchase of "certified organic" produce is important can shop at Rainbow secure in the knowledge that what they are buying is not only free of pesticides, but also full of vital nutrients because it is grown on healthy soil. In the housewares section, signs explain the ingredients and health implications of a variety of cleansing agents. It feels good to be able to refer friends who value organic produce and nontoxic cleansers to Rainbow General Store.

Place   Place, the second of the four P's of marketing, refers to the accessibility of your business, which we have discussed in general terms in Chapter 4. Looking at your business from your customer's point of view, though, how easy are you to do business with? Additional elements in this category refer to ease of parking, hours of operation, information on your product packaging, whether you have an 800 number, whether you make house calls, whether you are listed in all of the appropriate and logical places, your signage, and so forth. Being accessible means paying attention to all of the details, from posting your hours at your place of business to having a recorded message on your answering machine with clear instructions as to when you are available.

The idea is to make it easy for customers to find and use your business. If your business is out of the way, you will need to have a clear map on all your brochures, your business card, in the yellow pages, and so on. Include any nearby landmarks if possible.

If parking is a problem, be sure to identify any nearby parking lots and offer validated parking if possible, as well as identifying the best street parking and public transportation. Have maps printed to make it easy for customers to use your business.

Sometimes it makes sense to take your product to the customer by offering low-cost or free delivery. A massage therapist who makes house calls so her clients can skip the stress of driving home, a mobile auto-repair service that saves costly towing charges and inconvenience for his customers, a bookstore that allows customers to order current titles by phone, and a tax preparer who visits elderly and handicapped clients in their homes are but a few examples of bringing your business to the customer.

Price We provide an in-depth discussion of pricing in Chapter 4, but here we will look at it from the perspective of describing your business. The main questions to ask yourself regarding price are: Does your price reflect value? Is the price right for the product? Are your terms clearly stated and easy to understand? Is it financially easy to do business with you?

Promotion Promotion involves samples, direct mail, ads, annual planning, asking for referrals, getting testimonial letters, giving seminars, having open houses, public relations, graphics, and all collateral material. Although promotion is only one fourth of the business description pie, this is the slice that most people believe will make or break a business. Promotion *is* critical—a vital quarter of your marketing mix—but the other pieces of the pie are equally important.

Discover Your Clients

When you are new in business, any customer seems like a small miracle, and the notion that you could actually select customers seems like a fairy tale. After you have been in operation for a while, it becomes apparent that you do choose your customers. To remain enthusiastic and passionate about your business over the years, you must enjoy serving your customers. That means attracting the people

---

The Six Laws of Pricing

1. Pricing is more than just money.
2. Changing the price usually only changes who the customer is.
3. All prices are ultimately based on feelings, both yours and the customers. Set the price so you won't regret it either way.
4. The price you charge sends a hidden message, be sure you mean it.
5. People feel better if they sense that they are paying the right price for what they are getting.
6. If they don't like your work or product, don't take their money.

---

with whom you can build a long-term relationship and focusing on a specific segment of the public that would most benefit from your business.

As computer and training consultant Bill Dale puts it, "When I started I was glad of any work, but rapidly, within the first year or two, I weeded out my client base. I have been working for myself for almost fourteen years now, and within limits choose the clients I want to work with. For instance, I do not work for anyone that I don't like or whose company I regard as not worth supporting."

Roger Pritchard, who works in many areas of small business consulting, including socially responsible investing, is in his fourteenth year of business and has screened his clients from the beginning. "It has always been important to me to screen clients for ideological and personal fit. Philosophically I try to come from a place of right livelihood and full living and I attract customers that share my values so they are likely to be good customers in terms of how they deal with me. Some personalities just don't fit, and I shouldn't be working with certain people and they shouldn't be working with me. If you are in a common business that everybody does, it is much harder to screen for ideology and personal fit. If you're developing a niche and you have a large enough pool of people and you stay on your toes and you serve them, then it will work."

Do a Market Survey If you want to test a new business idea to find out how well it will sell, try doing a market survey. Your goal is to learn how many potential clients for your product or service inhabit the market you would like to focus on, and what the likelihood of their buying from you might be.

Your market is the industry segment or geographical trading area in which you want to do business. If you want to open a bookstore in a big city, you might define your market as one of the city's neighborhoods. If you want to sell used books, your market would be consumers who prefer to buy used books.

Your market survey would also include information from industry publications and sources about the industry you would like to enter. It would help you learn the answers to such questions as: How many consumers does it take to support a used book store? How many people live in the neighborhood where I would like to locate? How many titles do I need to carry and how many square feet of shelf space do I need to put them on?

Five components of a good market survey are: (1) determining the boundaries of your market or trading area; (2) studying the area's population to determine potential buying characteristics; (3) finding out the area's purchasing power; (4) getting some numbers on what businesses like yours are currently making from selling the product or service you want to offer; and (5) making an educated estimate of the portion of those sales that you can reasonably expect to get.

You will have to turn to local government and other sources to find much of this information. Maps of your trading area are available on a county and state basis from many chambers of commerce, city development commissions, and newspaper offices. Many local governments will have census tracts for your area as well. Publications like *Sales Management* magazine can also be helpful. Trade associations, business libraries, university departments, and market research firms are other sources of information. Almost every industry has one or more trade magazines that features stories on the kinds of things that are working well for people within that field.

No matter how unique you think your idea is, there is probably someone else who is running a business similar to yours, and we highly recommend interviewing as many people as you can in your field. There is no better way to learn the barriers and pitfalls than by reaching out to people within your industry.

When Paul Terry started his first business, which was a retail store, he got most of his information in two ways: "(1) I interviewed all the potential vendors that were going to sell to me and asked them what they would do if they were starting a business and what product lines they would have and how much of each; (2) I went to a competitor and said, 'I'm opening a business across town and I'd like to hire your manager for a week and get her to help me set this business up.' These were both incredibly effective. Not only did they figure out what my inventory was, they told me what kind of customers I was likely to get because of the area that I had chosen to open in."

Select Your Customers   A business selects its customers in a number of ways:

You select customers by the price you charge. A consultant who charges $1,000 a day will attract large corporations that operate in terms of day rates and long-term projects. A consultant who charges $50 per hour will attract small businesses that require his or her services for an hour or two at a time over a period of several months.

You select customers by your pricing schedules. A plumber with a $200 minimum will work primarily with construction contractors. An auto mechanic who offers a discount for large jobs will attract auto rental businesses rather than off-the-street clients.

You select customers by the type of service you offer. A fine printer will appeal to the poetry and specialty book trade rather than to mass-market publishers.

You select customers by rejection. A female criminal lawyer might have a policy of refusing to defend accused rapists. A dentist might refer alcoholic and obese clients to a specialist because he feels unqualified to treat people with special gum and heart problems.

You select customers by your attention and concern. Customers know when you like them and appreciate the special care you demonstrate by paying extra attention to their needs and idiosyncrasies.

One of the objectives in the conscious selection of your customers is to provide your business with a variety of income sources. As discussed in Chapter 4, having diverse sources of income is necessary to the financial health of your business because it assures you steady income. It also encourages you to upgrade your skills and to be prepared to respond to the changing nature of your business.

Retain Your Customers   Customer retention begins with the customer's first contact with you and continues for as long as your company is in business. According to marketing guru Jay C. Levinson, "Eighty percent of lost business is the fault not of poor quality but of failure to continue in the effort to maintain and build on customer satisfaction." Author Paul Hawken builds on this thought: "Our business lives, breathes, and dies according to one simple activity: repeat business."

Studies have shown that it takes five times as much money to attract a new client as to keep an old one. The Ford Motor Company estimates that a loyal customer is worth more than $100,000 in repeat purchases. It is clearly cost-effective to focus your marketing efforts on retaining clients.

Business consultant Roger Pritchard is a strong believer in retention marketing, "I think businesspeople tend to focus on attracting new customers rather than retaining old customers and keeping them coming back. I think people tend to focus too much on the new people and not enough on the old. One of the key things in small business is that once you understand how many customers you need, spending how much to support you, the income level you need, the profit level you need, you realize that often you don't need that many. Therefore, getting these limited number of people to come back more often becomes a much easier thing to do. But because the pervading ideology is expand, expand, expand, people don't look at how relatively easy it is to keep a relatively small number of people happy. The prime example of this is psychoanalysts. They need eight customers for five years. That's all they need. Once a day five days a week for five years."

Accountant Malcolm Ponder knows that keeping his clients happy is the key to success for his accounting business. "Keep your present clients happy and they become your best source of new people. Money is dramatically tighter now for most everybody I see. One or two hundred dollars to have your taxes done wasn't a problem for most people seven or eight years ago. Now it's a problem for a lot of people, and so keeping my client base and keeping them happy is something I pay much more attention to than I used to.

"The changes I see coming down in the future are that it's going to be harder and harder to make it. More and more attention is going to have to be paid by all of us to our client base: keeping them happy, keeping them with us, and keeping our own overhead low so we don't have to get into a high price realm and price some of our clients out of our services. And my existing clients are my best marketing tool. Absolutely. This fall I will do a mailing to my existing clients saying that there is room in the client base for friends of yours that might need my services."

Identify Your Supporters

By maintaining good marketing records and looking at them on a regular basis you will be aware of where your referrals come from. Usually it's a small group of people mostly consisting of customers, family and friends, and business associates.

We think of this base of support as *circles of intimacy*. Picture yourself as a jewel dropped into a clear warm pond. You are surrounded by many concentric circles rippling out from the center. The circles surrounding you represent the people who act as your referral base. The circles include close family members and friends, planning buddies and investors, vendors, distributors, and former school chums. The possibilities are endless.

Take a piece of paper and draw a small circle in the middle of it. Write your own name inside that circle. Now draw a slightly larger circle around that one. Inside the second circle write the names of the one or two or three people to whom you feel the closest. These are people who understand you and whom you understand. You enjoy sharing with these people and you can always count on them for support. These are your closest friends, your confidants.

Now draw a third circle around the second. Inside this circle write the names of people with whom you are not quite as intimate, but whom you can count on most of the time and whom you would be willing to help most of the time if asked. These are your friends.

Finally, draw a fourth circle around the third and write the names of groups that you are a part of: clubs, community groups, churches, schools, your job, your professional contacts, and so forth. These are your networks and associates.

The people within all of these circles are your personal grassroots community. They will be the resource pool from which you will build all the support you need to find and maintain your right livelihood. They will provide you with role models, mentors, and guides. They can give you friendship and nurturance, help in times of crisis, referrals to others who can help, and encouragement along the way. They will also be the primary source of most of your referrals to jobs, customers, or clients.

The idea is to market from the center out. As you move out, you gain practice in becoming clearer and clearer about your business identity, so that when you begin talking with those who know you less well you have figured out just what to say.

This approach can help you to identify the individuals who can best recommend you. Every business has a unique grassroots community. The closer to you people in the circle are, the more informal your marketing efforts can be. As you move into the outer rings you can formalize your marketing. In this way the circles of intimacy exercise can help to keep your marketing efforts focused and right on target.

Create a Marketing Calendar

Now that you have developed a clear and precise way of describing what you do, have decided what kinds of customers you wish to work with, and are confident that your business is in good order and you are focusing your marketing efforts on building relationships and stimulating personal recommendation, it's finally time to make a marketing calendar!

The first law of grassroots marketing is: *The best time to market is when you don't need more business.* One of the major reasons so many businesses fail is because they don't allow time and resources for marketing. If you wait until you need more customers it will probably be too late! If you are a seasonal business, market ahead of the season. A marketing calendar takes time to implement and must become an integral part of the rhythm of your business.

Veteran business consultant Paul Terry understands the tendency to procrastinate: "When we are busy we don't remember to market. And that's because we don't have a plan or a procedure that kicks in on a regular basis. When you use a certain number of copies in your copy machine, something kicks in. The cartridge says 'You are out of toner—replace me.' And so we don't have to write down on a piece of paper somewhere 'Remember to replace the toner,' because the machine takes care of that for us. But the marketplace for our business doesn't necessarily come back to us and say, 'Oh, by the way, you haven't contacted me recently. Pay attention to me!'"

So, now it is time to purchase a big wall calendar and to start scheduling your marketing activities. Your marketing calendar is a visual system for maintaining regular contact. When you are busy, it is tempting to neglect marketing. Inevitably, then, business will slack off, and you will wish you had marketing activities lined up. Plan activities throughout the year, leaving enough time in between to make them fun rather than a chore.

Prioritize your ideas and set deadlines for turning them into action. Once you have decided on dates, prepare a worksheet for each activity, detailing every important step and deadline: when the invitations must be at the printers, when the press releases should go out, when the flowers must be picked up, and so on. Note all of these deadlines on your oversized wall calendar, and hang it where you can't miss it.

The success of your marketing calendar depends on two things: the quality of your mailing list and your follow-up.

Follow-Up We cannot emphasize enough the need for follow-up. Monitoring the results of your marketing activities helps you plan for the future and is an important marketing activity itself.

Marketing without follow-up yields poor results when compared to marketing with follow-up. So, while we encourage any marketing activity that's fun and informative and reminds people about your business, to be really effective most activities should be followed by a phone call or letter.

Because you are a one-person business it will be relatively difficult to do follow-up, so try to think of it as an opportunity to learn more about your customers, their needs, and how can you can best serve them. Don't fall into the trap of viewing follow-up as merely a way to close a sale.

Mailing List The single most important marketing tool you have is your list of clients, prospects, and referral sources. This list is the basis for almost all your marketing activities.

The simple mailing-list management methods we describe in figure 9.1 are suitable for managing small lists of from a few to several hundred names. Beyond that you should computerize or hire an outside service. Whatever method you choose, make sure it is easy to use and keep it up to date.

Effective Use of Your Mailing List Once you have created an up-to-date and easy-to-use mailing list system (see figure 9.1), what do you do with it? Start using it. Get into the habit of mailing something of interest to everyone on your list at least four times a year. Perhaps your business can best communicate to customers through a newsletter. Or maybe you can send out samples of your work.

You can also use your list to make follow-up phone calls to your customers; see how they are doing with the product you sold them or with the results of your last consulting project for them. Ask them if you can be of any further service. And be sure to ask if they can give you the names of one or two other people who might be interested in using your services or buying your products.

Let clients know, too, when anything new or exciting happens in your business that might be of interest to them. For example, if you are a massage professional who has just learned a new technique for alleviating the inflammation of tennis elbow, you would naturally call your carpenter, firewood-dealer, and tennis-player clients to share your excitement. This is the most direct and spontaneous approach to marketing and one that we encourage.

Marketing with your mailing list also includes informing clients about classes or product demonstrations you are giving, and sending out promotional materials.

Fig. 9.1   Mailing-List Management Methods

Master-Sheet Method

Fine artist Bill Morehouse has assembled an impressive mailing list that includes people who have either purchased work or expressed interest, supportive friends involved in the art world, names of potential collectors given him by commercial galleries, and people who attend his showings.

Because he wanted to handle his own promotions efficiently, in addition to what a gallery would do, Bill decided to enter his mailing list onto a master sheet that he can photocopy onto labels.

His system works like this: Buy a box of three-up copier labels, the kind that has thirty-three labels in three columns of eleven on an 8½ × 11-inch backing sheet. A template is usually included with each box of labels; it has a grid laid out in exactly the same pattern as the labels. Place this sheet behind a blank piece of paper, then type all your names into the label-sized outlined spaces. These are now your mailing list masters.

When someone moves, merely cover the old address with a blank label and type over it directly onto your master.

Kate Bishop, who recently returned from a year's hiatus, uses the same system as Bill. "I have a primary mailing list file of approximately four hundred names that I update with each new client. I keep this file very current. I also receive five hundred to a thousand labels from the Bridal Fair, a trade show where I rent a booth every year. I send these prospects and the people on my primary mailing list an invitation to my once-a-year sample sale. If the prospects from the Bridal Fair become clients, I add them to my primary list. If not, they receive no future mailings. This year I was super-busy and for the first time used a mailing service. I didn't receive a single response. This has never happened before, and I can't help but wonder if they actually sent the invitations. If I ever use a service again, I will include my own name as a control.

"Several years ago I needed to drum up some business, so I went through my list and wrote notes to clients I had not seen in a while, letting them know about some designs that might interest them. It worked. I learned from that experience that by writing a personal note reminding people about my business, I could be sure of getting responses."

Although you can handle up to several hundred names manually, once your list exceeds five hundred it's time to explore the cost to hire somebody to help you keep it up to date.

When your list passes one thousand names, it's time for the services of a reliable mailing-list management business. This kind of service can create labels, stuff and label the envelopes, and take them to the post office much faster and with fewer errors than you can. And the price is usually low enough to be cost-effective.

Piggyback Method

While the master-sheet method is a good way to handle mailing labels, if you need to keep track of details about each customer or supplier, add the piggyback method. Here's how it works: Purchase 4-by-6-inch cards in yellow, red, and blue (or purple, pink, and green) along with a special kind of address label called piggyback labels. Arbitrarily assign, say, suppliers the yellow cards, prospects the red, and clients the blue.

Using the piggyback labels, type the name, company, address, and phone number of each prospect. Affix these labels to the prospect (red) cards. For supplier (yellow) and client (blue) cards, omit the piggyback label but write the same information directly on the front of the cards. The reverse sides of the supplier and client cards can be used to record calls, visits, names of the people who referred them, dates of sales, and so on. When a prospect (red) becomes a client (blue), give a cheer, peel off the piggyback label, and stick it onto a blue card. Any pertinent information contained on the red card can easily be saved by stapling the two cards together rather than copying it over.

Computerized Labels

When we wrote the first edition of this book, there were far fewer computer owners than today. Millions of people now own and use computers, and if you are one of them there is no reason why you cannot computerize your mailing list.

You will still use the combined master-sheet and piggy back methods, but you will let the computer do the sorting for you. In other words, you will use one of the many "flat-file" databases that come set up to handle mailing lists. When you enter the data you will categorize each name, as you did using the colored cards. When you want to do a mailing, you will print out labels directly onto the label sheets, replacing the photocopy step in the master-sheet method.

Three extra advantages of a computerized mailing list are that it allows you to print smaller parts of the list for specialized mailings, you can create personalized "mail merge" mailings, and you can sort by zip code to take advantage of bulk mailing rates.

The Five Laws of Grassroots Marketing

1. The best time to market is when you don't need more business.
2. The best source of new clients is old clients.
3. Market for quality, not quantity.

4. Your best marketing vehicle is a satisfied client.
5. Customer retention is the measure of successful marketing.

Choose Your Marketing Vehicles

Listings: The First Place People Will Look for Your Business It's important to distinguish between advertisements, which are constant bombardments over which you have little control, and listings of goods and services that customers seek out. It is extremely important for the one-person business to be listed in all appropriate directories or trade publications, and anyplace else where potential customers might expect to locate your services or products. Listings are the most effective marketing tool for attracting customers to a one-person business. Unlike advertisements, which interrupt and irritate, listings are well-placed gems waiting to be discovered by potential customers. Listings are placed where customers expect to find out about your business: the yellow pages, the Silver Pages for older citizens, various ethnic yellow pages, college bulletin boards, commercial directories and even the bulletin board at your local laundromat or grocery store.

As a photographer, Norman Prince is listed in both *Literary Marketplace* magazine and *Audio-Video Marketplace*, as well as in all the standard reference books in his field. Norman has given careful thought to the probable places someone would search for the service he offers, and these listings have paid off for him.

Artist Bill Morehouse also uses listings. "For years I resisted the careerism-in-arts attitude where both teachers and students are focused toward making a career of being an artist," he explains. "As a student of art, and as a young teacher, art had

---

Caution: Are You Ready for More Clients?

Before you attempt to create your marketing plan based on personal recommendations, take a critical look at your business. Is it operating well enough to accommodate new customers? If you do attract a lot of new customers, will you still be able to satisfy your steady clientele? Many a business has been sunk by an influx of customers when it wasn't prepared to respond.

Bill Dale, computer and training consultant, bases his marketing on personal references and has this good advice to offer:

"Do a small job very well first. Then go for the next one. Beware of trying to tie up a big deal before you know the business, before the client knows you, and before you know what is involved. You will end up regretting it!"

nothing to do with the vagaries of profit and gain. In recent years, however, I have more aggressively pursued the connections that would lead to sales of my work. I am listed both in the white and yellow pages of the phone book, under 'African and Contemporary Art.' Also I'm in an international art listing of artists and critics for all countries and cities. And in the *New York Art Review*. I also belong to an alumni club."

Samples and Demonstrations   Although it may seem farfetched that a one-person business could offer samples, like big companies do, the basic idea is an excellent one. Dress designer Kate Bishop, for instance, might want to send a recently dyed swatch of silk she is particularly proud of to her favorite customers. A caterer might call up some regular customers and offer to bring by her latest creation along with a price list. A printer might send out a sample of paper that he recently purchased in bulk and can offer at a good price.

Information is a different sort of sample that you can share with people on your mailing list, something business consultant Laura Golstein consistently pays attention to. Once a month or so, Laura reviews her most current inquiries, including referrals interested in her services and potential students interested in workshops. In addition, she reviews the folders of clients she has worked for in the last three months but hasn't recently communicated with. She calls these recent clients to see how they are getting along, and asks whether they need any additional consultation. Often, even though Laura's clients did have further need for her services, they were too caught up in their day-to-day business to give her a call. Even those who don't require any additional service always expressed appreciation for her taking the time to phone them.

Laura also maintains a computerized mailing list of about a hundred or so clients, two hundred students, and two hundred prospects to whom she occasionally sends out either a mailing about an upcoming workshop, or an interesting article about work she is involved in or considers relevant to the small-business owner. She does this both to keep her list informed and to remind them that she is still interested in their business.

Celebrations and Events   When Salli was the director of Farallones Institute, a California agricultural research project engaged in alternative energy and organic gardening, her group hosted a celebration-of-food event called Taste of Spring. This gala affair was sponsored by Wine Country Cuisine, a Sonoma County food distributor, and by the San Francisco Culinary Academy. All of the organic growers and distributors in the greater Bay Area were invited, along with local gourmet chefs who either already used, or were interested in using, organic produce. Students from the San Francisco Culinary Academy prepared gourmet delights from locally grown fresh produce. What better way to educate chefs that fresh organic food carefully prepared has no equal?

Another kind of marketing event can be planned around a significant change in your business. When you move, change direction, purchase some significant office equipment, or meet an important goal, it is beneficial and fun to celebrate the changes. A celebration will remind people about your business and its rule in their community. Whenever possible, celebrate at your place of business. If this is not possible, hold the event in a location that is strongly associated with your business. If you are a banking consultant, use a bank boardroom; if you sell art, use a gallery; and so forth. Keeping your community informed makes it easier for customers to continue referring other people to you. They will retain confidence in their referrals when they can participate in the growth of your business.

Equally effective is an event not directly related to your field or business at all, but which involves those who are in your field or customers of your business. For instance, Claude is an amateur photographer. He once held an event in which he invited a half dozen clients and suppliers who were also amateur photographers to exhibit their works together. Nearly 150 friends, peers, and clients attended the opening. It was a lot of fun, and everyone was surprised at the professional level of the work exhibited. Undoubtedly, the next time any of these people think about hiring a consultant, Claude will be likely to pop into their minds.

Promotional Material   When Norman Prince first started his photography business, he had an agreement in which he allowed the manufacturer of a high-quality color printing press to reproduce lithographs of certain of his photographs during trade show demonstrations. In exchange, Norman got several thousand copies of those same photographs made into greeting cards or postcards. Several times a year, if you are on Norman's mailing list, you can still look forward to receiving a small selection of these beautiful cards. Whenever Norman used these cards for promoting his photography he would include a cover letter like this one:

Dear [name]:

Enclosed please find some cards with a photograph of mine from [wherever the photo was taken]. This photograph was taken using [type of film, lens, filter and/or technique] for [client].

I hope that you enjoy these cards.

Sincerely,

Norman Prince

This is a wonderful marketing technique. The important point is that on the back of every one of these cards there was an imprint reading "Norman Prince,

Photographer, San Francisco, California." Even months after receiving a card, if anyone saw it and wanted to know who did the work, the name was clearly there. But this wouldn't have been an effective label unless Norman also made sure he was listed in the San Francisco phone directory, which he did.

Labeling Anyone who sells products to retail outlets has probably encountered the typical retailer's resistance to letting you label your product with your address and phone number. Naturally you want to make sure that the customer can continue to buy your product should the retailer drop it or go out of business. Most retailers won't object to a simple name, city, and state label such as Kate Bishop uses. Kate told us, "I went to a fancy business consultant who charged me $300 and gave me no other useful information except that, since my dress labels said San Francisco, California, I should be listed in the directories of San Francisco, Marin County, and as many other adjacent counties as I could afford. Otherwise the label would be useless. It was very good information, well worth $300."

Judgment Cards Judgment cards are a special vehicle first introduced to us by career counselor Shali Parsons. A friend of his who was looking for bookkeeping work had asked him for help. Shali recommended that she write down a clear description of exactly the kind of work she was looking for. Next he suggested that she type this description onto 4 × 6-inch note cards and pass them out to people in a position to refer work to her. The note cards made it easy for friends and associates to remember her when someone asked if they knew of a bookkeeper. The clear description on the card provided potential clients with a level of judgment regarding her skills that would otherwise have been impossible to obtain without calling her first.

Helen Hendricks, a therapist, uses a judgment card that includes the question "Are you crazy?" in bold print at the top. There follows a list of the symptoms of psychological stress and the conclusion that just because you are feeling some of these symptoms doesn't mean you've necessarily gone over the edge (see figure 9.2).

Figure 9.3 illustrates the judgment card that Charlie Varon used when we wrote the first edition of this book. Back then, Charlie's was a one-person editing business. Now that he is a legal word-processor, Charlie uses a judgment card that mimics the look of a legal brief. This card is a one-page graphic and type image that instantly makes clear what Charlie does as well as that he understands legal offices (see figure 9.4).

Résumé guru Yana Parker's Bookmark Mini-Guide tells you a lot about writing résumés and also gives you a pretty good idea of how good she is at her business (see figure 9.5).

Bodyworker JoanAnn Radu came up with a brilliant judgment card that provides a lot more information about her business than you can normally get across in a judgment card. If you look closely at figure 9.6, you will see (1) her name, company name, and phone number; (2) which days and times she normally takes appointments and which days she is not available; (3) the fact that she does workplace visits in which seven to ten people can get neck and shoulder massages; (4) that she attends a networking meeting once a month; and (5) that she has a couple of pricing options.

Photographer Harrison Judd's judgment card in figure 9.7 perfectly depicts the essence of his business. It is made to resemble a personal photo album with his business card on the inside cover page facing a mounted black-and-white photograph.

Many small businesses we're acquainted with have used judgment cards to excellent effect. The basic rules for creating a good judgment card are simple: (1) it should help a client judge your knowledge of your field; (2) what you say should be easily applied to you; (3) it should be absolutely clear what product or service that you offer; (4) the information should be presented in an interesting enough way that people will want to save it.

The note-card format, using interesting information or aesthetically pleasing images, encourages people to pin your judgment card on the bulletin board or near the phone, or to keep it in a wallet or purse for future reference. Small cards are also easy to pass from person to person. They can be like a mini-brochure, but much quicker to read.

PUBLICITY

Sooner or later the idea of attracting some favorable publicity for your business will begin to seem like a good idea. In a few rare cases you might be asked to appear on national TV or radio, and you would have to decide whether you could handle the resulting anxiety and attention. Although this once-in-a-lifetime publicity shot might be something to tell your grandchildren about, unless you are a writer or entertainer it might not do much to promote your business. Much more important to your business is publicity sought within your own community as part of a well-thought-out promotional campaign.

Publicity seems the mysterious province of a lucky few, something out of reach for a car mechanic, hairdresser, accountant, or doll restorer. Besides, you have also heard of people who have gotten hurt by bad publicity—"bad" meaning that they were quoted inaccurately, their business was presented in a misleading way, or worse. Yet people in the media are like people everywhere. Most are kind and want to do a good job of presenting your story to their public. After all, you are their bread and butter; too many inaccurate stories and the reporter or newscaster will be looking for another job.

The media are hungry for interesting stories. All you have to do is get their attention. Once you have it, respect those who want to spread the good news about your business: Be truthful, don't blow your own horn too much, and don't exploit coverage for personal gain.

YOU'RE NOT CRAZY.

Does this sound familiar?

☐ *You want to exert more control over your life.*

☐ *You have concerns about your social/sexual life.*

☐ *You have recently started or ended a relationship.*

☐ *You have a new baby and feel overwhelmed.*

☐ *You've been promoted to a new job, or . . .*

☐ *You or your mate have lost a job.*

☐ *You've recently lost a parent or friend.*

☐ *You or your family have had repeated illnesses.*

☐ *You want to learn about your stress and ways of utilizing it more effectively.*

You're not crazy if one of these life changes is getting you down.

Helen Jensen Hendricks R.N. (Ph.D. candidate) is a licensed Marriage, Family, Child Counselor who consults with business, industry and education. Call her. You can maximize your potential and manage life stress.

San Francisco

M.F.C.C. M2457

Insurance accepted.

Fig. 9.2   Judgment Card Samples

Ten Remedies for

WRITER'S BLOCK

1. Call a friend and explain where you're stuck.

2. Go for a walk.

3. Draw a "concept map," putting each idea, sub-idea, and pre-idea in a bubble and connecting the bubbles with arrows.

4. Give up temporarily.

5. Listen to music.

6. Write about how frustrated and stuck you are, using plenty of obscenities.

7. Write the opposite of what you're trying to say.

8. Try changing your audience—write your idea as a letter to a close friend, a *National Enquirer* story, or a Shakespeare soliloquy.

9. Write down and savor each critical thought that is getting in your way.

10. Yell, scream, growl, stamp your feet.

Charlie Varon's Wordworks
58 Gladys Street
San Francisco, CA 94110
415/648-7425

Charlie Varon's Wordworks
58 Gladys Street • San Francisco, CA 94110
415/648-7425

Editorial Services
from Light Editing to Collaboration

After a break of several years, I am back in the editing business! The services I offer range from brush-up editing to major rewriting and collaboration. I will:

— help you think through how to proceed on a writing project from its inception or at any point along the way

— edit or rewrite your manuscript to sharpen ideas and improve organization

— copy edit for grammar, spelling, and style

— interview you on tape to help you get past your blocks, and then transform the tape transcript into a manuscript

— write in collaboration with you

— work in concert with typesetters and designers

Credentials:
I bring to my work an inquisitive mind, a sense of humor, and eleven years of experience writing and editing for general and specialized audiences.
I am coauthor, with Fran Peavey and Myra Levy, of *Heart Politics*, published by New Society Publishers, 1986. Called "captivating" by *Library Journal*.
Since 1976, I have authored and coauthored numerous articles and humorous essays. Publication credits include *The Atlantic, California, The San Francisco Chronicle, In These Times, New Age Journal, San Francisco Focus, TV Guide,* and *Whole Earth Review.*
I worked for a year as copy editor and text editor for *San Francisco Focus*, a monthly magazine (circulation 150,000). I have also done freelance book editing and proofreading; credits include *Diet for a Small Planet: Tenth Anniversary Edition* by Frances Moore Lappé and *Working Fire* by John Burks.
I am familiar with many ways of working with words, and will tailor my services to your needs and budget.

Charlie Varon's Wordworks
58 Gladys Street
San Francisco, CA 94110

Fig. 9.3   Judgment Card Sample

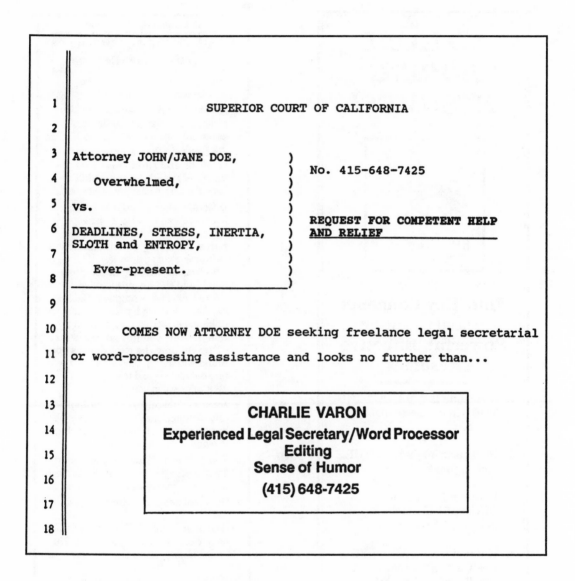

Fig. 9.4   Judgment Card Sample

NO MORE BORING RESUMES!

Four Key Concepts
crucial to writing
Powerful, Effective Resumes

1. **A resume is a MARKETING TOOL** (not a personnel document.)

   •

2. **It focuses on your FUTURE** (not on your past.)

   •

3. **It summarizes your ACCOMPLISHMENTS** (not your job duties.)

   •

4. **It documents SKILLS YOU ENJOY USING** (not things you did because you had to.)

- A Bookmark Mini-Guide -

SEVEN TIPS on Writing a "Damn Good Resume"

1 Always start with a clear, concise **Job Objective** - a job title if possible.

2 Identify about 3 to 6 **essential skills** required to do that job, or the most **essential functions** of that job.

3 For each essential skill or function, **recall several situations** where you successfully **used the same skill** or did something similar (for pay or not).

4 **Describe what you did in brief, lively statements.** Here's how:
   – In each statement, **focus on your part** in it, **leading off with an action word** identifying your role.
   – Spell out the resulting **accomplishment, and the benefit** to others.
   – Avoid using job descriptions ("duties included..."); instead, present your **uniquely effective way of doing things - how you got good results.**
   – **Present only the experiences you found satisfying**; omit (or at least play down) tasks and roles you don't want to repeat in your new job.

5 Arrange all this **either chronologically or functionally** — that is, by job or by essential skill/function, **keeping it lean** yet packed with useful info.

6 Top it off with a **Summary** (4-5 short lines) of your "juiciest" strengths & qualifications + one prime accomplishment.

7 **Get feedback** and revise as needed.

Taken from Yana Parker's books: *Damn Good Resume Guide* and *The Resume Catalog: 200 Damn Good Examples*

Ten Speed Press, Berkeley (415) 845-8414
Damn Good Resume Service (415) 540-5876
© 1989, Yana Parker

Fig. 9.5   Judgment Card Sample

Appointment Calendar • JoanAnn Radu • The Knead to Relax • 415/255-7520

Sun	Mon	Tues	Weds	Thurs	Fri	Sat
Sun 8/27 Day Off	**Mon 8/28** Day Off	**Tues 8/29** 2:30 PM: ★ 4:00 PM: ★ 5:30 PM: ★ 7:00 PM: ★ 8:30 PM: ★	**Weds 8/30** Day Off	**Thurs 8/31** 2:30 PM: ★ 4:00 PM: ★ 5:30 PM: ★ 7:00 PM: ★ 8:30 PM: ★	**Fri 9/1** Available for Massage at the Workplace (Neck & Shoulders) Minimum 7 people Maximum 10 people	**Sat 9/2** 12 NOON: ◆ or ★ 2:00 PM: ◆ or ★ 4:00 PM: ◆ or ★ 6:00 PM: ◆ or ★
Sun 9/3 Day Off	**Mon 9/4** LABOR DAY HOLIDAY 12 NOON: ◆ or ★ 2:00 PM: ◆ or ★ 4:00 PM: ◆ or ★ 6:00 PM: ◆ or ★	**Tues 9/5** 2:30 PM: ★ 4:00 PM: ★ 5:30 PM: ★ 7:00 PM: ★ 8:30 PM: ★	**Weds 9/6** 4:00 PM: ★ 5:30 PM: ★ 7:00 PM: ★ 8:30 PM: ★	**Thurs 9/7** 2:30 PM: ★ 4:00 PM: ★ 5:30 PM: ★ 7:00 PM: ★ 8:30 PM: ★	**Fri 9/8** Available for Massage at the Workplace (Neck & Shoulders) Minimum 7 people Maximum 10 people	**Sat 9/9** 12 NOON: ◆ or ★ 2:00 PM: ◆ or ★ 4:00 PM: ◆ or ★ 6:00 PM: ◆ or ★
Sun 9/10 Day Off	**Mon 9/11** Day Off	**Tues 9/12** 2:30 PM: ★ 4:00 PM: ★ 5:30 PM: ★ 7:00 PM: ★ 8:30 PM: ★	**Weds 9/13** 4:00 PM: ★ 5:30 PM: ★ 7:00 PM: ★ 8:30 PM: ★	**Thurs 9/14** 2:30 PM: ★ 4:00 PM: ★ 5:30 PM: ★ 7:00 PM: ★ 8:30 PM: ★	**Fri 9/15** Day Off	**Sat 9/16** Marianna Nunes Men's and Women's Spiritual Networking Breakfast 9:30-11:00 Press Club 550 Post St.
Sun 9/17 12 NOON: ◆ or ★ 2:00 PM: ◆ or ★ 4:00 PM: ◆ or ★ 6:00 PM: ◆ or ★	**Mon 9/18** Day Off	**Tues 9/19** 2:30 PM: ★ 4:00 PM: ★ 5:30 PM: ★ 7:00 PM: ★ 8:30 PM: ★	**Weds 9/20** 4:00 PM: ★ 5:30 PM: ★ 7:00 PM: ★ 8:30 PM: ★	**Thurs 9/21** 2:30 PM: ★ 4:00 PM: ★ 5:30 PM: ★ 7:00 PM: ★ 8:30 PM: ★	**Fri 9/22** Available for Massage at the Workplace (Neck & Shoulders) Minimum 7 people Maximum 10 people	**Sat 9/23** 12 NOON: ◆ or ★ 2:00 PM: ◆ or ★ 4:00 PM: ◆ or ★ 6:00 PM: ◆ or ★
Sun 9/24 Day Off	**Mon 9/25** Day Off	**Tues 9/26** 2:30 PM: ★ 4:00 PM: ★ 5:30 PM: ★ 7:00 PM: ★ 8:30 PM: ★	**Weds 9/27** 4:00 PM: ★ 5:30 PM: ★ 7:00 PM: ★ 8:30 PM: ★	**Thurs 9/28** Day Off	**Fri 9/29** Day Off	**Sat 9/30** 12 NOON: ◆ or ★ 2:00 PM: ◆ or ★ 4:00 PM: ◆ or ★ 6:00 PM: ◆ or ★
Sun 10/1 12 NOON: ◆ or ★ 2:00 PM: ◆ or ★ 4:00 PM: ◆ or ★ 6:00 PM: ◆ or ★	**Mon 10/2** Day Off	**Tues 10/3** 2:30 PM: ★ 4:00 PM: ★ 5:30 PM: ★ 7:00 PM: ★ 8:30 PM: ★	**Weds 10/4** 4:00 PM: ★ 5:30 PM: ★ 7:00 PM: ★ 8:30 PM: ★	**Thurs 10/5** 2:30 PM: ★ 4:00 PM: ★ 5:30 PM: ★ 7:00 PM: ★ 8:30 PM: ★	**Fri 10/6** Day Off	**Sat 10/7** 12 NOON: ◆ or ★ 2:00 PM: ◆ or ★ 4:00 PM: ◆ or ★ 6:00 PM: ◆ or ★

◆ = 75 minute massage for $70   ★ = 50 minute massage for $50 / Please note rate increase. (First one in over five years).

Fig. 9.6   Judgment Card Sample

Fig. 9.7   Judgment Card Sample

If you get on a television or radio show or find yourself being asked penetrating questions by a local reporter, remain calm. Most one-person-business owners love talking about their work. So just concentrate on what you love and not yourself or what you look like on the TV monitor. Usually, you can relax in the company of a professional media person, whose job it is to provide a good show or write an interesting article. Media professionals are dedicated to providing their audience with entertainment and information and they know their business. All you have to do is share yours.

Whether you are a foot doctor, a plant tender, a drum repairperson, or a stained-glass restorer, there are people interested in your business. These two facts should give you all the confidence you need to go for it: (1) you are interesting to others, and (2) the media has a lot of time and space to fill.

Once you have made it through your first interview, don't sit around staring at your clipping, or wear out your tape of the show. To be effective, publicity must be carried out on a consistent basis and is just one part of your promotional efforts. Make sure your business can handle the brief flurry of inquiries that is bound to result from, say, a feature story in the Sunday paper. Keep in mind that maintaining superior service, for old customers as well as new, must always be your first consideration. The best strategy is to maintain a regular, low-profile exposure, punctuated with an occasional bit of hullabaloo.

If you are interviewed on the radio ask them for a tape, and if you are on television be sure to have several people record the interview. Regardless of the type of media you are interviewed for, be sure to provide them with written information about where you can be reached. In the case of radio and television it's a very good idea to have ten written questions for yourself in case the host or hostess didn't have time to go over your material, which occasionally happens.

There is a domino effect at work in the publicity arena, and you can use tapes and articles written about you to generate more publicity.

Should you hire a publicist? Publicists are like bookkeepers. There are a lot of fine ones around and you can benefit from their expertise. But a one-person business should use both sparingly. Just as it may be a good idea to hire a bookkeeper to

---

Quotes from an "Expert in the Field"

Becoming known as an expert in your field is a big plus in attracting favorable publicity. If you can, write a column for your local newspaper or have a weekly radio spot where people call in with questions relevant to your business. People will begin to look to you for information. Ever notice how some people's names seem to show up repeatedly in your hometown newspaper? That's because the media is on an eternal deadline, and they will naturally call an "expert," because then they don't have to worry about the validity of the contribution. Writing an interesting response to the letters-to-the-editor section of your newspaper or trade journal is another way to become known as an expert in your field. Remember to identify your business and location.

help you set up a workable system, it may be beneficial to hire a publicist for a few hours to help you formulate some of your ideas and to provide you with contacts. But it's your business, and no one knows it better than you or can talk about it as enthusiastically. Besides you probably don't have a lot of money to spare. Although a publicist is invaluable for some businesses, such as for an author planning a promotion tour, for the typical one-person business it's neither necessary nor cost-effective to have one on retainer or hire one to run the whole show.

MARKETING CHECKLIST

In closing this chapter then, let us summarize: A good marketing plan is based on knowing everything there is to know about your business and the grassroots community it is nestled in. It's a commitment to continually improving and fine-tuning the four P's of marketing: product, price, place, and promotion. It's having a well-run business, offering an excellent product and superior service, including a written recourse policy. It means actively knowing your referral base, including satisfied customers, colleagues, and vendors as well as family and friends, and keeping them up to date on any changes in your business. It's having a well-thought-out calendar of marketing activities, using marketing vehicles that are appropriate to the circle of intimacy that you are targeting. It means active follow-up on all marketing activities.

Personal recommendation is the focus of grassroots marketing and is a superior strategy for the one-person business. By identifying the appropriate customers and building long-term relationships with them, you will gain their trust and their recommendations.

Grassroots marketing is an ongoing commitment to your personal community and to the most important asset of your business: your customers!

Finally, we leave you with this one-person-business marketing checklist:

Fig. 9.8   One-person-business Marketing Checklist

	My marketing concept is complete and the components fit together clearly. I can clearly describe my business and so can most of my customers, suppliers, and employees. People can easily tell what the product or service is.
	My product or service is the best it can be.
	My pricing is clear, complete, and fair.
	I treat everyone around me, including employees, suppliers, friends, and even those who dislike me, as honestly and professionally as possible. If they are unhappy with my products or services, or don't agree with my business practices, they have clear and easy recourse.
	I have developed a trustworthy openness regarding my products, packaging, educational information, ideas, physical premises, management style, and finances.
	My customers know as much as they want to about my product or service, including what is superior and unique about the way I conduct business.
	Old customers, current customers, and future customers find my business inviting and easily accessible.
	I have a complete and current list of customers and those in my business networks, and I schedule and carry out marketing activities of interest to them on a regular basis.
	I'm prepared to smoothly and efficiently handle an increase in the number of customers generated by my marketing plan.

RESOURCES

Barometer of Small Business. Accounting Corporation of America, 1929 First Avenue, San Diego, CA 92112.

Andreasen, Alan. *Strategic Marketing for Nonprofit Organizations*, 4th. ed. New York: Prentice Hall, 1990.

Brodsky, Bart, and Janet Geis. *Finding Your Niche: Marketing Your Professional Service*. Berkeley: Community Resource Institute Press, 1992.

————. *The Teaching Marketplace*. Berkeley: Community Resource Institute Press, 1991.

Levinson, Jay C. *Guerrilla Marketing for the Nineties*. Boston: Houghton-Mifflin, 1993.

Phillips, Michael, and Salli Rasberry. *Marketing without Advertising*. Berkeley, Calif.: Nolo Press, 1987.

Annual Statement Studies. Robert Morris Associates. Philadelphia National Bank Building, Philadelphia, PA 19107.

Sachs, Laura. *Do-It-Yourself Marketing for the Professional Practice*. New York: Prentice-Hall, 1986.

Sales Forecasting for Small Business. Small Business Administration. Publication 1.10/2:2, No. 48.

Withers, Jean, and Carol Vipperman. *Marketing Your Service: A Planning Guide for Small Business*. Seattle: Self-Counsel Press, 1987.

Steinhoff, Dan, and John F. Burgess. *Small Business Management Fundamentals*, 6th. ed. New York: McGraw-Hill, 1992.

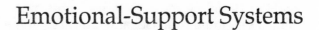

10

Emotional-Support Systems

A one-person business can fail for a number of reasons, a few of them obvious, such as lack of competence, lack of persistence, and severe illness. The most common reason, though, and the least discussed, is emotional stress. Emotional health is not usually considered a factor in the success or failure of a business. It's as if we believe life must be compartmentalized and a death in the family dealt with only at night or on weekends. No matter what happens, come Monday morning it's time for a stiff upper lip. Pretending that emotions have no effect on business is naive, and it definitely won't work in a one-person business.

A one-person business has to rely heavily on self-starting energy, which is usually in abundance unless things go wrong on an emotional level. If you are losing sleep worrying about something, there is no boss to pressure you into getting on with the day's business, and little motivation to get up and attend to what suddenly seems like an overwhelming number of details.

Only some parts of your business offer immediate and direct rewards, such as talking to an enthusiastic customer, giving a well-received speech, or mailing off your manuscript. Much of the work involves dealing with administrative details and requires pure self-starting energy—the kind that is drained by depression, grief, sorrow, or self-pity. Catastrophic events over which you have no control are bound to happen. Your spouse may leave, friends may die, illnesses may occur. A one-person-business owner has to acknowledge this and arrange for some sort of support in advance. The bills have to be paid, the late supplier checked on, the telephone messages retrieved and answered. There is no one to take responsibility but you.

As property manager Diane Stuart explains, "You have to have a real drive that comes from inside and propels you to do things. Once you reach that level of enthusiasm about what you're doing, you'll put out whatever energy it takes to make it work. Without that self-starting energy it's very difficult."

Before the Industrial Revolution, it might not have been necessary to make observations such as these. Most people belonged to the communities of family, clan, and village that included support structures. But the advent of large-scale centralized manufacturing led to a mass migration to cities and brought about a decline in this kind of community structure. Today we think of the nuclear family—mother, father, and children—as the basic social unit. But in fact, this has been true for only about the past two hundred years. Prior to that, (and still true today in many other cultures) the basic economic and social unit was an extended household. The typical household varies greatly from culture to culture, but the one constant is that the household's members work collaboratively to support each other—economically, socially, emotionally, and spiritually.

Because the support of the naturally larger household, clan, or community has been lost to us, we must consciously re-create it. As business consultant Paul Terry puts it: "Juggling the balls of how you run your business, maintain your relationships, get some exercise, and preserve some kind of spiritual awareness can be hard. Sometimes you feel like your business is working, but you never get any exercise; or sometimes you are getting a lot of exercise but ignoring your business; or putting a lot of energy into your relationships but not finding the time for contemplation of your spiritual life. Being a one-person business, you sometimes have to create your own environment, rather than having an environment created for you."

Fortunately, there are many ways to create this supportive environment and maintain the necessary self-starting energy to run a one-person business. We will discuss some of the typical dangers and concerns connected with running a one-person business and suggest ways of dealing with them, focusing on stabilization through routine, overcoming isolation, having fun, getting and getting support, handling emergency emotional needs, taking time off, active health practices, and concerns about old age.

STABILIZATION THROUGH ROUTINE

If you go to bed and get up at a different time each day, never eat regular food at a regular time, have no regular exercise, and in general lack any kind of dependable rhythm to your life, then you are bound to experience wide emotional swings.

On the other hand, if you decide on a certain routine and then simply do what needs to be done regardless of how you feel, you will soon find your emotions stabilizing. If this sounds too simplistic, you can easily check it out. Start by cooking yourself one meal, with forethought and awareness, at the same time each day. It doesn't take much observation to discover what psychologists have known for many years: Emotions follow behavior.

After you have gotten into the routine of a regular meal, add a daily constitutional or walk. Fifteen minutes is enough. Keep watching what happens to your mood swings as your routine builds momentum. Most people report an amazing stabilizing effect.

Our clients have found many ways to ensure emotional stability in their lives. Gift-shop owner Trish, for example, uses the requirements of her home and workplace to dictate her routine. "I get up every morning at the same time, make my husband breakfast, do the routine chores, and am at the shop by ten. I leave at five except on weekends, when I stay until six. Except for making up my money bag for the next day, I relax in the evening. I start out with the same amount of cash every day, so when I make up my money bag for the next day, I know what my profit was for today. Sometimes I work on my books in the evening also."

Shirley, who runs a word-processing business from her home, relies on a regular session in the garden each morning. Sandy, a successful potter, does meditation every morning and every Saturday drops in for lunch at a nearby meditation center. Five days a week, Michael runs at 6 A.M. Afterwards, he takes a warm shower followed by a cold one, and then goes to a coffeehouse to meet with friends before going to work. Charles, a computer consultant, gets up at the last minute, drinks several cups of strong coffee, and rushes to work. After dinner he always smokes an expensive cigar, and he spends his last waking hour reading up on his latest intellectual pursuit. (We include Charles to make it obvious that "healthy" and "spiritual" are not the only reasonable ways to build routine.)

The range of options is great: exercise, meditation, therapy, yoga, meeting with friends, as well as reading, eating, and even smoking a cigar. The key is to give high priority to the need for routine. Different people require more routine than others. For some, doing something once a week is enough. For others, it must be every day.

Observing and modifying the effect that routine has on your daily life is an activity well worth engaging in. David Reynolds, in his book *Constructive Living*, explains it like this:

> America is a land of freedom, we say. Yet all around us are restrictions on what we can do. Only designated persons can prescribe medicine, only certain drugs can be taken legally, streets should be crossed only when the traffic light is green, children under a certain age cannot work for wages, it is impolite to sneeze in someone's face, social greetings are required at parties, we are expected to speak on one level of formality to our bosses and another way to our friends. We are not entirely free in what we do, of course. And no one really wants to live an absolutely unfettered life. Children who are given too much leeway are miserable; they actually seek limits and direction from adults. Mentally disturbed people also seem more comfortable when a warm but firm hand limits the bound-

aries of their "crazy" behavior. Even artists are never truly free. They voluntarily take on the limits of the medium they use, the style they employ, the model, the patron, time constraints, the question of cost, and so on.

We are able to operate within these limits, even to enjoy some of them, because our behavior is controllable in a way that our feelings are not. There is a very special satisfaction for the Artist of Living who works within life's limits to produce a fine self-portrait. The more control we develop over our actions, the more chance we have of producing a self we can be proud of.

People find many ways to promote emotional stability through regular daily routines. And when you're your own business, doing this takes on a special meaning.

OVERCOMING ISOLATION

Every owner of a one-person business must contend with isolation. It's always going to be there, and you must give it some thought to make sure you don't find yourself staring miserably at the walls one day, with nowhere to turn. Isolation can be partially overcome by occasional get-togethers with peers or by structuring time to get out of the office every day, so that you see other people. But it's also important to take a hard look at your personality to see if you really can work alone. If you are super-gregarious, or have spent many years in a friendly office situation, you might decide that a shared business space is for you.

A wide range of shared business spaces exist, from business "incubators" at one end to full-service offices on the other. The different services fall into four major groupings: (1) business or office space with services and office equipment; (2) space and services rented to a group of businesses that are related or that share clients in some way; (3) services, shared clients, and some kind of an advisory service; and (4) services, shared clients, an advisory service, and start-up financing.

Each of these arrangements usually includes secretary and receptionist services, copy machines, and reception and meeting areas. They sometimes include computers, laser printers, fax machines, bookkeepers, accountants, and business lawyers. The last two types of shared space are sometimes called *incubators*. An incubator is any arrangement that offers some combination of financing and advice. Financing usually takes the form of a subsidy built into the rent, for the primary purpose of helping businesses get started. The subsidy may cease after a fixed period of time, or after the business gets going. Incubators are usually sponsored by local economic development agencies. Check with your local government to see if any exist near you.

Each of these four basic forms has advantages and disadvantages. The biggest overall disadvantage is the limited number of locations where you can find any type of shared business service. Among the advantages, aside from solving the isolation problem, is the smaller amount of money you need to invest in office equipment and office support services, because you are sharing. Also you often get access to meeting rooms or other facilities that you might not otherwise be able to afford.

Catherine Campbell, a family attorney, has her office in a shared space that includes some services. "My business is self-contained. I don't share my economic setup with any other attorneys, and I have no employees. I do share space with a group of other attorneys, and a receptionist and common secretarial pool. Within the office I have a "one on one" relationship, which is infinitely valuable for someone like me who has ethical and emotional problems in her work. It's just a very close, intimate friendship in the office that is available to me at any hour I need it. It is essential, the protein of everything there. It would be hard for me to live with the isolation I think I would experience if I didn't have that friendship within the office. In addition to that we have a professional relationship. We meet to discuss issues that come up in the office context. It would be difficult to deal with the internal politics of the office and the structural problems of the office and common needs and experiences that occur without that friendship."

If you only need occasional use of meeting space or support services, you can get them from companies that specialize in meeting space rentals or office services and use a different choice to overcome isolation. You can join a local professional or networking group for your business field. Teri Joe Wheeler, a designer of fine satchels, has located her home and studio on an isolated rural property a few hours drive from San Francisco. "I go for a run every morning, and on my run I check the phone machine, which is about a half mile from my studio. Then I spend some time enjoying the garden before going to work. Although I lack the access of people who live in an urban environment, I get inspiration from the land and have found ways to cope with the loneliness. I knew before I chose this lifestyle that I had the ability to spend a lot of time by myself. Another aspect is that I have to be disciplined. It's not hard for me to work; it's hard to know when to stop. I joined the San Francisco Design Network, which turned out to be a lot of fun. We get together once a month and I enjoy the various presentations and bouncing ideas off the other artists."

Fine artist Pam Glasscock volunteers in her local elementary school. "I actually feel very strongly about having something that I can offer that's interesting and intense and contributes to the school. I've also been playing piano with a friend, and it's such an enriching thing. I think, for me, one of the dangers is being isolated and depressed and overly self-critical, which probably happens to a lot of people who work for themselves. It's really nice to have dates where you go and do something together with other people, whether teaching at school or playing music with my friend Jane."

HAVING FUN

Few callings in life offer as great a chance to have fun as a one-person business. First, if you've taken the steps we suggest in Chapter 6, it is highly likely that the work itself will be fun. So you can just linger over the parts you love most. Second, you control the pace. If you follow the tips offered in this book, you should be able to slow down and do the diverting things that catch your eye at the moment: talk to the postmistress, watch a butterfly, play with a child you pass at the park, skip a rock across a stream. And spend an extra half hour getting to know a new person you met over morning coffee at the local coffee shop.

But to make this happen you must plan for it. At first it may seem contradictory to talk about planning your fun. Fun is supposed to arise spontaneously from other activities and it often does. But it is very easy to get so involved in the day-to-day operation of your business to the exclusion of everything else. One of the most frequent complaints we hear is, "I don't ever seem to have enough time for fun!"

The solution is to build in fun. Remember to add little pieces of time onto some of your business activities so that there's room for fun as well. If it takes a half hour to go to the post office, schedule forty-five minutes so you won't feel you have to pass up an interesting conversation with a friend you happen to meet there. If you can see a heavy day coming later in the week, schedule a movie for that evening as a reward for making it through the day. This way, you will keep your spirits high, be more likely to recognize those moments when they arise, and be able to take advantage of them without worrying about your busy schedule and the demands placed on your time by your business.

Here's how book designer and consultant Clifford Burke explains the importance of fun in his life: "I once spent three years having no fun in my work. The only fun was the work I was doing on my own time. Those three years of steady work were unusual for me because I had been an independent for so long. They really taught me that the most important thing is to have fun every day rather than wait for it on Friday. For me fun is more important than making a lot of money. It's not so much just having fun as feeling that my creative energies are driving the day, not some other demands.

"The biggest risk of the one-person business is overwork. You have to avoid burying yourself in work. It's not a pleasure unless you get off on overwork, and some people do, I guess. If your life is dedicated to the business and something emotional or spiritual or physical happens to jeopardize your ability to run it, there is nothing to fall back on. Human beings are just more complex than that. You can wake up fifteen years later and not know who your kids are. It took me a long time to learn to take time, to be lazy. Having learned it, I consider it a real treasure. I still work very hard. I just treasure my time."

For many one-person businesses, the fun is intrinsic in the business itself. Teri Joe Wheeler finds fun and excitement in all aspects of her work. "It's really fun when I walk into a store with a bag of my things and it turns into an 'ooh ahh' situation. I really adore fabrics, so it's exciting to have new ones. It's fun also because if someone is happy with their bag, then it's rewarding."

Even Don Anderson finds ways to have fun in his dental lab: "My wife's aunt, who is in her sixties, needed a crown. On the inside of the tooth, where you couldn't see it, I engraved under the surface where you could never scratch it the word *sexy* spelled backwards. Since it's backwards it's not readable except by the dentist when he puts his mirror in there. Her dentist loved it. And she has such a great sense of humor, she loved it too. She pulls her cheek back and shows everybody.

"My next-door-neighbor's daughter is a hawker with the Audobon Society. So I did this beautiful redtail hawk on a crown that she needed—very small—with its wings spread and a little red tail. I have fun with the engraving and I don't charge for it."

Maybe the real secret to having fun in business is best expressed by Pam Glasscock. "One thing that really influenced me was in college. I went to a lecture and the professor said something that really struck me. I think about it a lot. He said `You have to figure out what you love and do that.' That's rule number one."

GETTING AND GIVING SUPPORT

By experimenting with different systems for ourselves and by observing the ways our clients and the people we interviewed for this book gain emotional support, we have come up with four strategies that work for most people: planning buddies, business support groups, mentors, and business advisory boards.

Everything we need to support our one-person business will come from the people who surround us. In America, even the most liberal among us tend to idolize the cowboy, the self-sufficient loner, and this tendency keeps us from asking for help from fear that this would be a sign of weakness. And yet for anyone building a one-person business, it is not only impossible to live life completely alone, it isn't even desirable.

We spoke earlier about the necessity to consciously re-create our lost or weakened support structures. There are three effective steps to begin this process: (1) focus on the people in your life; (2) find the right people to support what you want to do; (3) give back more than you get.

Focusing on the People in Your Life

As we explained in Chapter 9, a good way to focus on the people who support us is in terms of circles of intimacy. Bring out the piece of paper you drew your circles on from Chapter 9, and review the results. Recall that the people within all of these circles are your personal community. They will be the resource pool from which you will build all the support you need to start and maintain your one-person business. They will provide you with role models, mentors, and guides. They can give you friendship and nurturance, help in times of crisis, referrals to others who can help, and encouragement along the way.

If you are not happy with the kind or number of confidants, friends, and network associates you have now, it is never too late to find new ones. Start by using this simple three-step process: (1) Get clear with yourself about what kind of people you want to be with. (What kind of character would they exhibit? What kind of people would be attracted to them?) (2) Ask yourself this simple question: "Where would a person like that hang out?" (3) Go hang out there yourself.

To get started on this, make a list of the characteristics you would like to find in the people who support you. Next to each characteristic, note the name of one or more supporters (friends, relatives, associates) who offer you that characteristic. Are there any blanks? Characteristics for which you have no supporters? If so, make a note of where people with that kind of characteristic would hang out. Make an appointment with yourself to find at least one person each week who might become a new friend if you would just spend some time with them building the friendship.

Remember though, support is not a one-way street. It won't work to simply seek out people who will take care of you. You have to first take care of yourself. Then you can seek out people with whom you can share a supportive relationship. Life within our personal community only works well when most of us are giving back to the well-being of the individuals and the group as a whole, without giving up our own well-being. In the final analysis, the support you receive will be in direct proportion to the support you give.

Managing Your Difficult Friends Make a list of relationships that are not supportive, the ones that are holding you back, the ones that never have anything encouraging to say. Choose a single action step that would improve these relationships, or decide to drop them.

Keeping the Support Flowing Make a list of friends, former coworkers, and others whom you need to catch up with. Who just needs a call? Who needs to be thanked for a recent favor? Who needs a favor returned? Make an appointment with yourself to contact at least one of these people each day until you are caught up.

Fig. 10.1   The Characteristics of Your Supporters

Characteristics	Who	Where	When
Always knows the right thing to say	Sheila		
Listens to my complaints without trying to fix me	Don		
Willing to share his years of experience	Bob		
Shares an interest in healthy activities, especially hiking and bird watching	Still looking	Sierra Singles	Audubon Christmas count on Grizzly Island

Finding the Right People

When we begin to make a conscious effort to build more support for ourselves, there are several different actions we can take to effectively organize our supporters. Among the many alternatives, four basic ones seem to provide both the most immediate results and greatest long-term effectiveness: (1) a *planning buddy*, (2) *support groups*, (3) *mentors*, and (4) a *board of advisors*.

The Planning Buddy The planning buddy comes from an idea first introduced to us by Barbara Sher in *Wishcraft*, where she describes what she calls the "buddy system."

Planning buddies offer each other a special kind of friendship that attempts to be unconditional. You agree with a close friend, or someone you can trust to keep agreements, to meet weekly and to serve as catalysts for each other. You also agree not to act as therapists or counselors. Your weekly agenda should have three parts:

1. Catch up on each other's activities in the preceding week. What you report may be either work-related or personal.
2. Allow each person to tell the other about any hard times: moments or events in the last week that were emotionally disruptive. This part of the meeting is not about fixing anything. The listener should just listen, and if the talker wants advice, he or she will have to ask for it. This is an important rule.
3. Tell each other what your plans are for the coming week, and use this opportunity to set a goal. The other person's job is not to punish or harass you if you don't meet your goal, but to help you put your goal outside of yourself, out into the real world. When you seriously tell someone what you want to accomplish, the chance that you will actually reach the goal increases. At the very least, you may see that the goal wasn't what you really wanted anyway.

Attorney Catherine Campbell feels that a planning buddy is the most important of all support systems. "There is a very strong series of overlapping circles that form a net that supports me in what I do and, of course, supports everybody else involved in similar kinds of work. The 'one on one' is the most important of the support systems. All the social networks in the world would not be enough if I did not have that one close friend with whom I could talk and plan."

Humorist Charlie Varon has taken the planning buddy idea one step further. "I have found over the years that if there is someone to whom I am accountable or who is giving me support, then I will pursue things that I otherwise might not. I need to have someone who is sort of my sounding board and support person. Since I'm involved in lots of different projects, instead of one planning buddy for everything, I have a 'contact person' for each project. For instance, I have a friend who is head of a theater department, and he supported me in teaching a class for extended education. I knew it would be good for business but I just couldn't get to it. His enthusiasm encouraged me to work ten minutes a day writing my class proposal. It took several months of ten-minute days until it was done. But then it was done. Now I am going to teach this class in the fall. Without him it would have just been another idea."

Support Groups Support groups are especially important to one-person businesses. There are many different types of support groups, differing mostly in focus or agenda. The basic support group is usually made up of friends or carefully chosen associates who get together from one to four times per month. At these meetings, you listen to one another's work or personal problems and successes, share concerns and useful information, and give each other emotional support. As with the buddy system, an important value comes from getting your plans, dreams, and hardtimes out on the table. But the support group differs from the planning buddy in two ways. First, because there are more people involved, you get more support. Second, support groups can be made to focus more on work-related goal-setting than on emotional issues if that is the focus its participants need. Planning buddies, by contrast, are usually specifically focused on emotional needs, with work as a secondary agenda item.

In a support group there is usually more brainstorming to find solutions, and more checking in to see how well group members are accomplishing things on their to-do lists. And setting a goal in front of a group seems to be even more motivating, leading to even more goal completions.

For instance, at one meeting you might hear, "I want you all to know that I will make four phone calls a day to my prospect list until our next meeting." And at the next meeting, that person might report back, "I did it, and I'm proud of myself—I got two new clients." Although this is a lot like the third item on the planning buddy agenda, setting a goal in front of a group seems to be even more motivating, leading to even more goal completions.

A support group can provide emotional support too, like a planning buddy, but with an important difference: It is unfair to expect one single person whom you see every week to be always upbeat and strong emotionally. The group spreads support responsibilities around, making it easier on everyone.

Mentors There are always other people who know more about some aspect of work or life than you do. If you can figure out who they are, and find that you enjoy spending time together, then you have found your mentors.

The mentor relationship is a delicate one and needs special attention. You must be careful not to overstep your welcome in asking for help. Generally a mentor should be the last person you go to, when your planning buddy or your support group has been unable to come up with an answer. But sometimes a mentor is the first person you go to, especially if you have a problem in the day-to-day stuff of work and you know that one of your mentors would know the precise answer. The general rule for treatment of mentors is to respect them and value their time as you would your own.

Advisory Boards   A business advisory board differs from a business support group in that it meets only as frequently as necessary and consists, in addition to some of your usual advisors, of people with expertise that is valuable to your business. It might include your local banker or a loan officer from the branch where you bank; your accountant and perhaps a business lawyer; one or more of your special advisors; one or more of your suppliers; and so forth. This group is not for emotional support, although you might find them supportive, given the interest that these people will have in your business. The primary purpose of an advisory board is to meet with you once or twice a year at crucial times: to help guide your business as it grows, to help you through a business crisis, or to help you find answers to business problems that you have not been able to resolve elsewhere. Your job is to do your homework, including extensive library and real-life research. When you convene your advisory board, you should be fully prepared to answer any questions they might have about your problem.

Examples of Sources of Support

Kate Bishop uses a planning buddy in addition to networking with other designers for support. "I have a situation with another designer that I enjoy a lot. We have a semiformal agreement to spend time at each other's studios about once a week. We bring whatever we're working on, or work on something together. We set challenges for each other, like homework assignments that we have to show each other at a certain time. It's really stimulating. It's also fun and we learn from each other.

"I've been doing a lot of networking with other designers. I belonged to the San Francisco Design Network for about a year and a half, and I found it real inspiring. But the Design Network wanted to be on the cutting edge of fashion, and I was sort of an outcast when I didn't do the latest look. That experience helped me define my own style better and my own needs. Now I've replaced that association with networking with designers who have the same needs and goals that I do. I call them up and say, 'I'm Kate Bishop. I've heard of you. I'd love to see your studio. Where do you get rhinestones? How do you handle this problem or that? We must have a lot of similar business problems, since we're both working by ourselves. Let's get together and talk.'

"I take single-handed responsibility for getting the designers in my area to know each other. I make an effort to get to know other designers and to share as much as I can with them."

Business advisor Paul Terry uses all of the emotional support methods we recommend. "Isolation is not something I can avoid. It happens to me and my clients. Ironically, it's like the wounded healer—giving advice to clients on how to deal with isolation when you yourself are dealing with the same issue. I think that's part of my strength as an advisor; often I am dealing with or have dealt with exactly what a client is going through.

"I deal with isolation by trying to involve myself in relationships that will have a positive effect on my business. I've had two or three different support partners on an ongoing basis, I've been involved in three support groups, and now belong to a support group that meets weekly. I use business advisors, people whom I call for things that I'm stuck on or need help with. Emotional and psychological needs can be met by support partners or groups if they are open enough to deal with those things. Staying in touch with friends is important too. Sometimes I have to put a lot of energy into just arranging to have breakfast or lunch with someone or making myself go to certain events or get involved in activities that are helpful in dealing with isolation. It can be something as mundane but as fun as playing softball on a regular basis or having a tennis partner or running with somebody."

Suzanne, a job-development researcher, relies mostly on friends. "I have a rich circle of friends who have kept me alive for years. Women who work and are up and down with it all the time. Recently I've developed a relationship with a woman who does what I do in a very similar situation. We've decided it would be helpful to communicate more.

"The woman who turned the business over to me is definitely a mentor and has played a big part in my life. The counselor I work with isn't an advisor, but his respect for what I do and his appreciation keep me going. Whenever I give him a lead he says, 'Nice work!' Then there is another counselor who is always there to answer questions. And that's important because when I jumped into this, I knew nothing, and she is the one I can turn to."

Take a moment to look again at your circles of intimacy map. Do you have a planning buddy, support group, mentor, or board of advisors? What's missing? Which could use improvement? Describe an action step for each category that might have immediate results. Pick a target date for completing each step.

THE IMPORTANCE OF TRUST IN MAKING SUPPORT WORK

The most important underlying element in the giving and receiving of support is trust. You trust yourself when you believe in your ability to make judgments about what will be good for you. You demonstrate trust for others when you believe in their judgment and integrity. Others learn to trust you when you show that you are open to their input, willing to listen, and concerned about the impact your decisions will have on them.

When you and those you work and live with trust each other, you create an atmosphere in which people can be open and honest. You build a strong team spirit that permeates all your work and play together.

Fig. 10.2   Using Support Networks to Overcome Isolation

1. The Challenge	Tradeskills & Isolation
2. Needs	• Sociability & Fun • Moral Support • Assertion of Values: rituals, symbols, and so on • Good Information & Connections • Pool of Role Models and Peers • Technical Assistance & Other Help
3. Forms of Delivery (From simplest to most formalized)	• Buddies • Support Groups • Advisory Boards & Boards of Directors • Incubators • Role Models & Mentors • Support Networks • Formal Associations (such as Trade Groups or Chambers of Commerce)
4. Network Organizing Issues	• Informality • Simplicity • Leadership Style • Services Offered • Practical Learning • Group Recruitment • Ideological Compatibility • Modification/Termination of the Network

Based on personal communications with Roger Pritchard, Berkeley, Calif.

How can you begin to build trust or improve the level of trust in an existing situation? Beyond honesty and openness, beyond the willingness to listen, and a concern for the future welfare of those around you, it is important for you to get clear about your own goals and to communicate your goals to those around you.

The single most important factor in building and maintaining trust is consistency. It is difficult to build trust and extremely easy to lose it. If you want people to trust you over the long term, you must remember never to leave them out of the loop. If you make just one decision that you expect others to carry out or support you on, and you fail to give them the opportunity for input, expect the worst.

Fig. 10.3 The Rules of Good Networking

1. Be useful.	Be useful to yourself and let others be useful to you.
2. Don't be boring.	Don't overwhelm your audience by showing off your ability to come up with contacts. Allow for reciprocity and don't exploit.
3. Listen.	Let the speaker know you're listening. Listen as if you are going to learn something. Listen equally to people you both agree and disagree with.
4. Ask questions.	Ask challenging but friendly questions. "What is important to you?" "How do you know that is true?"
5. Play the wild card.	Don't assume someone can't be useful or that you can't be useful to them. Almost anyone can surprise you with contacts and information gleaned from friends, relatives, coworkers, or from just living a full life.

Some Networking Tricks

1. Make a wish list of things you need and things you might offer someone. Keep the list updated with the help of people who know you.

2. Take the time to find how you can be useful to someone before you ask for a favor. The more important the favor is, the more useful you might consider being.

3. You don't have to file every scrap of paper in triplicate in order to be a useful networker. Stay loose—you will never get on top of all the information in the world, so don't try.

4. Take off your blinders. Don't neglect to network for fun when you are job-hunting—or job hunt while you are having fun. Networking allows you to treat your life as a whole.

5. Don't expect to save people. Networking is not the same as being a counselor or a social service agency.

6. Don't feel bad if you have to say no. Networking should not make people feel guilty or obligated.

7. If you find someone interesting to talk with today, you don't have to monopolize his or her time. Get a phone number and call next week.

Based on material from Pat Wagner and Leif Smith, Pattern Research, Denver, Colorado.

The greatest enemy of trust is failure to keep your commitments. When you make a promise to yourself and fail to keep it, you undermine self-trust. When you make promises to others and don't keep them, you undermine their trust in you. When others make promises to you and don't keep them, you stop trusting them. A simple rule to remember is "Life works when we keep our promises."

Next time you make a promise to yourself, write it down. Then look at the promise in detail until you see its smallest parts. Every time it occurs to you to do what you have promised, make it a habit to at least do some small part of it. Even though you don't feel like it, even if you are tempted to just sit there, do something.

For example, if you promise yourself that you will start exercising each day, write it down. With only a few moments of thought it is easy to see that exercise is made up of a lot of little movements: movements of your head, your arms, your legs, and so forth. From the moment that you write down your promise to exercise, you are committed.

To keep your commitment you must follow this simple procedure: Every time you think of exercising get up and move. Even if all you do is turn your head from side to side, or lift your arms up parallel with the floor that is ok.

The secret here is that if you think of exercising and then do even the simplest movement you will be creating an experience of movement associated with the thought of exercising. If you don't get up and move you will be creating the association of lethargy with the thought of exercise.

The same thing holds true when you make a promise to others. Even if you can't complete the whole promise at the moment you are thinking of it, try to do some tiny part of it, or at least make an appointment with yourself to do it. After all, setting aside time is one of the small parts of keeping any commitment.

Make a list of promises that you need to keep in the coming week. Separate them into smaller parts, and make as many appointments with yourself as necessary to begin doing those parts. Actually write your appointments down in your appointment calendar. If you don't have an appointment calendar, use a wall calendar or go buy one.

GIVING BACK MORE THAN YOU GET

The most important step in building support for your one-person business is giving back more than you get. It's not really a matter of keeping track in some kind of accounting ledger. It's more a function of the attitude that you adopt in the way that you treat yourself and those around you. People tend to mirror the way that they are treated:

- If you show an interest in helping and sharing, those around you will start helping you and sharing more with you. If you empathize with other peoples' situations, they tend to empathize more with yours.

- If you work with others to solve a problem you have, by sharing information and creating a collaborative solution, they will start including you in their own problem-solving efforts.
- If you give those around you the latitude to solve problems in their own way, rather than telling them how to do it, they will start letting you solve problems in your own way.
- If you give others factual descriptions of what bothers you, rather than blaming them, they will respect you more and be a great deal less defensive.

The key is to take action. Look for opportunities to cooperate. With a proactive attitude of supporting others, you will seldom experience a shortage of support from others.

Make a list of five people with whom you feel some rapport. Make contact with them. Take them to coffee or lunch. Let them know how things are going in your life. Make an effort to empathize with their situations. If an opportunity to support them arises, choose to help. You don't have to give yourself away to the point of exhaustion. Just commit to some small, but helpful thing. Keep your commitment.

One caution, though. Many of us suffer from the tendency to give too much. We stumble from one-sided relationship to one-sided relationship, wondering why this "give more than you get" thing isn't working. The solution to this is to learn to be clear about boundaries—learn to say "No." The next time you find yourself in what feels like a lop-sided relationship, ask yourself if the support you offer is truly serving your long-term goals. If it isn't, extricate yourself as quickly and politely as possible. To help you remember this point we've thought up this little aphorism: "Give more than you get, but not more than you've got!"

HANDLING EMERGENCY EMOTIONAL NEEDS

Sometimes an emotional crisis, either in your business or your personal life, can be so critical that it needs special attention. Forming an ad hoc emergency support group, which we call the personal intervention resource group, or PIRG, can provide just the kind of short-term support that you need to meet these crises. The PIRG is designed to nurture and aid individual efforts with the help of friends and associates.

The PIRG appears when you need it and requires no maintenance when it is not in use. You call it together to meet a particular need and disband it when that need has been met. In fact, the PIRG doesn't work well if you try to make it an ongoing thing.

In addition, unlike a support group, the PIRG has a binding, two-way nature. If you call your friends together to help you manage a personal crisis, it means you are going to take seriously what they tell you to do, and it also means that they have a responsibility to give you their absolute best.

When Should You Use a PIRG?

A PIRG can be especially helpful in getting through two difficult life situations that occur more and more frequently today: personal transitions (career change, divorce, life-threatening disease, and so on) and business crises. Whatever the situation that moves you to call a PIRG, be sure you are ready to accept your friends' advice and to act on it.

Phillip, for example, was encountering clear-cut cases of theft and fraud at work. He had pointed them out to his superiors, but they made it clear they wanted him to look the other way. He didn't know what to do. His integrity required him to stick with this problem until it was corrected, but if he did, he stood a good chance of losing his job and creating a public scandal. His PIRG supported him in the best possible way. They told him to resign and then tell all that he knew to the proper authorities. Without the support of his friends and their confirmation of his values, taking this course would have been much more difficult. And his friends knew that in making that recommendation, they would also have to be there for Phillip afterwards when he was trying to continue his career on some other path.

PIRGs can also be useful for less drastic life issues. Nan was having trouble controlling her spending habits. She met monthly with a group of friends to share business financial statements, and this helped her see where her money was going. Later, because she was still having difficulties with impulse buying and spending money in response to stress, she started a PIRG. She got members of her PIRG to form a two-person committee to act as her money governor. Whenever she felt the need to spend more than $50, she agreed to call these two friends. Surprisingly, she never needed to call them at all. Just knowing they were there allowed her to control her spending.

Whom Should You Invite?

The membership of your PIRG is crucial. It is important that the friends you pick have similar enough values to arrive at a consensus. Ralph invited six close friends who turned out to be incompatible. Because they had conflicting values, they couldn't agree on an appropriate action for him to take. This left Ralph without the help he needed.

How Big Should It Be?

We've seen PIRGs ranging in size from one to ten. The size that works best is about four to six. More than that requires someone to act as a group facilitator to make sure that everyone gets heard and to keep track of the time. With four to six, members of the group tend to take care to hear each other, each taking responsibility to see that something comes of the meeting in the time allotted.

How Long Should It Last?

For your PIRG to work most effectively, you do not want it to be a burden on your friends. But you do want them to come up with recommendations that will be meaningful to you. If they spend less than an hour, you'll probably question the usefulness of their advice. On the other hand, we've heard many reports that nothing gets accomplished after the first two hours of a meeting. You are left with the conclusion that a PIRG should last somewhere between one and two hours.

What Structure Should You Use?

Once everybody is gathered together and ready to work on the problem, it is up to you to present the issues clearly. Make sure you provide enough background material for your advisors to understand the situation. Ask if they need more information. Make sure they understand what you want of them. Then leave. Go for a walk. Go make some phone calls, do anything, just so you let the group have time alone to speak frankly about what to recommend.

Return at the appointed hour and make a written list of the recommendations. Ask questions if anything recommended is not clear. Set a date for a follow-up meeting at which you can report your progress. Then go out and do your best to implement their advice.

What Should You Do if Your PIRG Doesn't Produce the Kind of Advice You Had Hoped For?

Question yourself deeply about your willingness to listen. If you're sure you are open to receiving advice from your friends, then look closer at who you asked to be in the group. But first, reexamine the way you presented the problem. Were your friends underinformed? Did you make it clear what you wanted from them?

If you do not feel you can follow their advice, thank them for their efforts. Think it over for a few days, and then give it a try anyway. If you find it simply isn't working for you, schedule a new meeting to discuss your doubts and clear up the difficulties.

If it seems that you made a mistake in your choice of PIRG members, think about it for a few days, then start over with a new group.

Once you master clarity and the art of choosing the right people, you will find the PIRG to be an indispensable tool for work on life transitions and crises. If you decide to try setting up your own personal intervention resource group, let us know about your successes, or your difficulties.

TAKING TIME OFF

Taking time off is not only a wonderful idea, it is also good business strategy. It not only lets you recharge, but also offers the chance to review your vision, purpose, and goals and return to work with a renewed commitment. Every one-person business should build four kinds of time off into its calendar: energizing time, no-agenda time, relationship time, and vacations.

Energizing Time

Human beings are not by nature meant to spend eight hours every day doing the same thing. To work at your maximum effectiveness it helps to break the day up into several short segments of no more than two or three hours and to separate them by doing something energizing. This could be a quick walk around the block, some stretching exercises, or a body practice like tai chi or chi kung. Whatever it is, the important point is to do it several times throughout the day so that you can return to your routine refreshed and alert.

No-Agenda Time

What we call no-agenda time also has a magical, rejuvenating effect. With no-agenda time, you set aside part of a day, a whole day, or several days, and when you enter that time, you have one simple rule: It doesn't matter what you do as long as it wasn't planned.

Claude sets aside every day ending in zero as a no-agenda day. On the tenth, twentieth, and thirtieth of each month he makes no appointments, not even appointments with himself. He gets up at his regular time, but instead of rushing out the door to his first meeting or sitting down at the computer, he enjoys a leisurely breakfast and over coffee decides what he would like to do most that day. Because he enjoys his work very much, it is inevitable that sometimes he will choose to work. But he may also go to the beach, or drop in on friends, go shopping for new clothes, or do whatever else meets his fancy. A useful effect of no-agenda time is the perspective it gives you on how you feel about the rest of your time. If you wake up thinking that you really should do that report or box up those ceramic mugs that have to go out, and the overriding emotion is one of resentment, this is a warning signal you should pay attention to. Maybe you only need a vacation, but you might also need to reexamine your long-range goals.

Relationship Time

If you don't tend to your primary relationships, if you don't practice the behavior that creates friendship, if you spend no time on community building—well, you can guess the eventual results: no primary relationships, no friendships, no community. The relationships of love, friendship, and community are the foundation of your support. So be sure to plan time for them.

Vacations

Vacations are a longer version of time off. They are among the most effective contributors to emotional stability. As tension and stress accumulate over time, a vacation that offers a complete change of setting and freedom from responsibilities can alleviate many problems. Afterwards you can return to your business with a fresh perspective, full of vim and vigor.

The function of a vacation is clear from the Latin roots of the word *vacatio*, meaning to be free, to be empty. Yet the most common vacation, spent at or near ones home, is also the worst possible one for building emotional stability. We call it "taking a bath with your clothes on." This is because you will not stop thinking about work or being stimulated by it unless you are well away from it.

Many people won't take vacations because their identity is so tied to their work that they can't imagine themselves without it. Ralph, a real estate financier and workaholic, is a good example of this. Every time he plans a vacation, something comes up at work that forces him to cancel. His identity is too weak for him to feel comfortable on a vacation, so work always takes precedence. He isn't alone; many people who appear to be wrapped up in their jobs are really just uncomfortable on their own.

Admittedly, during the first few years of starting a business there is often too much work to do and too little revenue. It may not be possible to take a vacation during this time. But the main reason one-person proprietors give for not taking vacations is that there is no way to deal with the business that comes in while they are gone. They fear that their business's momentum will be lost and that customers will begin to view them as unreliable. There are two answers to this: One is to create and use backup support, which we talk about in Chapter 11. Another is to plan something to inject new life into your business upon returning, such as the kind of marketing events or community parties that we talk about in Chapter 9.

To take a real vacation, get far away from your work geographically—into a different climate, different air, and a different colored sky. Get far away in time as well. Taking four days off to rest is a good idea, but don't call it a vacation. Your mind takes that long to stop thinking about important issues. Two weeks may be an emotional minimum; much shorter than that may not be worthwhile. In fact, too short a vacation may make matters worse if you return without the emotional renewal needed to handle the work that accumulated in your absence. Consider that it takes at least three days to let go of your worries and three more to prepare to return to the work world. So if you take only one week off, you will get only one day of real vacation.

Lastly, don't plan a vacation that is more work than what you left behind. Even if the work is different, it shouldn't be without relaxation. Property managers

Ted Rabinowitsh and Diane Stuart have a prescription that works well with their type of business. "We work on a project until it gets done, starting early and ending late. But when we go on vacation, we usually go for two or three months."

Musician Alicia Bay Laurel schedules her vacations for her business's slow period, in May and September. "Being an entertainer in Hawaii, I'm always at work when other people are vacationing or playing. During some periods there are hardly any tourists, so sometimes I'll plan to travel off the island then and just cancel whatever work might come up, because that's when I'll take the smallest amount of loss. I have friends who live all over the country and I don't get to see them all that often, so every couple of years I like to take a month or two off and go visit them."

These three elements—change of geography, enough time, and a change of pace—are each an important part of emotional renewal. If you have never taken a vacation that involved a change of geography, at least two weeks off, and a change of pace, try it. It is hard to appreciate without having experienced it once.

ACTIVE HEALTH PRACTICES

Learning more about how to take care of your health is a major weapon against disease and emotional turbulence. Many people's first reaction to pain is to go straight to a doctor to have the pain removed. We recommend that you pause for a moment and ask yourself a few questions: Where did this pain come from? What is going on emotionally? What have I done or eaten recently? What are the strategies that I have used in the past to handle this kind of problem? In this way you will be actively taking responsibility for your own health. The answers will tell you whether it is really necessary to go to a doctor. Moreover, taking control of the healing process will raise your self-esteem, again contributing to emotional stability. In taking charge of your health, exercise and diet are two of the most important factors in helping to maintain emotional stability.

Exercise

The specific form of exercise you engage in is less important than doing it on a regular basis. You need not become a marathon runner or spend two hours a day in the gym doing aerobics or weight-lifting. Something as simple as a brisk fifteen-minute walk around the block every day can be an effective way to help maintain your emotional stability. If you wish to be more physically fit, the American College of Sports Medicine recommends from fifteen to sixty minutes of walking, jogging, cycling, or swimming three to five times per week.

At the very least, take breaks and go for a walk. Part of the benefit comes from the increased circulation and exposure to sunlight. But also important is the regularity. Regularity is a very effective tool. It creates a kind of rhythm that gives you a sense of stability, even in the midst of the periodic chaos that can arise in successful businesses. Regular physical activity is also one of your best investments for health in old age.

Dr. Tom Ferguson works out in the late afternoon or early evening. "Usually I go walking, and I have an exercise bike. Depending on the weather or if it's dark or not will decide what I do. In good weather I like to go walking outside or occasionally ride a real bike. My exercise bike is in a room where I have a TV and a tape player with earphones. I like to listen to tape-recorded books while I exercise. I also find it very useful to go for a walk in the evening by myself. Sometimes I really get some great ideas.

"I think one of the most important things you can do for your health is the work you really love. I walked away from a guaranteed six-figure income in medicine to be a penniless writer. And I have not regretted it once. I imagine the people reading your book would have a sense of that and that it would be one of the reasons they are interested in being a one-person business. I urge you to encourage them to do it. It's simple: If you can tap into something you're really interested in and set up your life to work in a way you really like to work, it's probably one of the best things you could do for your health. My college roommate and I always used to say that we were going to find work that was play. Well, this is it for me."

Diet

Diet goes hand in glove with regular physical activity. As with exercise, eating meals at regular times is almost as important as what you eat. Having established meal regularity, you can go on to review the nutritional content of your diet. You can also promote stability by taking the time to prepare your own food. Careful preparation of meals requires planning and a different pace from that required for managing your business. It can be a rejuvenating experience to pause for an hour to prepare a meal with care and then eat it—much more so than rushing out to a restaurant or fast-food outlet. Part of the reason for being in business for yourself is to be able to set and enjoy your own pace. So think twice about letting the urgency of your business force you to eat out, or gulp down a quick meal before rushing back to the fray. Don't just take our word for it. Spend one week cooking all your own meals at home, with planning and forethought. See if it doesn't provide the emotionally stabilizing effect we describe, not to mention the soothing effect it will have on your digestive system.

Insurance

The issue of insurance is so complicated it would require an entire book of its own to explain it adequately. We can only cover the principles behind insurance here and make some recommendations about how a one-person business might best think about insurance for the long run.

Insurance is a cooperative device for sharing risks, which assures a sum of money to meet the uncertain losses resulting from damage to, or destruction of, life or property. Insurance transfers the risks of many persons to an insurance company. This is accomplished by means of a contract between the company (the insurer) and the individual (the insured). In the contract, the company promises to pay a stated sum of money if and when the event insured against occurs. The money may be paid to the insured or to persons designated by the insured (the beneficiaries). In the contract the insured, or someone who has an insurable interest, agrees to pay periodically a sum of money (the premium) to the insurance company.

There are many types of insurance: property, accident, health, life, liability, disability, workers compensation, and so forth. Social Security is a type of insurance too. But if you exercise and eat regularly and sensibly, you will probably find yourself in good health, both physically and emotionally. If so, you may never need to make a claim on an insurance policy of any kind.

It is likely, therefore, that you will buy insurance almost entirely because it increases your emotional stability by decreasing your worry about what to do if you get sick, are in an accident or experience damage or loss of some kind. You will evaluate all forms of insurance from the point of view of "in the unlikely event." Their main value is that you will worry less about how you would cope with a disaster or untoward event. And when you are healthy you can reduce the cost of health insurance premiums by buying policies with large deductible.

CONCERNS ABOUT OLD AGE

People have many reasons for being afraid of old age, and these worries affect emotional stability. The most common fears are of physical disabilities and infirmities, being a financial burden to family and friends, and being overly dependent on others for getting around.

Most people respond to these fears by saving as much money as possible. As a one-person-business owner, you may be able to take an approach that is not so dependent on savings, and the need to save money for old age might be satisfied with a more modest amount.

Calculating the savings needed to generate a desired retirement income is simple. At age sixty-five an annuity that will pay you $250 a month for the rest of your life costs $30,000. At $40 per month it would take thirty years to save this much, including five percent interest compounded monthly. So you would have to begin by age thirty-five, or else increase your monthly savings accordingly. If you want more than $250 per month when you retire, you will have to save proportionally more.

People who own businesses need less savings for two reasons. First, if your business can be sold, and most can, the best savings plan would be to invest in the business. Second, many people view retirement as an escape from their job. But, if you are already doing what you love, what is there to escape from?

The main question you should have about investing in your own business is not whether the investment will yield a high enough return, but whether you will ever get your capital back. In other words, can you someday sell your business for a good price? Although one-person businesses as we know them today are a new phenomenon, in traditional fields such as dentistry, medicine, insurance, law, and accounting, it has long been easy to sell a good practice. The keys to getting a good price are all the points made in this book: loyal clients, good service, superb record-keeping, good backup for overflow work and vacations, and a diversified customer base. So if you put your money into making your business better in these ways, you'll be likely to get your capital back in the future.

Are a one-person-business owner's concerns about old age the same as those of a salaried worker? No! A salaried person usually has no chance to earn a few extra dollars, no chance to earn money in new ways in changing times, and very little control over the cost of living. A salaried person is often uneasy at the prospect of life without a steady income. Except for occasional dabbling in real estate, most salaried people have no fallback position if inflation hits or the unexpected happens.

You, on the other hand, have the most useful of all human skills—the ability to make money with your own resources. If you can do it now, you can do it until infirmity sets in. So you probably have much longer to save for "retirement." And for you, "retirement" will mean you've reached the point in your life where you can no longer care for yourself and must hire help.

Your skills as a sole proprietor will get better the longer you are in business and the older you get. Your earning power will steadily increase. So, with good health and careful planning, you can create a different pattern of saving: one that requires you to start out saving little and gradually increase your savings rate as you become better at your business.

The most important planning you can do for old age is thus to continue to improve your business skills, diversify your business into new directions as times change, and be flexible in changing markets.

On the whole, the idea of retirement should probably seem ridiculous to you. Salaried people retire to do the things they have always dreamed of: hobbies, reading, treasure hunting, leisure, travel, or starting a business. But you are already doing what you dream of. That is what your business is about. And when your dreams change, you can change your business. So retirement hasn't the same meaning for you.

Robert Kourik, the author of several books, including the classic *Designing and Maintaining Your Edible Landscape Naturally* (Santa Rosa, Calif.: Metamorphic Press, 1986) and countless articles about environmentally sound horticulture believes, "You can't find an ecological model for a retirement plan. Expect to work until you die. Retirement is an unnatural construct of an environmentally unsound society and has no historical basis. The baby boom can't make enough babies to support itself. I haven't thought about it enough, but if you look around, what animal says,

'Okay, I'm a bobcat. I've lived eight years so I should just take it easy for the next three years and have somebody bring me my dead rabbits.' Fat chance! Dead bob-cat!"

Instead of talking about retirement, people who have their own businesses talk about learning new skills and practicing them in new parts of the world, trying out business ideas that have been on the back burner, or adding some social action to their work that is important to them.

Eileen Mulligan, landscape gardener, knows she won't be able to continue in this line of work when she's old. "I own my own home, which is important, and I also have two children who I put a lot of juice into. If they don't take care of me when I'm an old lady, I'll come after them. I know how to grow my own food. I'm strong and healthy."

Alicia Bay Laurel, musician, also thinks of doing something different in her old age. "The other things that I have done to make a living are more appropriate for that time of my life. I write and paint and draw. I think that in old age I will be more reclusive and will spend a lot more time doing those things. I look forward to that. I look now at my art and writing projects and wonder why I don't get around to them. I know it's because I have this fire inside to get out there and play music. So when that fire is spent, which I assume will be sometime in my fifties, then I'll be able to turn my attention to these other things that have been on the back burner."

Ted Rabinowitsh, property manager, says, "What we're doing is better than anything else because we're creating something that can supply us income. I mean you build up equity so you can sell properties. We don't qualify for Social Security, Medicare, pensions, or anything, so it's completely up to us. Now we have Blue Shield, with a real high deductible." For Diane Stuart, Ted's partner, "Retirement is not a goal. I can't imagine not working on something at any given time."

Norman Prince, photographer, feels the same. "I believe that as long as I am not disabled, I will continue working as a photographer, a teacher, and a consultant, and I'll keep marketing my stock photos for the rest of my life. I don't intend to stop. I like a lot of my work, and I like to think that part of my future income will come from resale of my pictures for use in new editions, new books, etc. Also from future sales of pictures from my stock files through subcontractor agencies in this country and overseas. Since I've never really worked a regular job, I don't have any of the advantages of it, but I don't have any of the disadvantages either—like compulsory retirement or being forced out of business or losing my job because the company is moving or shutting down."

Social Security

Automatic saving occurs on your behalf when you pay your Social Security tax. The amount you will receive depends primarily on your earnings from age fifty to sixty-five. As of 1987, Social Security pays $230 a month based on average annual net earnings of $3,600. For the next $15,000 earned, you would get $410, and so on.

Although the limit is now around $600 a month for one person, all the proportions will increase steadily when adjusted for future inflation. In the year 2011, however, the retirement age will be increased to sixty-six, and twenty years later to sixty-seven.

Most people are eligible for Medicare coverage even if they paid into Social Security for only one three-month quarter in their lives. Through Social Security, nearly everyone is covered for major medical expenses with a plan that has a 20 percent deductible. Two drawbacks to Medicare are that it can only be used for traditional forms of medicine, which doesn't include many holistic practices, and it won't cover extraordinary needs such as traveling long distances to see a particular specialist.

On a positive note, medical care has been changing rapidly and is increasingly considered a fundamental human right in much of the world. This means that with every passing day it is more likely that the quality of medical care for the aged will improve and be more readily available. The lag between the introduction of new medical practices and their widespread availability is only a few years. So it is only a matter of time before today's expensive "special" treatments become tomorrow's affordable standard care.

Keoghs, IRAs, and SEP IRAs

A sole proprietor can set money aside under a Keogh Plan, an IRA, or a SEP IRA. These funds are tax deductible until you draw on the account. You could well pay lower taxes the last few years before you retire, by making your earnings taper off, putting yourself in a lower tax bracket. Any financial institution, such as a bank, an insurance company, or a stockbroker, can help you set up one of these plans. The amount you can set aside is substantial.

RESOURCES

Anderson, Nancy. *Work With Passion: How to Do What You Love for a Living*. New York: Caroll & Graff, 1986.

Barnett, Frank and Sharan. *Working Together: Entrepreneurial Couples*. Berkeley: Ten Speed Press, 1988.

Brill, Jack A., and Alan Reder. *Investing from the Heart: The Guide to Socially Responsible Investments and Money Management*. New York: Crown, 1992.

Jaffe, Dennis T., and Cynthia D. Scott. *From Burnout to Balance*. New York: McGraw-Hill, 1984; out of print.

Phillips, Michael, and Catherine Campbell. *Simple Living Investments: for True Security and Adventure in Old Age*. San Francisco: Clear Glass, 1988.

Reynolds, David K. *Constructive Living*. Honolulu: University of Hawaii Press, 1984.

Sher, Barbara, and Annie Gottlieb. *Teamworks: Building Support Groups that Guarantee Success*. New York: Warner, 1991.

———. *Wishcraft: How to Get What You Really Want*. New York: Ballantine, 1986.

Siegelman, Ellen Y. *Personal Risk: Mastering Change in Love and Work*. New York: Harper & Row, 1983; out of print.

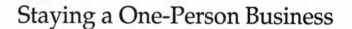

11

Staying a One-Person Business

As a one-person business you may encounter such problems as having more business than you can handle, getting sick, or needing a vacation. Because you are almost certain to find yourself in at least one of these circumstances, it is essential to understand the need for backup, the perils of managing others, the importance of good suppliers, the value of client contracts, and how to stay current in your field.

THE NEED FOR BACKUP

Occasionally, you just won't be able to do all your work. You'll face a too tight deadline, get sick or emotionally overloaded, want to take a vacation, or have to deal with a family emergency. At such times you are going to need backup. Having a backup system already in place will help you weather these challenges.

There are two ways to plan for *backup* before you need it. One is to have a good referral system, the other is to have your office systems in such good order that someone else could easily run your business while you are away. If you have taken the advice and words of wisdom offered in Chapters 5, 6, 7, and 8, your business is probably so well organized that any competent person could fill in for you.

Referrals

Referring work to others can be a touchy subject for a one-person business. Insecurity creeps in. What if your client prefers the person you recommend and wants to switch? Or, worse, what if your backup does a bad job? Not only might you lose the client, but word could get around that you are not very professional.

You can do little about losing a client except presume that you will also inherit clients from others. Console yourself with the thought that the change of clients would eventually have happened anyway if the match with your substitute was really more appropriate. As in any relationship, holding on isn't worth the energy if the other person isn't interested.

Most of the businesses we have worked with find that better than 80 percent of the clients they refer elsewhere in emergencies or peak periods return to them. Given this figure and considering that you might lose clients anyway if you don't make referrals when you can't handle the work, you might as well take the plunge. With experience will come the confidence and knowledge that you really are the best choice for certain clients.

Trisha, the gift store operator, can turn to her husband for backup. "He knows the business, and I keep everything up to date. I also have a friend who has worked for me a few times who could help in an emergency. My store is like a big baby to me, and the first time I had my friend mind it, I would pop in all the time to make sure everything was all right. Now I have confidence that she could cover for me if I needed her."

Book designer Clifford Burke finds that he increasingly needs to do referrals. "There was a time when I hated to refer anybody to anyone. I wanted to do everything! Now there are lots of things that I don't *want* to do. I'm realizing that I need a good referral list and I will have to go out and build one. If somebody comes to me for something that I can do and I don't have the time, finding somebody else that can do what I can is hard. Finding somebody who can do what I can't do isn't so hard. How do you find another me?"

In computer and training consultant Bill Dale's business, other team members can take his place. "They have already done so on one occasion so that I could represent my old school in a golf tournament. My criteria for choosing other consultants to work with are that I must have firsthand knowledge of their work, they must work to a high standard, they must understand what I expect from them, and they must be capable of working with minimal supervision."

"This office works by a process that's simple and clear," states Paul Terry, small-business advisor. "If someone had the skills to do business consulting, had values and philosophies similar to mine, and could use a computer, they would find it a fairly straightforward job to answer the phone, see clients, and generate information and reports. I know two or three people who could come in and do that."

For unusual businesses, finding a substitute is obviously harder. Nevertheless, it is important to have a list of back-up people ready in advance. Just as you appreciate it when a retail business tells you where to buy something that they don't have, so your clients will appreciate your concern for their needs.

Subcontractors

In the appendix on start-up and legal matters we talk about who is and who is not an independent contractor. This is a matter of law and ruling by the IRS. Here we are going to talk about working with other people from a completely different perspective. So don't get the words "subcontractor" and "independent contractor" mixed up. You may find yourself paying some subcontractors as employees because that may be what the law requires. You should still heed the advice we are about to give.

Subcontracting is an agreement in which you promise to pay someone else for services to you or on your behalf, or for manufacturing a product or parts of a product for you. The promise can be in writing or it can be verbal. In business it is often verbal.

When you offer a high school student $10 to fold and stuff a pile of envelopes, you're hiring a subcontractor. When you leave a stack of pages overnight at a copy center and ask for one hundred copies each, you're hiring a subcontractor. And if you are a small publisher who hires a book distributor to fill your bookstore orders, you're hiring a subcontractor.

The first two agreements are probably verbal, the last almost certainly written. All three are bona fide contracts. And even with simple examples like these, the key to making them work is to be absolutely clear about what each party expects of the other.

The Importance of Clear Agreements

Business has a long history of conflict, antagonism, and mutual distrust among participants. Even if you are not part of this picture, it still needs to be faced. Clear agreements offer the best way of avoiding unpleasantness and having open, honest relations with people. And the best way to keep the agreements clear over time is to write them down. Some people think that a written agreement is to protect against untrustworthy subcontractors. This couldn't be further from the truth. *You shouldn't do business with someone you can't trust.*

Drafting a written agreement reminds you to think of *all* the dimensions of the agreement, be it a single transaction or an ongoing relationship, and to make sure that both parties genuinely understand what is expected. Most of all, a well-written agreement, complete with a mediation clause, provides a simple, unemotional remedy for the countless little things that might go wrong.

A written agreement is a contract and as such should always contain certain basic elements. The most important part of any contract is the mediation or arbitration clause. We recommend including a list of friends and associates who have agreed to participate as mediators or arbitrators should you have a disagreement. This is effective because by showing the contract to several people in your community, you have made your agreement public. Making the agreement public has two advantages: (1) you will make sure that it is a good agreement before you sign it; and (2) you will be less likely to succumb to the all-too-human tendency to remember past agreements in your favor. Of the many agreements we have seen that were submitted to potential mediators before they were signed, not one has gone to mediation after it took effect.

The next most important part of an agreement is a statement of the personal reasons for engaging in the agreement. Don't list the profit motive here. Rather, list why you enjoy working together, the values you share, the results you each and both want to achieve, and so forth. This part of an agreement is important because it will remind you later of the goodwill you felt towards each other at the time and why you entered into the agreement in the first place.

The other parts of an agreement are fairly standard and include explanations of how things will be done, how much money people will get, and how many of what will be delivered by when.

When to Use Subcontractors

Robert Kourik's experience with subcontractors is a good example of the circumstances under which this practice might be appropriate. "I've learned since my experience with employees to hire subcontractors. I now have a shipper eight hours a week total who is a subcontractor. I believe it's cost-effective to subcontract what you have no desire or aptitude for, within a reasonable budget. For example, I hate balancing a checkbook. I pay for six to ten hours a month for a skilled bookkeeper to reconcile the checkbook, to enter all the income and expenses into the computer and to explain what it all means to me. Then I do the business projections. I also use a CPA at the end of the year because even a good bookkeeper doesn't have enough skills for the fact that I have two different limited partnerships, a sole proprietorship, and my own personal business. I need someone who knows a lot about the tax code. But no bookkeeper or shipper or CPA can find new markets for my services or write any of my books or articles. So that's how I spend my time."

The two major reasons for using subcontractors are *overflow* and *project work*.

Overflow Work   Subcontractors come in handy when you have more work than you can do, or when you begin to get clients whom you would rather pass on. If you pass on work without putting yourself in a position to supervise or review it, it

Figure 11.1 Sample Subcontractor Agreement

ARTICLES OF AGREEMENT

This agreement is entered into and effective as of September 15, 1995, by Claude Whitmyer and Gail Grimes. Claude and Gail wish to enter into an independent contractor relationship as follows:

PERSONAL

Claude: I am presently developing contract technical writing as a part of my consulting practice. I wish to engage in this kind of work with those who are already experienced and can lead me through it in a mentoring capacity. Gail is a top-notch motivational writer in the fund-raising arena, so I am anxious to work with her as much as possible in order to learn this type of writing.

Gail: My consulting practice is growing and I need more independent contractors who can create the same caliber work as I provide for my clients on an everyday basis. I know that with a minimum of instruction and feedback that Claude can do this kind of work. I look forward to developing an ongoing subcontractor relationship with him.

HOW IT WORKS

Working on a project-by-project basis, Claude will do contract writing for Gail. Gail and Claude will draft an agreement before the onset of each project covering goals, objectives and deliverables, time schedule, and any particulars specific to the project. Gail and Claude will review ongoing work every thirty days, at which time Gail will give a verbal evaluation of Claude's work. Changes may be made at any time by mutual consent. This agreement shall continue for ninety days. Either party may terminate this agreement with thirty days notice to the other, in writing.

Payment will be handled in the following way: $50.00 per hour unless otherwise agreed.

GOALS AND EXPECTATIONS

Claude: My goal is to provide a quality first-draft writing product, while learning to improve my technical skills in the arena of motivational writing for fund-raising. In the interest of this goal, I would like to receive more detailed feedback about my work product than might ordinarily be extended to a subcontractor.

I expect Gail to clearly communicate assignments and deadlines. I will set my own work schedule and work in my own office space, in order to complete the assignments and meet Gail's deadlines. Gail will be responsible for all client contact, and will provide me with enough background information to do the job. She will be available by phone during the writing process to answer questions and provide client contact should I need it.

Gail: For each project, I expect Claude to study the background material I provide and write a first draft as I specify. Claude will provide me with a typewritten or computer-printed copy of his work, as well as an electronic copy on media and in a format that I can use with my personal computer and word-processing package.

Claude will make no effort to contact my clients directly, as a part of this work, and he will relinquish any public recognition of the work product done. This is "work for hire," and ownership of the work product is entirely mine.

MEDIATION

If we disagree on any matter regarding the terms of this relationship we will each choose one person from the following list, or any other person we wish, to choose a third person and mediate our disagreement. The recommendation of this team of three shall be binding.

Claude Whitmyer	Gail Grimes

Date	Date

MEDIATORS

Paul Terry
Salli Rasberry
Becky Jaggers
Gwen Vollan-Johnson

is best to put the subcontractor in direct contact with the client and take a referral fee, if appropriate.

Book designer Clifford Burke describes the most sensible approach to using a subcontractor when you don't want the work for yourself. "I try to find a subcontractor and hire him or her out through the person who will actually be paying him. So I don't take a cut. I prefer not to handle other people's money. If you want to make money off other people's money, then you have to handle it in order to strip a little away as it goes by."

Landscape gardener Eileen Mulligan agrees. "I subcontract out if something comes up that I'm not really good at. I'll find a person to do it and then put them in direct contact with the client. I prefer for them to relate directly rather than for me to be in the middle."

In some overflow situations, however, you may want to maintain control of the work, perhaps even asking your subcontractor to bill or submit sales invoices through you. In these cases you should review the work or products for quality and completeness as the project proceeds. Remember to allow time for the reviews and for any necessary corrections so that you can keep your promise to meet the client's needs by the deadline date.

Project Work   Project work can be any service or product venture that has many parts to it. You hire subcontractors for project work when you want people with special expertise to complete some of the parts. If you are a small book publisher, you might hire one person to design your book layouts and covers, another to do all your typesetting, and another to do the printing and bindery work. If you are a market researcher, you might contract with a recruitment agency to locate your subjects, a special facility to provide space for holding your focus-groups, independent focus group moderators to lead the groups, and a videographer to tape the sessions. All of these are examples of project work, as are any of the many kinds of contracting such as landscape, building, plumbing, electrical, and so on.

Written contracts are especially useful for project work because they help explain exactly what you need. When a need reoccurs, you can review the previous agreement, and it will help you judge what worked and what didn't.

Avoid becoming too dependent on one person or one business to meet your subcontracting needs. If that person or business unexpectedly has a problem, you will have one too. For example, suppose you have been using the same mail-order fulfillment house to handle your address list and the mailing of your product for several years. A week before your next big mailing must go out, you find out that the owner is out of town, the operation is in chaos, and nobody knows where your client list is. This could be a big problem. The best safeguard against sudden changes in the quality or availability of work from subcontractors is to try alternative helpers from time to time and to rotate your work among the good ones.

Some Simple Rules for Subcontracting

1. When possible, use a written contract. Many people feel uncomfortable about written contracts. They fear that insisting on a written contract indicates a lack of trust. As we said earlier, a written contract has nothing to do with trust. It would be absurd to use a subcontractor you didn't completely trust, whether you had a written contract or not. A contract won't make an untrustworthy person be trustworthy. In the end, you would be left either with a court battle or a feeling of great disappointment.

The purpose of a written contract is to make as clear as possible what you want and what the subcontractor is expected to do. By clarifying all aspects of the work, you will avoid errors, confusion, forgetfulness, and recriminations, even among friends. (See the Nolo Press books *The Legal Guide for Starting and Running a Small Business* and *Simple Contracts for Personal Use*, which together have sample forms for almost every business arrangement imaginable.)

2. When dealing with a written contract, always read it. And read it carefully enough to spot anything that could go wrong.

3. Be prepared to routinely pay more to your subcontractors for the extra attention that you need as a one-person business: faster service, emergency or overtime work, or priority.

4. Always pay promptly. Never dawdle in paying your supplier and subcontractor invoices if you want to continue to get the best from them.

5. Always reward good work, not just with pay, but with imagination, personal concern, and appreciation. When a printer does a flier for you faster than you expected, or prints 20 percent extra as a gesture of goodwill, it is common to just say thanks and take it for granted. But for a one-person business, any extra service needs to be recognized and rewarded, even when it's not so important to you at the moment.

6. Don't ask for exclusivity. Many businesspeople are very possessive about their work. Exclusivity is usually aimed at keeping other businesses from taking away your clients, or at keeping the competition from finding out your special way of doing things. This looks logical on the surface, but the effect is just the opposite in almost every instance. You lose touch with your market, and sooner or later you lose clients.

THE PERILS OF MANAGING OTHERS

Managing other people adds a significant complication to a business, making it much more difficult to run. Even one additional person means a major increase in complexity. It changes you from being your own boss into being a manager, which is an additional skill that you may not have. Once you become a manager, you will have the same state of mind whether you manage one person or five. Your freedom of movement and financial flexibility can be severely restricted.

Alexandra Hart started Folkwear Patterns with two other people. "I liked the creative process of working with others. In the course of a year, however, we went from a very low capitalized business to a concern with an international product. Our product was in *People* magazine and *Women's Wear Daily*. Letters came in from all over the world. At one point we had thirty employees. Near the end I could no longer do any creative and design work; instead I was a businesswoman responsible for all these other people." Alexandra decided to become a one-person desktop publisher, which allows her to use her impressive talent as a designer without the burdens of a larger business.

Kate Bishop's story is more complicated. "When I was manufacturing I had nine employees. When I realized it wasn't working very well for me financially—everybody was making a living except me—I just laid everybody off. Then people started calling me up looking for dresses they hadn't seen in the stores lately. I would make appointments to see them and eventually these commissions turned into my custom business. I'm doing a lot better now by myself.

"Employees have to be paid once a week, which is a headache. I sold my goods on net thirty day terms. People usually paid me in sixty days, if I was lucky, and sometimes not at all. So there was always a cash flow problem. The financial statements looked good, but there was never enough money. I always paid my employees, but sometimes that meant I didn't get my draw. It was always a source of anxiety.

"For each employee there is waste. With two employees there is twice as much. Once I started taking on more of the responsibility, I realized that some of our standard methods were geared to make a perfect product. But not necessarily economically. The people who developed the methods weren't paying the bills. I found I could cut an awful lot of corners. When I sat down at the sewing machine to produce a garment, one that took 3½ hours on the books actually took me two hours and forty-five minutes. I also found that I could get a lot more yardage out of a bolt of silk when I was cutting it myself because I'm the one paying for it. And instead of abandoning garments that had a mistake, I would just correct them. When I went through my scrap boxes after a year of working by myself, I found literally hundreds of garments worth of scraps!

"Because of all the federal regulations and employee taxes and benefits and all, if you eliminate employees you cut your overhead way down. When I had employees it took a lot of work just to keep them all busy. I had to plan and organize so that everybody could have something to do when they arrived at work. In order to get to a point where I could make money and pay my employees, I had to produce about $50,000 a month. This meant more employees, a bigger facility, bigger debts. I decided to get smaller, and it's worked out wonderfully for me."

Author Robert Kourik had fewer employees than Kate, but his experience was similar. "I had a lot of employees during the publication of my *Edible Landscape*. I employed one person four days a week for about three or four years. Near the end, it swelled to eight or nine employees. I got nothing but positive feedback from the people that worked for and with me, overall. I developed tremendous debts during this project." Kourik has since returned to being a one-person business. "When in doubt, stay a one-person business. There is no reason to have more than one person in your business unless you really want to go nuts. Somewhere between four and eight people is the minimum jump you have to make before you make anything extra yourself. As far as I can see, in a lot of businesses, when you have three employees you're making no more money than when you started and you have three times the potential for headaches."

Running a one-person business is a luxury that you shouldn't give up lightly. If you are ever tempted to hire an employee, it's important that you carefully consider the downside. With employees, you have to put a goodly amount of time into supervision and associated recordkeeping. Remember that the one-person business has the strategic advantage of lower overhead and no employees to manage— meaning it is easier to start and maintain your business. If you are on the verge of bringing in an employee to help with the business, remember the litany of ten reasons for not doing so in figure 11.2.

You should not conclude from the downside arguments in figure 11.2 that employees are never the right choice. But when the moment comes to decide if employees are the right next step, you must be prepared to give the extra effort it takes to make a business with employees work. You must be prepared to give up many of the advantages offered by the simple one-person business form, and you must have managerial skills.

Working with Part-Time People

One transition step you can make without fully committing to the life of an employer is to hire part-time people only when you really need them. There are two reasons you might do this. One is when the extra work that requires additional help occurs irregularly. The other is when you get the chance to use a part-time job to train someone to be a subcontractor.

When you aren't sure if the extra work load you're experiencing is permanent, it is hard to know how to respond. The most reasonable response to an unexpected increase is to work longer hours yourself trying to maintain the higher pace long enough to know whether or not it will be temporary. This situation is quite different from that of people who know they will have an extra seasonal load, say before

Fig. 11.2   Ten Reasons Not to Hire an Employee

1. Loss of emotional freedom. When you hire an employee, you add a whole new dimension to your own work. Now you must concern yourself with making sure that your employee's job is both interesting and meaningful. You may find yourself thinking about this dilemma late at night and into the wee morning hours.

2. Administrative responsibility. Not only must you concern yourself with creating an interesting job for your employee, you must also plan his or her work loads to maximize output and minimize cost. Usually, simple general instructions only work for the most mundane tasks. Giving good instructions for more complex tasks—the kind that would leave you free to work on other projects—requires careful thought. Which brings us back to reason number one.

3. Financial responsibility. The responsibility of regularly paying someone else to work for you can become a horrible burden. You must figure out how to maintain an even, stable work flow so that you can provide the steady flow of income needed to pay your employee. As a single person, you can roll with the fluctuations in work, perhaps even taking advantage of slow periods to take time off or do neglected self-development work. With an employee, you must make sure that regular income is there to make the regular paycheck.

4. Less time off. As pointed out in No. 3, gone are the days when you could use slow business periods to relax, take vacations, catch up on backlogged work, or learn new skills. You must now spend that time keeping enough work going to pay your employee, or supervising what your employee is doing. With an employee you may have to eat into savings, drum up more work than you would need just to support yourself, and live with the anxiety that doing this might cause you.

5. The delegating work blues. In theory, delegating sounds like a good thing. In practice, it is often more difficult than it sounds. When you give someone else work, you have to figure out how to measure whether the work is being performed completely and correctly. Because another person isn't you, and doesn't think or do things the way you do, you might experience a nagging feeling of doubt and anxiety creeping in as you start noticing little signs that your employee might be making mistakes or taking too much time.

6. Wasted time. Not only do you have to recruit an employee, you have to do the training too. If he or she leaves before a year has passed, the chances are pretty high that you will have wasted your time. The value of the time you spent getting a new employee to the point of productivity is almost always much higher than the added productivity you received from your employee in the first year.

7. You are on trial as a good example. To expect an employee to do good work, you have to set a good example by constantly working hard. This forces you to give up the greatest advantage of a one-person business: flexible time. If you decide to spend the morning reading back issues of trade journals or taking a walk in the park, what do you think the employee is going to conclude about working habits? With an employee, being able to goof off from time to time or to set your own schedule could become a thing of the past.

8. Wrong pace. From the first day of hiring an employee, you have to give up your own pace for the employee's pace. You can't expect the employee to come in at 5 A.M. just because that is when you are most productive. You must now schedule your work in a more normal way. Soon you will be asking yourself, "Didn't I start this business to escape the nine-to-five rat race?"

9. Quality control. If someone else works for you, you have to make sure that everything is right before a client sees it. This makes a lot more work but you can't afford not to do it. You must develop systems and procedures to assure that only the highest-quality work or product ever reaches your customers or clients.

10. Profits. The greatest profitability in business comes from maintaining a low overhead and keeping costs down. A highly talented one-person-business owner, working cooperatively with others as subcontractors, can handle large or complex jobs far more efficiently than a comparable number of employees. And have more fun earning much more money doing it.

Christmas, or New Year's, or at tax return time. They expect the increase and can prepare themselves and hire help if necessary.

Consider a refrigerator repairwoman who normally has three to five customers a day. Suddenly she finds herself dealing with six to eight, which keeps her working into the evenings and all day Saturday. She doesn't know whether this is a temporary increase in business or a real one that will continue because she is finally getting known. If this level of work continues for some time, she will know that she has to figure out an alternative. If the work does let up, and she goes back to three to five customers a day, she has worked hard and saved herself the agony of training and supervising another person for the extra business that has now evaporated. In addition, she doesn't have a payroll to maintain.

An increased work load that turns out to be permanent can be an important crossroads in a one-person business. You will be faced with having to make a few choices. One option is to turn customers away, either by referring those you don't want to someone else or by asking them to wait until you can help them. In some businesses people can wait, in other they can't and they will go elsewhere.

A second option is to become much more efficient so that you can handle the increase in business. This can be done in a wide range of ways, one of which is to make your management systems more effective, including your use of time. Another is to find ways for clients to do more of the work themselves so that you need do only the part that you are best at. For example, as we mentioned in Chapter 5, your incoming telephone tape for new and inquiring prospects can list five of the most common problems your clients have and explain how to handle them. This tactic can eliminate many wasted phone calls and meetings. Another possibility is to mail customers a checklist of the information you need in order to work more efficiently, before they come to see you. However, until you can determine whether the extra work is permanent—and whether you want it—you may decide to hire a part-time person to help out.

Temp Workers   The obvious and probably best source of temporary workers is from a temporary employment agency. Using an agency has three big advantages: First, there is no ambiguity in the employee's mind or in yours that the relationship is temporary, so there will be no problem when you no longer need the help. Second, you don't have to concern yourself with employee benefits (which are handled by the temporary agency). Third, you can get a well-qualified person without going through classified employment listings, personnel interviews, or long delays. If one temporary person doesn't meet your specifications, you can phone the agency and request someone else. Using a temporary employment agency has one other advantage. If the expense of hiring the temporary helper turns out to be more than $600, you won't have to file a 1099 form at the end of the year (as you would have if you had hired the employee directly). Because your helper works for the agency, the IRS won't question whether he or she is an independent contractor. Temporary employment agency personnel may be more expensive than people you hire on your own, but the extra cost is nearly always worth it to avoid the many problems associated with being an employer.

If there are no temporary employment agencies in your area or if we haven't convinced you to rely on them, at least be aware of the three risks you face by hiring a part-time employee: (1) You may become accustomed to having an employee, especially if the first person you hire is good. Then you will no longer enjoy the benefits of a one-person business. (2) During the period you have a part-time employee, you will have to act like an employer, which will take work time that you thought you were saving. You will need to do income tax withholding and tax filing on your temporary employee. If you hire an immigrant, you will have to comply with Immigration and Naturalization Service requirements, including filling out an I-9 form. (3) Part-time employees can rapidly come to depend on you and fool themselves into believing that the job is permanent. Then, when the work runs out, you have the miserable job of letting them go.

You can do two things to avoid the last problem. First, hire someone who can't possibly become a permanent employee: a teacher who is on vacation, a pregnant woman who intends to be a full-time mother, a neighbor's relative who is visiting for a short time, a student on summer vacation, or an airline employee with short stopovers in your town. Second, write an employment contract that clearly lays out the situation (see figure 11.3).

It is not enough to have employees simply sign such a contract. You must also make a point of meeting with them, as agreed in the contract, to review how much longer you will need them. This discipline is a courtesy to them and it also helps you keep uppermost in your mind that the job is temporary, created to give you time to figure out whether an increased volume of work is permanent or not.

Apprentices

If you can find someone who is well matched to you and interested in learning some of what you know, you can not only contribute a great deal to this person's life and the betterment of your community, but you can also send this person out into the world as a living representative of your business.

Hal Howard, a floor finisher, has trained dozens of apprentices in the last twenty years. His community regards him as a master at floor refinishing because of the high-quality work that his former students continue to do. As a result, instead of creating an army of competitors, he has created a large group of loyal supporters, and he has more work than he can handle. His former students get much of his overflow work, so it is a mutually beneficial situation.

In San Francisco, an organization called the Apprentice Alliance has been matching apprentices with small-business masters since 1983. For a one-person business, taking on an apprentice can be an excellent way of getting part-time help in exchange for sharing what you know about your particular field. Here are some typical comments from masters in the Apprentice Alliance:

Fig. 11.3   Sample Employment Contract

Temporary Employment Contract

_____	_____
Temporary Employee	Employer
_____	_____
Address	Address

References:

_____	_____	_____	_____
Person to Phone	Phone No.	Person to Phone	Phone No.
_____	_____	_____	_____
Person to Phone	Phone No.	Person to Phone	Phone No.
_____	_____	_____	_____
Person to Phone	Phone No.	Person to Phone	Phone No.

I, _____, accept employment from _____, with full recognition that this work is of a temporary nature.

My pay will be $ _____ before taxes and withholding, and my net take-home pay at _____ (intervals) will be $ _____ .

My employer, _____, will review with me every (day or week) the amount of work remaining to be done and give me a reliable estimate of my expected tenure, so that I will be able to plan other work or activities on my own behalf.

I agree to let my employer, _____, know with reasonable advance notice when I have other commitments that will affect my availability to work. I am aware that I will receive no benefits, such as vacation pay, private retirement pay, and health coverage, during my employment.

_____	_____
Employee	Employer
_____	_____
Date	Date

The apprentice and I clicked, and the apprentice and gardening clicked. We were very straightforward with one another about our wants and needs. And we were both flexible about schedules. The work was held back at critical times by the need to explain and supervise, and by the slower pace of a nonpaid person, especially while learning. We developed a friendship and had a common interest and caring about plants. The apprentice was willing to do quality work. All in all, the match was excellent and of lasting value. The only improvement I could recommend would be on my part, to decrease my work load so there would be more leisurely periods for better training.

I had an excellent apprentice in nonprofit management. She was willing to learn, share, and work independently. She has helped to make the operation more streamlined. I helped her to gain skills and she put her skills to use for the organization. It was a mutual-gain situation. She was treated as a very trusted and responsible member of the staff.

THE IMPORTANCE OF GOOD SUPPLIERS

Suppliers are one of the most important resources you have. We use the word suppliers to include all of the people and businesses that supply you with goods and services. This means accountants, lawyers, landlords, the post office, copier technicians, gardeners, and the utility company, in addition to the manufacturers, distributors, or retailers that provide you with any products you resell.

Relying on your suppliers as a key source of information is a wise strategy. If you need to know what package to put your product in, ask a box manufacturer. How should a newsletter be laid out? Ask your printer. Most suppliers are willing to provide you with information, especially if they feel it will lead to repeat business for them.

One-person businesses are especially dependent on suppliers for several reasons. One is that bigger businesses often can afford to keep a larger inventory of supplies and materials on hand than you can, and they can more easily survive a supplier problem, argument, or strike if necessary. Another is that your business frequently offers qualitatively better service, which, when translated, means faster, more flexible, and more tailored service. You need the same characteristics in your suppliers.

Consider whether the prospective supplier will be able to develop a personable and friendly relationship with you, preferably a long-term one. Will you be an important client to the supplier, based on your average volume of business over a year, or for some other reason? Will you be important enough for them to do a little extra? Weigh a quick response to your needs and greater flexibility against physical inconvenience and higher price. For most one-person businesses it is preferable to drive an extra ten minutes to pick something up, and to pay full retail price, if the supplier meets these criteria. You gain longer evening or weekend hours in exchange for quick response time and quality work the first time around.

Creating good supplier relationships is something that satchel designer Teri Joe Wheeler has thought a lot about. "I want the best raw materials possible with the shortest delivery time. My hardware, buttons, and so on come mostly from overseas and can take up to six weeks to arrive. It's a lot easier when I can just call an 800 number and my material arrives the following week. I pay my suppliers immediately, as if it was COD. In getting to know the people behind the supplies, I have settled into doing business with people I like. I also am open to other sources. I have four accounts for fabric, and three for hardware. And I still shop around.

"I stay in touch with my suppliers and try to communicate to them that I appreciate what they do. I relate to them on a people level, which makes it more fun for me, and for them, I hope."

Clothes designer Kate Bishop uses a similar approach. "I do all my research by phone now. In the early years, I spent a lot of time driving around or flying around locating suppliers. Because silk is not produced in this country, you have to deal with what few importers there are. I have found the five or six that are the best for me, where salespeople are easy to work with. This is almost more important than what they have to offer.

"At one point, my customers were slow in paying, and I got into trouble with my suppliers. I kept communicating with them, though, and they were really generous. I don't know why. At one point, I owed $15,000. That took me a year and a half to pay off, and they still do business with me. If I buy net thirty now, I try to pay it immediately. I pretend that it's COD and send a check out as soon as the invoice comes."

Trish deals with many different suppliers in order to keep her little gift shop well stocked. She too feels it is important to pay promptly and to treat suppliers well. "I have all open accounts, net thirty days, and I always pay the full amount. I never pay the minimum. The suppliers are very good to me because of that, I think. When they come in, I always give them a sample of taffy and that seems to please them. I am always nice. A lot of store owners don't treat their sales reps very well. That's a mistake because you need a good relationship with your suppliers. I use maybe twenty suppliers at various times of the year. After a while, you learn who gives you just what you ask for. Some suppliers will stick things into your order that you didn't really want in the first place. If they keep doing it, even after you tell them about it, you stop dealing with them. In the gift business there are lots of places to buy from."

Landscape gardener Eileen Mulligan focuses on information and service as the major criteria for choosing a supplier. She also agrees that good relationships are important. "I go to Harmony Farm Supply because they have the best information I know of, and they have good-quality stuff. It's more expensive than going somewhere else, but the service is wonderful. Otherwise, I go wherever the plants and prices are good and I have a nice personable relationship with the salespeople."

And finally, a word from mail-order publisher Bear Kamoroff. "I think the United Parcel Service is the world's greatest invention for small businesses. They are more expensive than the post office, but they are more reliable, and faster, and they will come up to my house in Laytonville. And they will come up any day that I call. I'm not big on big corporations, but I love my UPS driver—he's the nicest man I've ever met.

"The fact that I pay my bills in five days instead of thirty makes every one of my vendors love me and trust me completely. They are happy to do business with me because they know I pay my bills. Some of them give discounts for early payment. If you have large bills, it never hurts to ask if your vendor will give you a discount for early payment. With one supplier, I save $300 just for writing a check ten days early."

THE VALUE OF CLIENT CONTRACTS

Everything we've said about the importance of contracts with your subcontractors applies to your clients too. Written contracts make it clear what you are going to provide to the client by when and what you expect from the client along the way and at the end. Again, by clarifying all aspects of the work, you will avoid errors, confusion, forgetfulness, and recriminations, even among friends.

When you are selling tangible goods your contract is usually a combination of a purchase order from the client or customer and an invoice from you. The purchase order tells you what the client wants, how many, at what price, and by when. You may have to negotiate modifications to the purchase order because it may not match exactly what you have to offer and you will want to inform the customer of that before delivering the goods. Once you have the customer's agreement, you finalize that agreement by making up an invoice. That's why the stock invoices and purchase orders in office supply stores look so much alike. They serve as an interactive contract for the sale of tangible goods.

When you are a consultant or provider of nontangible services, the contract is usually what we call a statement of *terms and conditions*. Terms and conditions spell out the same set of variables as purchase orders and invoices: what service you will provide (what the client wants, presumably), how long it will take (how many), what it will cost (at what price), and when the service will be complete (by when). (See figure 11.4.)

Computer and training consultant Bill Dale relies on contracts in the form of written letters or proposals to his clients. He makes some very good points about the process of creating a contract. "Detailed contracts are more trouble than they're worth, in my experience. I recommend trying the following instead:

- Meet to review needs.
- Develop an outline showing how you could meet needs.
- Agree that the outline is okay in principle.

Fig. 11.4   Sample Terms and Conditions with Accompanying Letter of Agreement

Terms and Conditions

1. **Fee Structure:** All time spent on the project, including travel hours, will be billed at the rate of $75.00 an hour.

   Rush work will be billed at 1.5 times the regular charge. Rush work is any work that must be completed in less than the usual amount of time. Rush charges will be applied at our discretion. Hourly rates will be adjusted semiannually to reflect changes in the cost-of-living index.

   Unless otherwise stated, any cost estimate presented verbally or in a proposal is for budgetary purposes only and is not a fixed price. Client and Consultant will review the progress of the project from time to time and adjust the budgetary estimates when needed.

2. **Reimbursable Expense:** The following expenses will be billed at direct cost:

   a. Travel expenses necessary for the execution of the project, including airfares, rental vehicles, and highway mileage in company or personal vehicles, which will be charged at 25 cents per mile. Air travel will be by the lowest fares available at the time of the booking.

   b. Telephone charges.

   c. Postage and couriers (messengers, Federal Express, UPS, Express Mail, etc.).

   d. Photocopies, printing and reproduction.

   e. Outside computer services.

   f. Other expenses directly attributable to the project.

3. **Invoices and Payments:** Invoices will be submitted as the work progresses, at least monthly, and payment is due on receipt of invoice. A 2% per month service charge will be added to all delinquent accounts. In the event that the Consultant is successful in prosecuting any suit for damages for breach of this agreement, including suits for nonpayment of invoices, to enforce this agreement, or to enjoin the other party from violating this agreement, Consultant shall be entitled to recover as part of the damages any reasonable legal costs and expenses for bringing and maintaining any such action.

4. **Warranty:** Our services will be performed in accordance with generally and currently accepted professional principles and practices. This warranty is in lieu of all other warranties either expressed or implied.

5. **Limitation of Professional Liability:** The Client agrees to limit any and all liability or claim for damage, for cost of defense, or for any expenses to be levied against Consultant to a sum not to exceed $5,000, or the amount of our fee, whichever is less, when such claim arises from any error, omission, or professional negligence on the part of Consultant.

6. **Copyright:** Consultant holds copyright on any product that results from the project. Client is entitled to utilize all or any part of such product for the purposes intended, and may adapt the product to related purposes, but may not sell or give away all or any part of such product.

7. **Other Document:** Consultant letter to Client dated _____ is hereby made a part of this document.

8. **Acceptance:** Client, by signing below, hereby agrees to these terms and conditions:

   Client Organization
   Client Address
   City, ST Zipcode
   Telephone

   By:

   _____

   _____
   Client Name, Title

Accompanying Letter of Agreement

Date
Client Name, Title
Client Organization
Client Address
City, ST Zipcode

Dear [Client Name]:

This letter is to summarize our discussion of [Date] and to outline my recommendations for how to proceed in evaluating your approaching need to upgrade the computer systems used by the Shelter, Membership, and Accounting departments of the [Client Organization].

Your major concerns seem to lie in three separate areas: (1) When would the best time to upgrade be? (2) What should the future configuration look like and how much would it cost? (3) Will it provide a solution to the problems of processing speed, number of terminals, and present conflicts of use experienced by the Shelter, Membership, and Accounting? I propose to interview the parties affected, do some secondary research on the hardware and software alternatives, and make a recommendation on how to proceed based on my findings.

As always, we will give priority to cultivating practical use of existing computer resources before asking for additional hardware or software. The outcome of this project will be an update to my previous detailed inventory of the computer hardware and software being used by the Shelter, Membership, and Accounting; a clear description of the proposed upgrades; and a recommendation as to how and when to do the proposed switch-over to a new system.

I will call you to discuss the steps outlined in this letter. If you approve, I can begin this project the week of [Date]. It will take approximately two weeks to complete at a cost of $2,200.00. Expenses such as mileage, phone, photocopies, and postage will be billed separately. Payment will be made one half on commencement of the work, and one half on completion. Additional consulting time will be billed at $75.00 per hour.

If you have any questions, please call me at your earliest convenience.

Sincerely,

- Confirm the needs, methods, and agreement in writing, including a detailed financial section giving your work effort, your fees, and the return on investment to the client.

- Follow up the letter on the phone. If it is fine, go ahead on this basis; if not, determine what is needed and amend the agreement if you can. If you can't, find some other project.

"Beware of selling a client on your services if there is no real need or if they do not recognize the need. You will spend all your time justifying the project, even when it is successful. Also, don't undertake projects that are not in the client's interests, even if they want you to. Think carefully before committing to something, and then *keep your word*."

Business advisor Paul Terry's approach is even less formal, but still relies on most of the same steps. "I used to have no contract situation at all. Now I do a verbal contract over the phone. Then I send them a basic terms and conditions page, which tells them who I am, what I do, who I've done it for, what I charge, what time they have to be here, what charges will be involved, and so on. It's very clearly marked, and I make sure that they have either received it in advance of coming to the office or read it when they come. So there is a verbal understanding, a contractual relationship in the sense that they have received something and have agreed to the terms. Sometimes if the issue is more complicated, or if I'm dealing with a larger client, I write them a contractual kind of letter saying, "Based on our conversation, it is my understanding that this is the work that we plan to do together," etc. They may sign it and send it back, or not. The larger the client and the more complicated the issue, the more likely that we will need something in writing before the work gets done."

HOW TO STAY CURRENT IN YOUR FIELD

Most service industries offer an abundance of regular seminars and classes for those in the field. Product industries have trade shows where wholesalers present their wares to retailers and the public. When you find such offerings in your field, we encourage you to go to as many as you can.

Seminars, classes, and trade shows in general are good places to meet your peers and learn from them. Those who have more experience in the field and are friendly can give you valuable tips about operational questions affecting your business. In most fields people in their first year could handle a much greater volume with the same effort if they possessed the knowledge of someone with many years' experience.

From a marketing point of view, your peers can refer their overflow business to you, if they know and respect you. Conversely, you may meet new people entering your field or others who can handle your overflow or act as backup. These reasons for attending professional or trade meetings are additional to the technical information you may gain. Being in the company of people who share common interests while you learn new aspects of your field is a useful diversion from your day-to-day operations. Trade shows present a similar opportunity for making contacts and acquiring information, but they also offer a powerful sales opportunity. In most business fields, trade shows seem to work well for the selling participants.

Lastly, staying current on developments in your field can give you the confidence to teach classes and seminars yourself. This is a prime source of new business, and a potential forum for gaining the respect of your peers. It also exerts a subtle pressure to keep yourself current in your chosen livelihood.

Self-care advocate Tom Ferguson stays current by reading a lot and talking to people: "I subscribe to a lot of magazines, journals, and newsletters. I have maybe a 25 or 35 percent turnover per year in my information sources. I'm always stopping some and starting new ones. I go to the library pretty often. Also I go to meetings and trade shows because that's a good way of meeting people and keeping up on what's new."

Book designer Clifford Burke says, "I read journals as necessary, and I stay good friends with a computer nut. I'm teaching him typography so that he can produce more books in the future, and in exchange, he passes on information to me. In terms of selling one's own talent, I operate on the rule that I don't turn down opportunity. Part of that strategy is going to new things to find opportunities. I did a seminar recently, and as it worked out, it didn't actually cost me money but I did not get paid either. The pay came in new contacts and new offers of work. Hopefully, these will lead to more work. While manufacturers work on accrual of capital and inventory, free-lancers work on accrual of recognition and connections."

Mail-order publisher Bear Kamoroff keeps an open channel to the outside world: "I always try to go to the American Booksellers Association convention, which is a big annual get-together. I hang out for two and a half days with all the people in the book world and hobnob and shoot the breeze with them—say hello to all the wholesalers, the other small book publishers, bookstore owners I know, and the graphic artists.

"I subscribe to a lot of business and publishing publications that are applicable to me and I skim them all. I also subscribe to a bunch of tax publications so I can keep up with the tax laws.

"Whenever I'm around people involved in business and books, I keep my ears open to hear what they have to say. I'm always open to ideas and suggestions. It's so easy to expand your business if you have time to do it. And it's so easy to just keep exploring and looking for new avenues, especially in mail order. I'm sure I could double my business if I just sat down and took the time to do it. But I don't want to take that time for my business right now. Some people feel that if you're not growing you're dying, but I don't agree with that. As long as you stay on top of things, there is no reason to keep growing unless you want to or need to."

RESOURCES

Steingold, Fred. *The Legal Guide for Starting and Running a Small Business*. Berkeley: Nolo Press, 1992.

Elias, Stephen, and Marcia Stewart. *Simple Contracts for Personal Use*. Berkeley: Nolo Press, 1992.

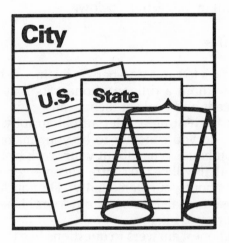

Appendix

Start-Up and Legal Matters

Every business has a start-up phase and therefore requires some help in sorting our all the details of getting going. In this chapter we will talk about the importance of self-assessment before you begin, the steps you must follow to create a successful launch, the myriad legal obligations you must meet, including your legal obligations to the people you work with. We will also address the business form you choose and its tax implications.

BUSINESS START-UP BASICS

While this book is intended primarily for ongoing businesses, we would be remiss in our responsibility to those of you who are not yet in business, but who think you might like to be if we didn't at least mention the steps necessary to starting up a business. So here is a list of what to do if you decide to take the plunge:

1. Assess your tradeskills.
2. Do your market research.
3. Create a business plan.
4. Check zoning restrictions, obtain the necessary licenses and permits, register your fictitious name, and register to pay sales taxes.

5. Open a business bank account.
6. Hire your personnel.
7. Develop and execute your marketing plan.

We will touch on each of these steps in this chapter and cover numbers 4 through 7 in some detail in the sections below.

Assess Your Tradeskills

Do you have what it takes to run a one-person business? Too many people launch a one-person business without a diligent, honest look at their own strengths and weaknesses and the needs and goals of their family.

You might begin by writing a brief autobiography. What have you done in your life so far? What do you consider to be your major accomplishments? How much education do you have? What about your work history? Do you already possess a specialized skill that will be the central income-generating aspect of your proposed business? How about your personality? Do you like to work with people? things? data? machines? animals? indoors? outdoors? Does your proposed business offer enough of the work you like?

If you begin with honest answers to questions like these you will quickly begin to see and feel whether your one-person business proposal and you truly fit together. For a more detailed assessment Douglas Gray's *The Entrepreneur's Complete Self-Assessment Guide* and Colin Ingram's *The Small Business Test* are especially helpful.

Do Your Market Research

The very first thing to do after you come up with a new business idea is to find out how feasible it will be. In addition to verifying the availability of the products you want to sell or the raw materials needed to make your product, you must also determine the need or desire for your products or services. This is called a *market survey*. A market survey tells you how many potential customers or clients for your products or services there are in the market you would like to focus on and what the likelihood is of their buying from you.

Additional market research steps are covered in Chapters 3 and 9.

Create a Business Plan

We've provided a general description of a business plan in Chapter 3, with enough detail to get you going. So we'll just summarize the process here, with these six basic steps to creating your business plan:

1. **Do your market research.** This is the step we just discussed. (See Chapters 3 and 9.)
2. **Create a cash-flow projection.** Determine the profit you need to cover the income you want to make, as well as the return you expect for any capital you have invested. (See Chapter 3.)
3. **Prepare an opening day balance sheet.** This will include a list of equipment and assets, as well as the money spent to get to opening day, that can be directly attributed to the business. (See Chapter 3.)
4. **Find the appropriate location and prepare a layout plan** for how the space will be used. (See Chapter 3.)
5. **Set up your books.** (See Chapter 2.)
6. **Develop your marketing and merchandising plan.** How will you display, promote, and sell your products or services? (See Chapter 9.)

Check Zoning Restrictions, Obtain Licenses and Permits, Register Your Fictitious Name, and Register to Pay Sales Tax

All businesses are set up according to certain broad legal definitions—basically as either sole proprietorships, partnerships, or corporations. A one-person business can be any of these, but by far the largest number are sole proprietorships.

Check Zoning Restrictions If you run your business out of your home you risk violating local residential zoning ordinances. Zoning is radically different in every single community and city in the U.S. In some exclusive suburbs with gates and guards, a graphic artist with a work table in the house would be in violation of the code and subject to a $5,000 penalty. By contrast, in the back counties of some states you could sell purebred horses out of your living room with no problem—at least no zoning problem.

Because of this national variation it is important to get the facts. Don't assume that zoning laws will be logical. Zoning is based on history, political structures, and social perceptions, not logic or necessity.

To get good advice, you should talk to a local person with political and zoning experience. Give him or her a few statistics about your operation, including how many people a week will come to your house and where they will park; how often you will have UPS package pickups and deliveries; and whether any visible equipment will be used in your business (such as a three-hundred-foot antenna or an eighteen-wheel truck).

If what you do is not legal for the zone you live in, learn what the penalties are before proceeding. Always assume that at some time you will be reported; you don't want to have to move at a time not of your choosing.

Obtain Licenses and Permits Many cities and counties require that you obtain a permit or license to operate. Check with your local government to find out whether your business is subject to this requirement. You may also need to get a state business license. In addition, all businesses, even one-person businesses, are required to have a federal ID number. In many cases you may use your personal Social Security number for this purpose. To obtain a separate federal ID number (called an employer identification number, or an EIN) file Form SS-4 with the IRS.

Register Your Fictitious Name If you wish to operate your business using a name other than your own, you may be required by your state or local government to file a DBA ("doing business as"), or "statement of fictitious business name." This usually involves registering with the appropriate government agency and then publishing your intent to use the name in a local newspaper. Regulations may vary depending on where you live, so check with your state or local government.

Register to Pay Sales Tax Most states, and some local governments, require you to apply for a permit to sell taxable products or services. This regulation may apply to wholesalers, retailers, and consultants. You may be required to make a security deposit against future payments for the taxes you are supposed to collect.

Open a Business Bank Account

It is highly desirable to have a separate checking account for your business. This will help you more easily track income and expenses that are only related to the business.

Hire Your Personnel

Locate the subcontractors and/or employees that you intend to use, if any, and negotiate your working relationships. Get all agreements in writing (see Chapter 11 for subcontractor agreements).

Legal Obligations with Personnel For tax purposes, when you hire part-time workers you may have to treat them as employees, whether they really are or not. If so, you will have to withhold taxes for them and pay several forms of tax in addition to the wages you pay them. If you wish to avoid employees, you should understand the way in which federal and state agencies view the different individuals you might hire to work with you. Then you can protect yourself by establishing clear relationships. Workers who are not employees can be roughly grouped into five categories: casual labor, rented labor, partner, or independent contractor.

Casual labor is any person that you hire to do a short, one-time job, such as chopping wood, hauling an old sofa, or washing windows. You don't pay them very much, and you probably don't hire them more than once. If you pay them more than $600 in a single year you must file a 1099 report with the IRS.

Rented labor is a person you get from a temporary agency such as Kelly, Manpower, or Daisy; he or she is really an employee of the agency. You may hire temporary personnel for an hour or a month and you may have them come back repeatedly. But they are still not your employees, so you do not have to file 1099s for them.

Partner refers to a real partner in a legal sense. They are not employees and they do not receive 1099s from the partnership. (See below for more on partners.)

True *independent contractors* include your lawyer, accountant, foot surgeon, and chimney sweep. They have their own businesses and their own tools, are their own boss, and almost always have clients other than you. These are the folks for whom you must file 1099s.

The rules and regulations about who is and who is not an independent contractor are numerous. On the list of jobs or occupations that have been denied withholding exemption, you will find many of the same jobs or occupations that have been granted the exemption (see "Independent Contractors," page 269). However, the general guidelines are pretty clear. For additional information, get Circular E, *Employers Tax Guide,* from the IRS, or you can file a Form SS-8 to obtain a ruling on a specific case. Your best insurance is to ascertain that all of the independent contractors working for you act like individual businesses. Ask them if they keep books and regularly file a Schedule C: Profit or Loss from a Business Profession, on which what you pay them is included. Explain to them that you will be filing Form 1099 (explained below) to report your payments to them to the IRS.

The biggest problem with being unclear on the independent contractor versus employee issue usually comes up after you have stopped working with someone and you find out that he or she has filed an unemployment claim. Suddenly you are faced with an audit of your practices regarding independent contractors. To avoid this, be sure to discuss the issue openly with any subcontractors about whom you have doubts. Explain that, as independent contractors, they will not be eligible for unemployment compensation. This kind of frank discussion should give you a feeling for whether they understand what being an independent contractor means, and whether you are going to have a problem later. Try to hire only people who seem to take being in business for themselves seriously enough to file all the correct tax forms, and who are unlikely to file for unemployment later.

The government keeps tabs on the amount of money paid to independent contractors by having you report it on Form 1099. Every January you are required by federal tax law to fill out 1099 forms and mail them to each independent contractor you hired in the previous year. You will need to include their tax ID number or Social Security number on the form. The only exceptions are if (1) your total payments to them were under $600 during the year, or (2) they are a corporation.

It is a good idea to keep track of the money you spend on every independent contractor as you go along, so that you don't have to burn the midnight oil in

January to get the forms out. You might keep a separate file labeled 1099, and when a payable is going to someone for whom you will have to write a 1099 in January, you can drop a copy of the check or invoice into that file. You must also remember to forward a copy of all 1099s to the IRS; use Form 1096 to do this.

Develop and Execute Your Marketing Plan

This is covered in Chapters 3 and 8.

THE LEGAL FORM OF YOUR BUSINESS

In business you usually start off as a sole proprietor, regardless of whether you have employees or run your business with a spouse. You may, however, form a partnership or a corporation through certain legal procedures; you can operate several different businesses with one or more as sole proprietorships and the others as partnerships or corporations.

Sole Proprietorship

The definition of sole proprietor is primarily meaningful in a tax context. It means that you file a Federal Schedule C (Form 1040), "Profit or (Loss) from Business or Profession," in addition to your Form 1040, "U.S. Individual Income Tax Return." The categories of the Schedule C are similar to those in the monthly records that many small businesses use, and it is easy to use the same expense categories in your monthly financial sheets and just transfer the yearly totals to your tax forms (although some might be irrelevant to your particular business).

Net earnings from a sole proprietorship are calculated on Schedule C and then reported on the front page of Form 1040. These business net earnings are taxable, like any other form of earnings. The same is true for earnings from a partnership, which are recorded on an adjacent line. Sole proprietor income, partnership income, and income from one kind of corporation (called a Sub-Chapter S) are all treated for tax purposes in the same way; you report your net earnings from them and pay regular income taxes on them as an individual.

Partnership

A partnership is any business relationship done jointly with other people, except as a corporation. From a tax point of view, a partnership is almost nonexistent. The only thing required is the filing of a simple annual notice of the revenue distributed to the partners (called a K-1). To do a K-1, a tax ID number is needed, which can be obtained simply by filing a request for a federal tax ID number.

From a legal point of view, a partnership is a real entity, whether a written partnership agreement exists or not. Unfortunately for many small businesses, a

Independent Contractors

Here are some excerpts on independent contractor status from the *Federal Tax Coordinator*, a publication used by accountants to stay current on tax law:

In general, an individual who is subject to the control and direction of another only as to the result of his work, and not as to the means, is an independent contractor and not an employee. Physicians, lawyers, dentists, veterinarians, contractors, subcontractors, public stenographers, auctioneers, and others who follow an independent trade, business, or profession in which they offer their services to the public are usually independent contractors according to the Treasury regulations.

A "free-lance worker" may or may not be subject to withholding. If the relationship between such a worker and the person paying for his services is such that the latter has the right to tell him what kind of work to do and how to do it, the worker will be considered an employee. But a person who works at home on a piecework basis is considered an independent contractor if he is subject to another's control only as to the result of the services and not as to the method of performing them. (He's nevertheless subject to FICA withholding.)

A general contractor wasn't the employer of the employees of its subcontractor even though it occasionally gave instructions directly to these employees and the subcontractor generally followed its advice as to hiring and firing. The subcontractor had full control of its employees and the fact that it chose to defer to the general contractor for business reasons didn't give the latter control.

Similarly, a subcontractor was an independent contractor and not a joint venturer with the general contractor where the latter only advanced funds which would be due at the completion of the job; shared in profits only because it advanced funds; didn't share losses or have any personal liability; and didn't have common management and control.

In determining whether an individual was an independent contractor, a district court considered the following factors: (1) Whether the person receiving the benefit of the service has the right to control the manner and method of performance; (2) Whether the person rendering the service has a substantial investment in his own tools or equipment; (3) Whether the person rendering the service undertook substantial costs to perform the services; (4) Whether the person performing the service had an opportunity for profit dependent on his managerial skill; (5) Whether the service rendered required special training and skill; (6) The duration of the relationship between the parties; (7) Whether the service performed is an integral part of the recipient's business rather than an ancillary portion; (8) Whether the person rendering the service had a risk of loss; (9) The relationship which the parties believed they created; (10) Whether or not the person who performed the services offered such services publicly and practiced an independent trade; (11) Whether the custom in the trade or industry was for the service to be performed on an independent contractor or employee basis; (12) Whether the person who received the benefit of the service held the right to discharge without cause the person who performed the service; (13) Whether the person who performed the services had the right to delegate his duty to others.

Conceivably, an individual may be both an employee and an independent contractor with respect to the same party. If, for example, an employee, in addition to his regular work, contracts with his employer to sell the company's product on his own time, he may be considered to be an independent contractor with respect to the work performed under that contract. At the same time, of course, the wages paid him for his regular work as an employee would be subject to withholding.

Many agent-drivers, full-time salesmen and industrial homeworkers are treated as employees under social security, even though they are independent contractors under the control test. However, "control" remains the test for withholding purposes. Such an individual is still exempt from income tax withholding as an independent contractor if he is not subject to another's control.

written document often does not exist. Partnerships should always be in writing. The key items to include are (1) the purpose of the partnership, (2) the distribution of earnings and responsibilities, (3) dissolution procedures, and (4) a mediation clause. An excellent reference on this subject is *The Partnership Book*.

One form of partnership exists solely for investment purposes: the limited partnership. It is made up of one or more partners who run the business, called the general partners, and the people who contribute only money, called the limited partners. The designation *limited* means that these people are legally liable for any actions of the partnership only to the degree of business ownership that their contribution of money represents. They must also have nothing to do with running the business. If the business is forced to settle a lawsuit, they can lose the money they invested.

Corporation

A corporation is treated like a living being under the law. It can be taxed, sued, forced into bankruptcy, and adopted by another being (in a merger). It differs in that it can't die of old age, and it can be sold.

If you are considering incorporation, keep the following points in mind. Because a corporation can be sued, the law generally protects the owners of the corporation, as individuals, from suit for the same actions. Even if you and the corporation are really one and the same, which is only possible in a few states, such as California and Maryland, the corporation is sued for its actions and only its assets are vulnerable in a settlement. The exceptions are if the corporation was improperly formed in the first place, or if you fail to hold regular board meetings and keep good minutes, or otherwise run it improperly. As a one-person-business owner, it is wise to remember that although forming a corporation may protect you from liability for the corporation's actions, you must still defend yourself against the suit, which can bankrupt you personally. A more useful perspective is to focus on the tax benefits of incorporation, which under the Tax Reform Act of 1986 begin to occur after you are generating about $300,000 or more in annual income.

Because it is taxed, you have to file separate state and federal tax returns for the corporation. Corporate taxes are calculated on net earnings before payments to the owner, and these earnings are then taxed again as personal income to the owner — in other words, you are taxed twice. The salary to an owner is taxed only as salary. The exception to this rule is the Sub-Chapter S Corporation, which is allowed to pass profits through to the stockholders, where they are taxed only once as stockholder income.

Tax laws for corporations change occasionally and unexpectedly. In addition to the concerns already mentioned, you should note two important items that influence some people in their decision to incorporate. As the tax laws change, either of these items may change in such a way as to harm or benefit your business.

1. Corporations have a minimum level of net earnings on which they pay taxes, and you may expect to earn below that level.
2. Certain expenses related to health insurance and care, life insurance, and pensions that are not deductible as business expenses to sole proprietorships or partnerships are deductible as business expenses to corporations.

Corporations can be bought and sold in whole and in part a little more readily than other forms of business. Corporate ownership is in the form of stock certificates, which can be traded without affecting the business. The stock certificates may contain provisions requiring all other existing shareholders to bid on stock before it is sold to new people. The corporation can also promise to buy the stock back for a fixed price in the future, and retail markets can be created to sell corporate stock. (In the latter case, be careful: Securities and Exchange Commission laws govern all aspects of stock sales, even the "prospect" of a stock offering to another person. The lawyers who deal with this issue are expensive but should be consulted if you are considering selling stock.)

Relative Merits

In the final analysis, the sole proprietorship represents the simplest form to choose and maintain for most one-person businesses. A partnership may be beneficial from time to time when collaboration for a longer period seems desirable or as a source of financing. A corporation requires the most work to maintain, and its true benefits do not begin to show themselves until you are generating a larger amount of income than most one-person businesses anticipate.

RESOURCES

Clifford, Denis, and Ralph Warner. *The Partnership Book*, 4th ed. Berkeley: Nolo Press, 1991.

Gray, Douglas. *The Entrepreneur's Complete Self-Assessment Guide: How to Accurately Determine Your Potential for Success*. Seattle, Wash.: International Self-Counsel Press, 1990.

Ingram, Colin. *The Small Business Test*. Berkeley: Ten Speed Press, 1990.

Internal Revenue Service. *New Business Tax Kit*. Contains information about taxes and tax forms, as well as a comprehensive guide to federal taxation of small businesses. Available in local IRS offices.

Kamoroff, Bernard. *Small-Time Operator*. Laytonville, Calif.: Bell Springs Publishing, 1993.

Index

Note: *page numbers for figures are in bold.*

About the Authors

Claude Whitmyer is associate professor and program director of the Master of Arts in Business program of the School for Transformational Learning at the California Institute of Integral Studies. He has more than fifteen years of experience as an owner of several small businesses including a natural-cosmetics manufacturing company; a wood-burning-stove distribution company; and an urban-oriented, alternative-technology retail store and fifteen years as a technology and growth-management consultant to large corporations, small businesses, and nonprofit organizations.

Salli Rasberry is a member of the adjunct faculty in the Master of Arts in Business Program of the School for Transformational Learning at the California Institute of Integral Studies. She is a prolific writer and a popular public speaker. She has successfully run a dozen small businesses in fields as varied as book fairs (the first San Francisco International), publishing companies (New Glide Publications and Freestone Publishing), documentary films, business consulting, and nonprofit management.

For the last twenty years, we have been privileged to be part of the growing community of one-person businesses around the world. We have been lucky enough to visit many one-person businesses in Brazil, Canada, England, Mexico, and Sweden, and throughout the United States. Many have called on us in Northern California from as far away as Argentina, Australia, Japan, Kenya, New Zealand, South Africa, and Uganda. We have taught the contents of this book to hundreds of students in the San Francisco Bay Area; Portland, Maine; Toronto,

Ontario; Plainfield, Vermont; Seattle, Washington; and electronically on the Whole Earth 'Lectronic Link (WELL).

It is clear to us that the one-person-business phenomenon is worldwide and growing, but there is still much to learn and share about what works and what doesn't for this new business form.

Today's one-person business is very much a product of our rapidly changing economy and the so-called information age. Downsizing and downshifting have meant more and more individuals leaving the corporate environment and launching one-person businesses of their own.

Our experience in teaching, writing, and publishing, as well as managing small businesses, both for-profit and nonprofit, has helped us to present this material in a form that is both detailed and practical.

If you would like to respond to what you read here, ask any questions, or keep abreast of the changing developments in the one-person-business arena, please write to us in care of The Center for Good Work, P.O. Box 77086, San Francisco, CA 94107; (707) 823-2207.